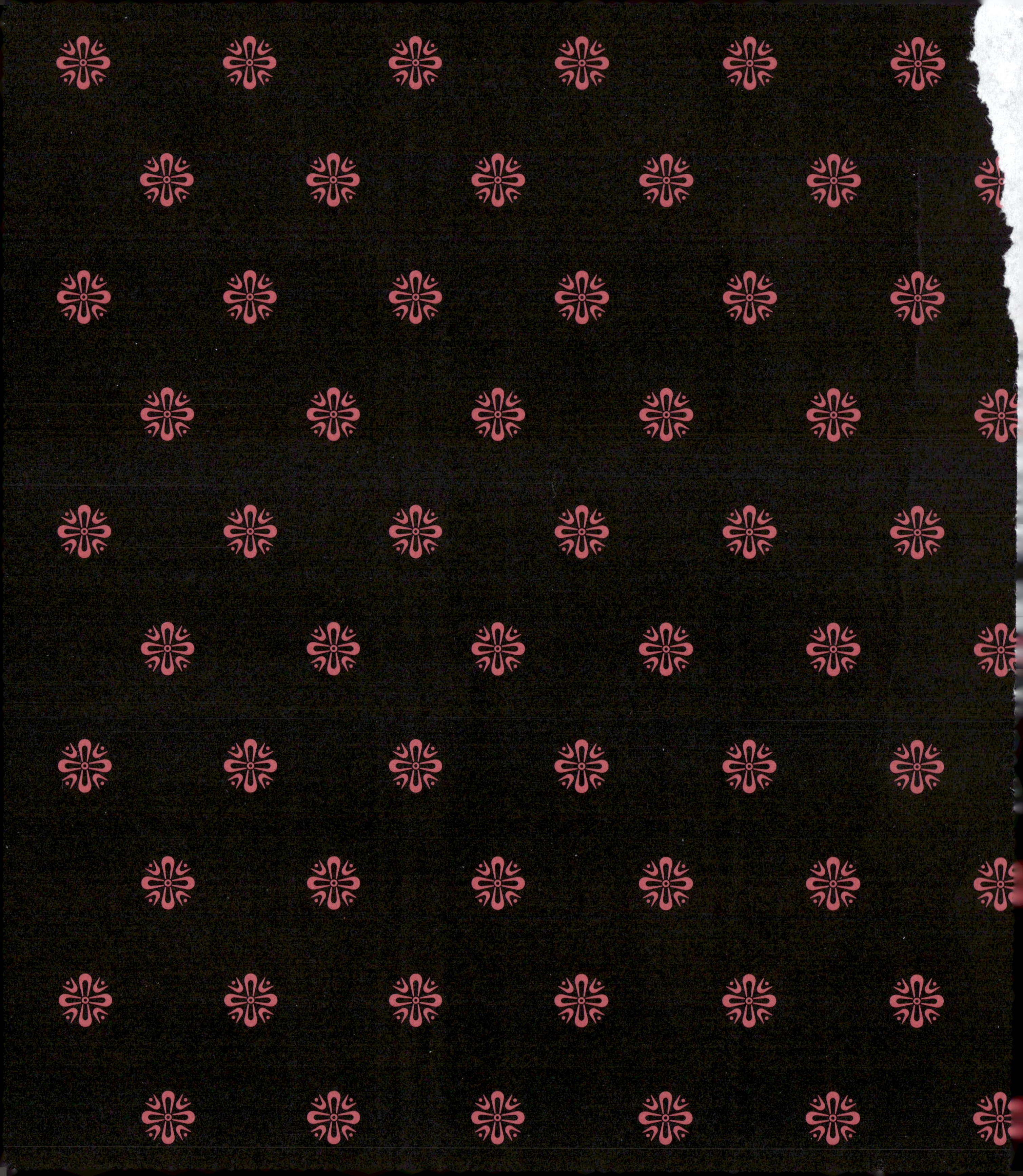

Bouquets of Art

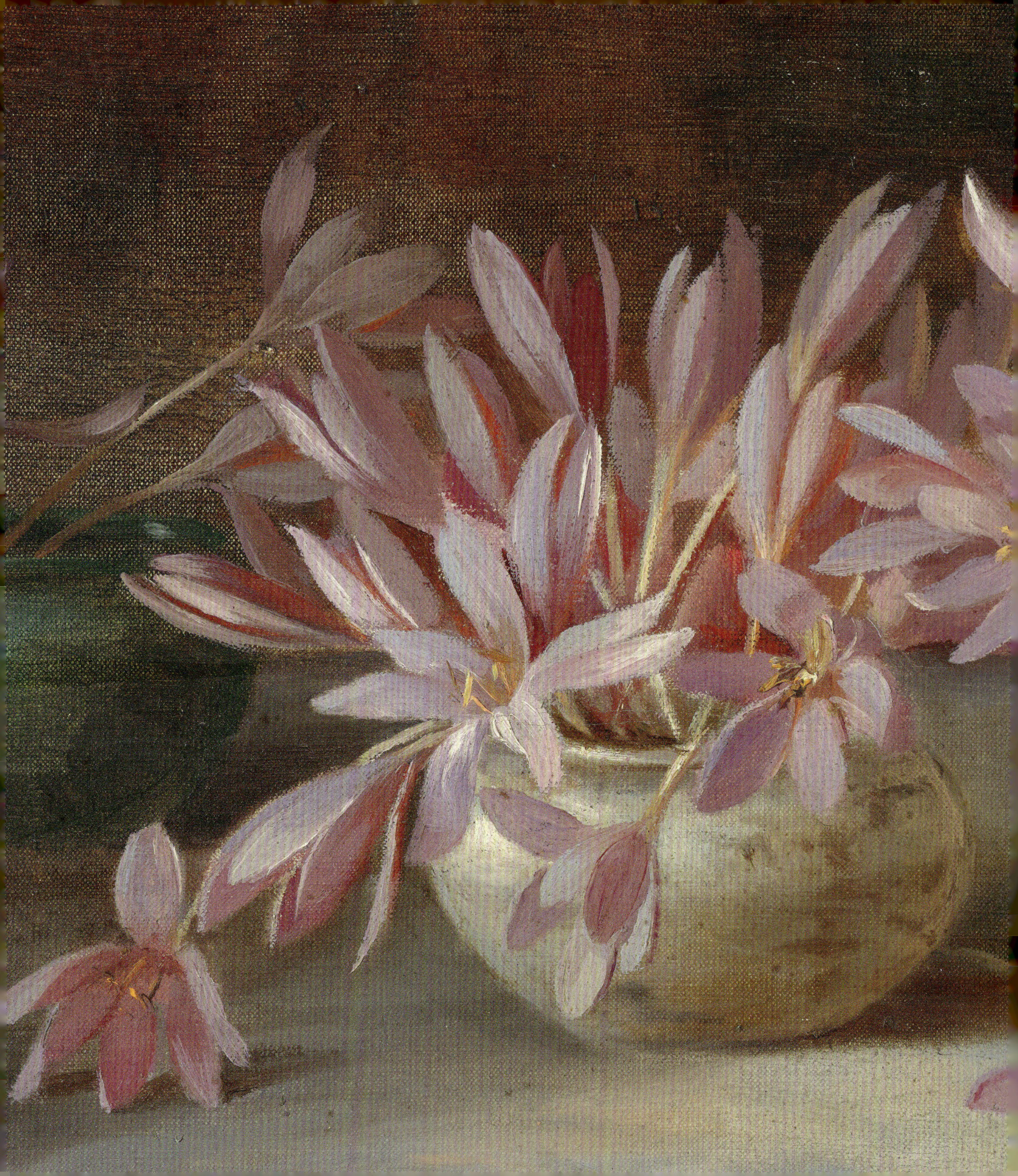

Bouquets of Art

A FLOWER DICTIONARY
from the
FINE ARTS MUSEUMS OF SAN FRANCISCO

Lauren Palmor

Fine Arts Museums of San Francisco
Cameron + Company

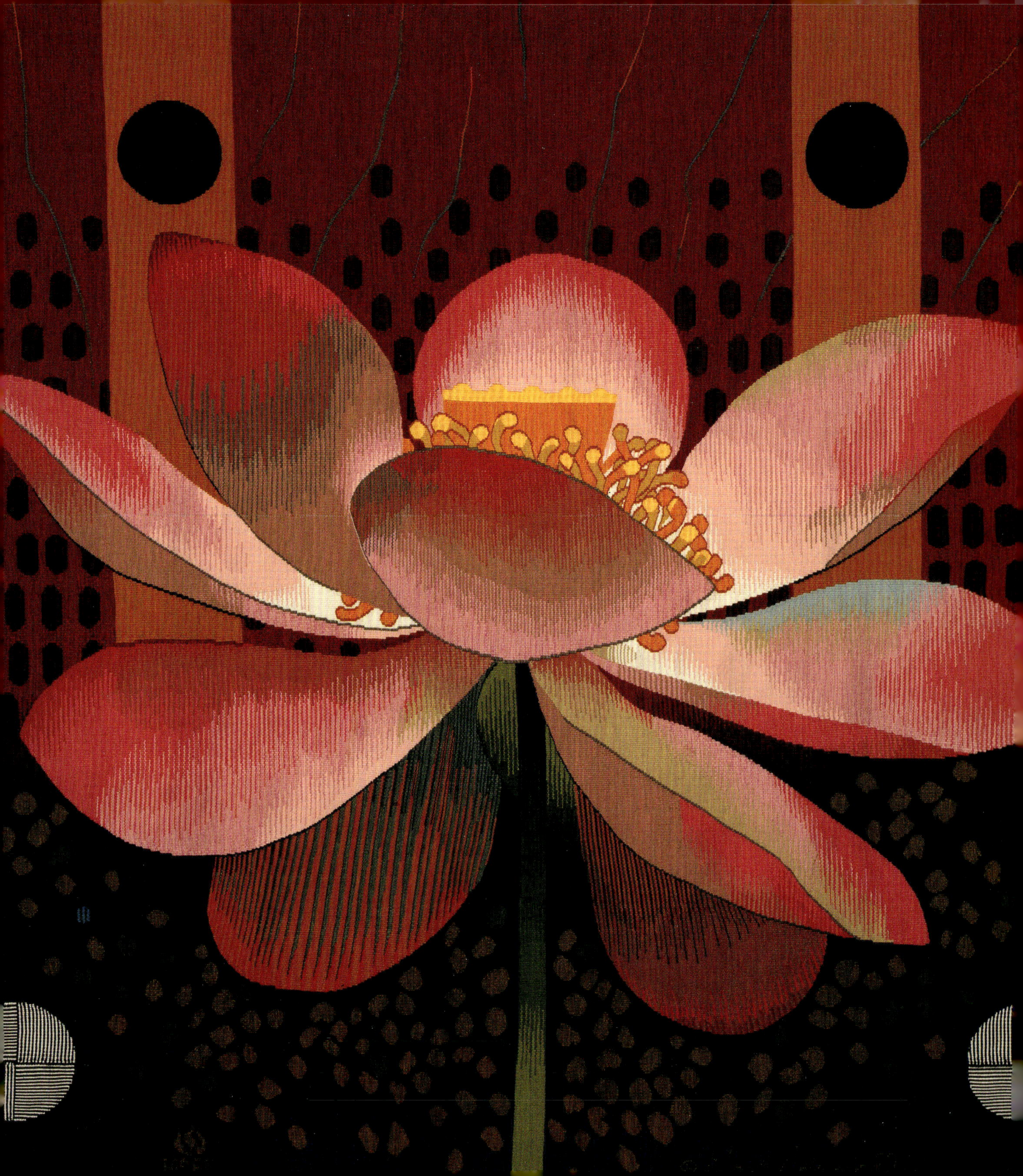

Contents

Foreword

THE DE YOUNG AND THE LEGION OF HONOR — the two museums that together form the Fine Arts Museums of San Francisco — feature a wide range of floral imagery in works spanning a diverse range of cultures and epochs. We celebrate these richly varied floral artworks each year during Bouquets to Art, the Fine Arts Museums' annual floral takeover that inspired the present volume. *Bouquets of Art: A Flower Dictionary from the Fine Arts Museums of San Francisco* pays tribute to this celebrated visual spectacle and beloved Bay Area tradition.

Since 1985, Bouquets to Art has been presented annually by the San Francisco Auxiliary of the Fine Arts Museums. Over the course of a week, tens of thousands of visitors enjoy floral arrangements by leading Bay Area designers and garden clubs, who interpret and complement objects from the Museums' permanent collection in arrangements composed of fresh flowers. In addition to the floral installations in the galleries, Bouquets to Art also offers floral-themed programming, including lectures, demonstrations, and focused online features offering closer engagement with the permanent collection. Bouquets to Art is the largest fundraiser held to benefit the Fine Arts Museums of San Francisco and is one of the country's premier floral events. Proceeds help underwrite essential activities at the Fine Arts Museums, and to date the event has raised more than seven million dollars to support the Museums' exhibitions, education programs, and conservation projects.

Bouquets to Art frames flowers and art as parallel artistic phenomena. Through their floral reinterpretations, guest floral designers often expand upon a single element of a composition that may otherwise go unnoticed. While an arrangement may complement a work of art as a whole, these responses to the microcosm of a single element also offer moments of surprise and delight. The aesthetic, visual, and sensual pleasures of these in-gallery encounters are self-apparent, but one of the additional benefits of these interactions is the manner in which they foster close looking at art objects in a new, specific way. Many Bouquets to Art visitors who love flowers come for the event and stay for the art.

Bouquets of Art: A Flower Dictionary from the Fine Arts Museums of San Francisco offers a dynamic exploration of the Museums' collections inspired by this cherished annual celebration. This volume draws upon the richness of floral symbolism to reinterpret works featuring floral imagery selected from across cultures, time periods, and media, encompassing American art, works on paper, costume and textile arts, European painting, and European decorative arts and sculpture. Entries are organized not by artist or period but by floral variety, inviting readers to draw new connections between the blossoms that fill these pages. A Pre-Raphaelite tapestry (Bluebell) is followed by a contemporary print (Bleeding Heart), and a still-life painting set within a tropical landscape (Orchid) precedes a hat decorated with silk flowers (Pansy). This spirited format suggests a multiplicity of fresh ways to approach familiar artworks with new questions and perspectives.

Our catalogue celebrates fifty works that demonstrate the cultural and visual diversity of the floral compositions in the Museums' permanent collection. We hope that this book will not only serve as a contemporary guide to the Victorian language of flowers, but also offer a method for approaching long-familiar floral artworks anew. Just as art is a language, flowers also offer a means for communication, and this guide invites deeper engagement with just one of the components that can enrich any museum visit. Perhaps this volume may serve as a reference for future encounters with Bouquets to Art, enabling visitors to appreciate a particular artwork and its companion floral interpretation, as well as the various ways in which the particular flowers in the arrangements on view represent their own worlds of meaning.

THOMAS P. CAMPBELL
Director and CEO
Fine Arts Museums of San Francisco

Bouquets of Art

LAUREN PALMOR

"Flowers were the first decorative implement for the earliest attempts of man to adorn himself; they grew all around him and were his just for the taking. . . . The fertile human mind assigned the medicinal and nutritious properties of plants, the beauty and fragrance of their leaves, flowers and blossoms as floral symbols."[1]

THIS VOLUME DRAWS upon the rich history of floriography — the language of flowers — in order to offer a new perspective through which to explore the permanent collections of the Fine Arts Museums of San Francisco. Featuring a sampling of floral imagery spanning diverse cultures, periods, and media, this guide builds on the methods of floriography as a means for navigating how the collection's expansive array of objects intersects with the rich histories of floral symbolism and communication.

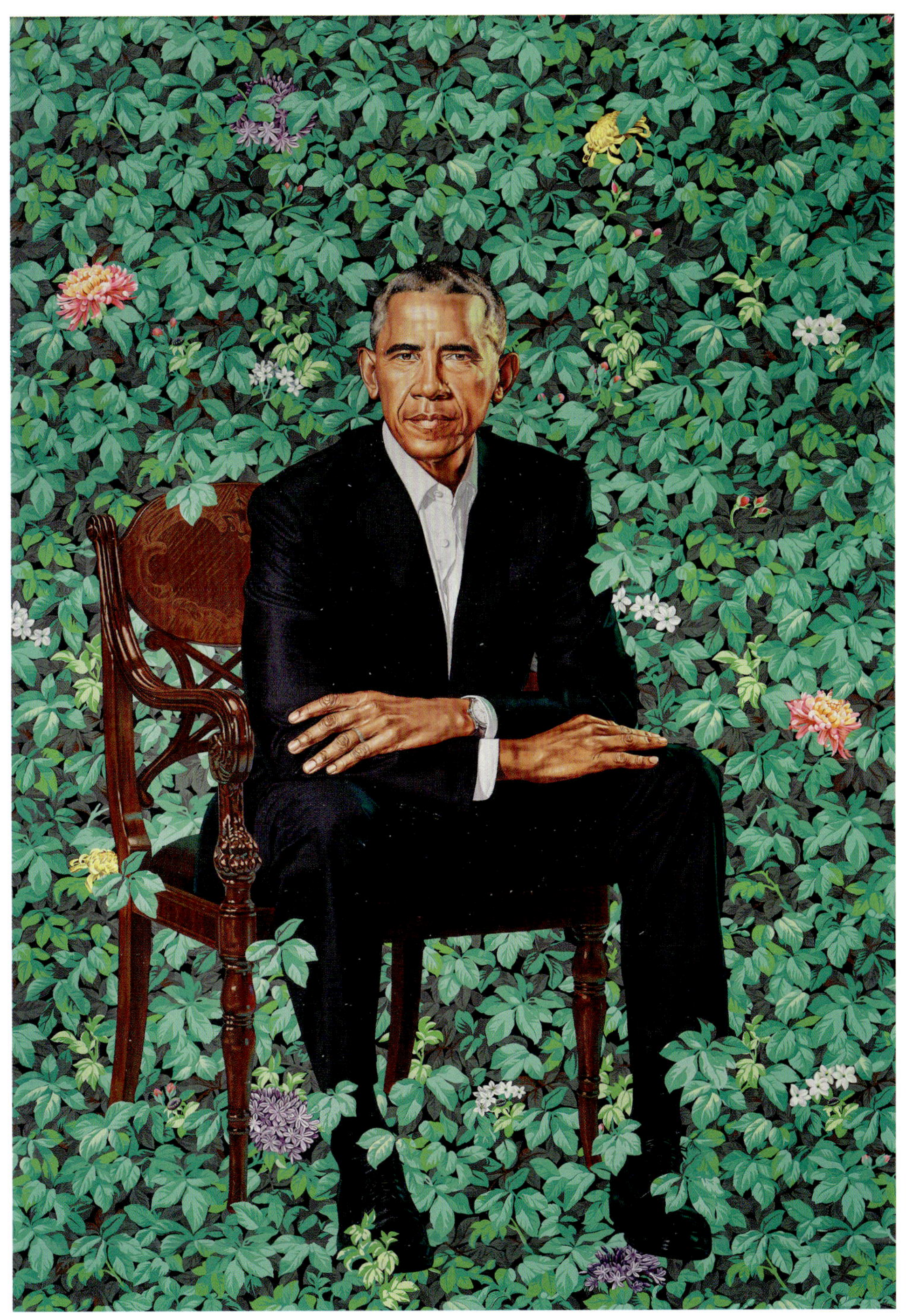

FIG. 1. Kehinde Wiley (American, b. 1977), *Barack Obama*, 2018. Oil on canvas, 84 1/8 x 57 7/8 in. (213.7 x 147 cm). National Portrait Gallery, Smithsonian Institution, Washington, DC, NPG.2018.16

Looking across the Fine Arts Museums' holdings of American art, works on paper, costume and textiles, European painting, and European decorative arts and sculpture, this selection of fifty floral-themed objects presents the collection from a fresh perspective. Entries are organized according to the format first popularized in the nineteenth century, with objects arranged in alphabetical order by floral variety. The accompanying texts explore some of the diverse histories of each flower's symbolic associations by addressing a rich variety of source material, including poetry, etymology, folklore, botany, popular music, biblical verse, mythology, histories of exploration and colonization, and systems of belief. These sources suggest many fresh ways to approach familiar artworks with new questions and points of view informed by the language of flowers.

The Language of Flowers: A Brief History

On February 12, 2018, President Barack Obama's presidential portrait was unveiled at the National Portrait Gallery in Washington, DC. In his near life-size depiction of the forty-fourth president of the United States, artist Kehinde Wiley departed from traditional, staid models of political portraiture; Obama is shown seated, his chair seemingly floating before a lush vertical garden. Although the space is dominated by greenery, the verdant backdrop is punctuated with bursts of color provided by purple, white, yellow, and pink flowers. Wiley utilized a distinct language of flowers to suggest the president's biography through geographic allusions: the purple African blue lily symbolizes the Kenyan heritage of his father, Barack Obama Sr.; white jasmine represents Hawai'i, his birthplace and childhood home; and chrysanthemums stand for Chicago, the city where Obama met his wife, Michelle Obama, and launched his political career.[2] Each flower illustrates an essential aspect of the former president's life, demonstrating the indelible power of floral symbolism to efficiently convey complex narratives to those who know how to read such details.

The Obama portrait fits within a much more expansive chronicle of the ways in which humans have always used flowers to tell multifaceted stories. Across millennia, flowers have become inextricably intertwined with diverse systems of belief and cultural expression. For instance, floral symbolism can be found in the visual culture and funerary practices of ancient Egypt, where the lotus flower served as a symbol of life, immortality, and resurrection.[3] Various flowers appear throughout the biblical Old Testament, and the poetry of the Song of Songs exalts the lily of the valley and rose of Sharon.[4] Flower lore can be found in such diverse contexts as Roman and Nordic mythology, early Christian symbolism, decorative patterns in Islamic art, Hindu religious practice, ancient Chinese verse, and traditional Japanese arts — their various innumerable attributes representative of deities, omens, seasons, heraldic devices, emblems of feasts and ceremonies, and expressions of desire.[5]

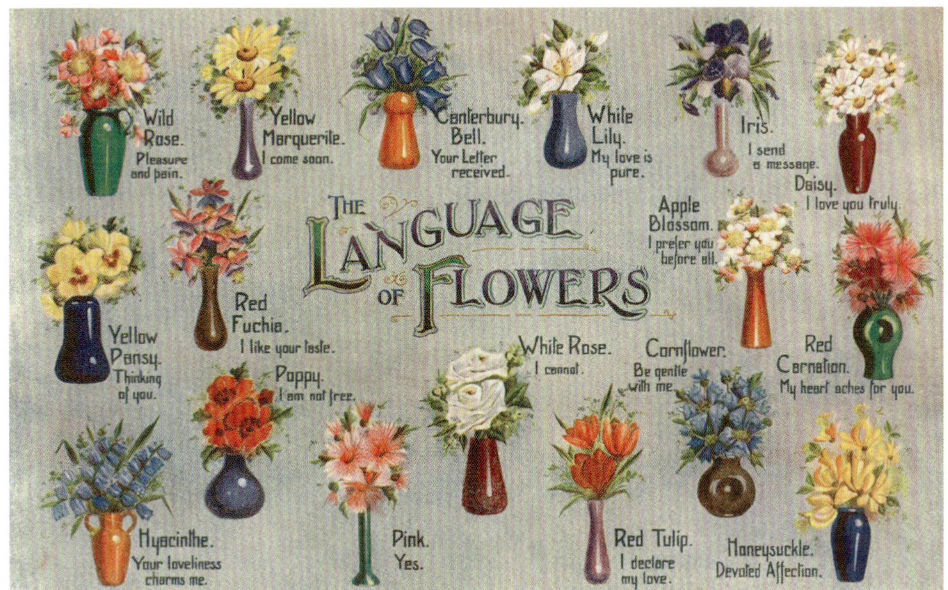

FIG. 2. Regent Publishing Co., Ltd., *The Language of Flowers*. Postcard, 3½ x 5½ in. (8.9 x 14 cm). Dumbarton Oaks Archives, Ephemera Collection, 054.SUZ.02.PCbox.094

The spiritual and emblematic significance of flowers stretches back to prehistory and the inception of nature worship: blossoms have historically adorned altars and shrines, their remnants discovered in ancient tombs dating back as far as fourteen thousand years.[6] Our contemporary understanding of diverse ancient cultures includes various symbologies of flowers, which have been associated with the seasons, virtues, life cycles, or political and regional alliances. Due to their radiate appearance and biological processes, flowers are also suggestive of primeval forces and the cosmic order of the universe. The study of various ancient cultures has revealed myriad ways in which floral communication has been linked to social practices, with rules prescribing the variety, color, and number of flowers selected for particular observances.[7]

Throughout the classical world, specific flowers were associated with particular gods and goddesses. For instance, Ovid's epic poem, *Metamorphoses*, relates the Greek myth that associates the hyacinth with the tale of Apollo and Hyacinthus (cat. no. 20). Other myths relayed by Ovid address crocuses, lilies, and violets to similar effect. In ancient Rome, the lily served as the emblem of Juno, goddess of love and marriage.[8] Later, early Christians absolved certain flowers of their pagan associations and ascribed to them qualities associated with Jesus Christ and the Virgin Mary — some emblems, including

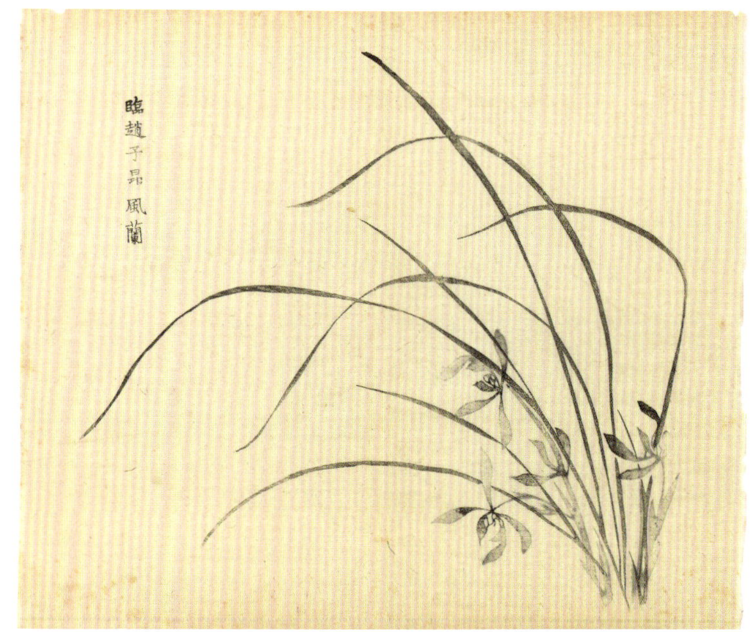

FIG. 3. *"Orchids in Wind," Four Flowers at Right*, no. 23 from *The Volume on Orchids* from *The Treatise on Calligraphy and Painting of the Ten Bamboo Studio*, ca. 17th century. Woodcut, 9⅜ x 10⅞ in. (23.8 x 27.5 cm). Fine Arts Museums of San Francisco, Achenbach Foundation for Graphic Arts, 1963.30.19378

particular flowers, were used more covertly to conceal their faith from nonbelievers.[9] A rich symbolic language continued to evolve in tandem with the flowering of Christian ideology. After the twelfth century, the intended Christian meanings of particular flowers were well established and widely understood: the white lily was affiliated with the purity and chastity of the Virgin Mary, the violet an emblem of Christ on Earth.[10] Roses came to decorate stories of the lives of the saints — as symbols of chastity or divine love, they were often incorporated into the hagiography of pious martyrs.

Different symbolic systems evolved in Asia, where the meanings of specific flowers were widely influenced by the teachings of the Chinese philosopher Confucius (551–479 BCE). For example, Confucius suggested that chrysanthemums be used as an object of meditation and praised the orchid as an emblem of the ideal man, noble and studious.[11] Confucian values and the metaphorical associations possessed by certain flowers in Chinese culture informed the development of a related symbolic language in Japan, where the Nara (710–794 CE) and Heian (794–1185 CE) periods saw the evolution of an intricate and enduring vocabulary inspired by the natural world.[12] The Japanese language of flowers developed in conjunction with the popularization of ikebana, the Japanese art of flower arranging that originated with sixth-century floral offerings made on the altars of Buddhist temples. Over the centuries, a rich tradition of ikebana practice grew to include more than a thousand schools and a wide variety of styles and design principles.[13]

In medieval Europe, illuminated manuscripts featured a rich language of flowers that was derived from biblical sources and influenced by pagan legend and contemporary botany.[14] In fifteenth-century Europe, botanical references also increasingly featured in stained-glass windows and liturgical garments, deepening parishioners' association between nature and the realm of the church and reinforcing wider understanding of Christian floral symbolism. During the Renaissance, the fervent innovations that transformed the fine and decorative arts further enshrined particular flowers as emblems of the Christian faith.

In sixteenth- and seventeenth-century Europe, exotic flowers were increasingly cultivated by those who had access to the worlds of global exploration, colonization, and commerce. Plants that were newly introduced to the West became highly prized as desired objects and fashionable additions to elite gardens. In terms of floral symbolism, these new varieties were ascribed novel associations that originated in classical and Christian thought.[15] Still-life paintings of the period provide rich source material for those seeking to understand the botanical world, as Western cultures created new floral meanings in parallel with their growing awareness of new floral varieties. The particularly arresting and detailed Dutch and Flemish flower paintings of the era provide evidence of idealized bouquets, which celebrate contemporary developments in floriculture as well as the rich symbolic and material associations possessed by individual blossoms.

Although the language of flowers is global, with variations on floral symbolism spanning centuries and cultures, the Victorians had a particularly well-documented, formalized system of floriography that provides a compelling entry point for the language of flowers as it is known today. Floriography most often describes a language of flowers that was largely disseminated during the Victorian period through prescriptive texts such as floral dictionaries, etiquette manuals, and women's magazines. In nineteenth-century England, France, and the United States, an audience comprising mostly upper-middle-class and upper-class women attempted to establish a Western language of flowers in which each flower was assigned a specific meaning.

The Victorian language of flowers has its origins in the eighteenth-century *Turkish Embassy Letters* of Lady Mary Wortley Montagu (1689–1762), a British aristocrat who lived in Constantinople. Montagu wrote about an alleged coded language of flowers that she observed in the Turkish *sélam,* or harem.[16] In her letters, which were published posthumously in 1763 and widely translated, she provided specific examples of this floral vocabulary, such as a jonquil to signify "have pity on my passion," and a rose, meaning "may you be pleased, and all your sorrows be mine."[17] Although Montagu provided just sixteen examples of this floral code in a letter written from Constantinople in 1718, her missive efficiently promoted the concept of this rich, cryptic system, and the idea took hold and spread widely among the French and British upper classes.[18,19]

FIG. 4. Workshop of the Master of the First Prayer Book of Maximilian (Flemish, active about 1475–1515), *Saint Clara with a Monstrance*, from *Spinola Hours*, ca. 1510–1520. Tempera colors, gold, and ink on parchment, 9⅛ x 6⁹⁄₁₆ in. (23.2 x 16.7 cm). The J. Paul Getty Museum, Los Angeles, 83.ML.114.267v (object number), Ms. Ludwig IX 18, fol. 267v (manuscript number)

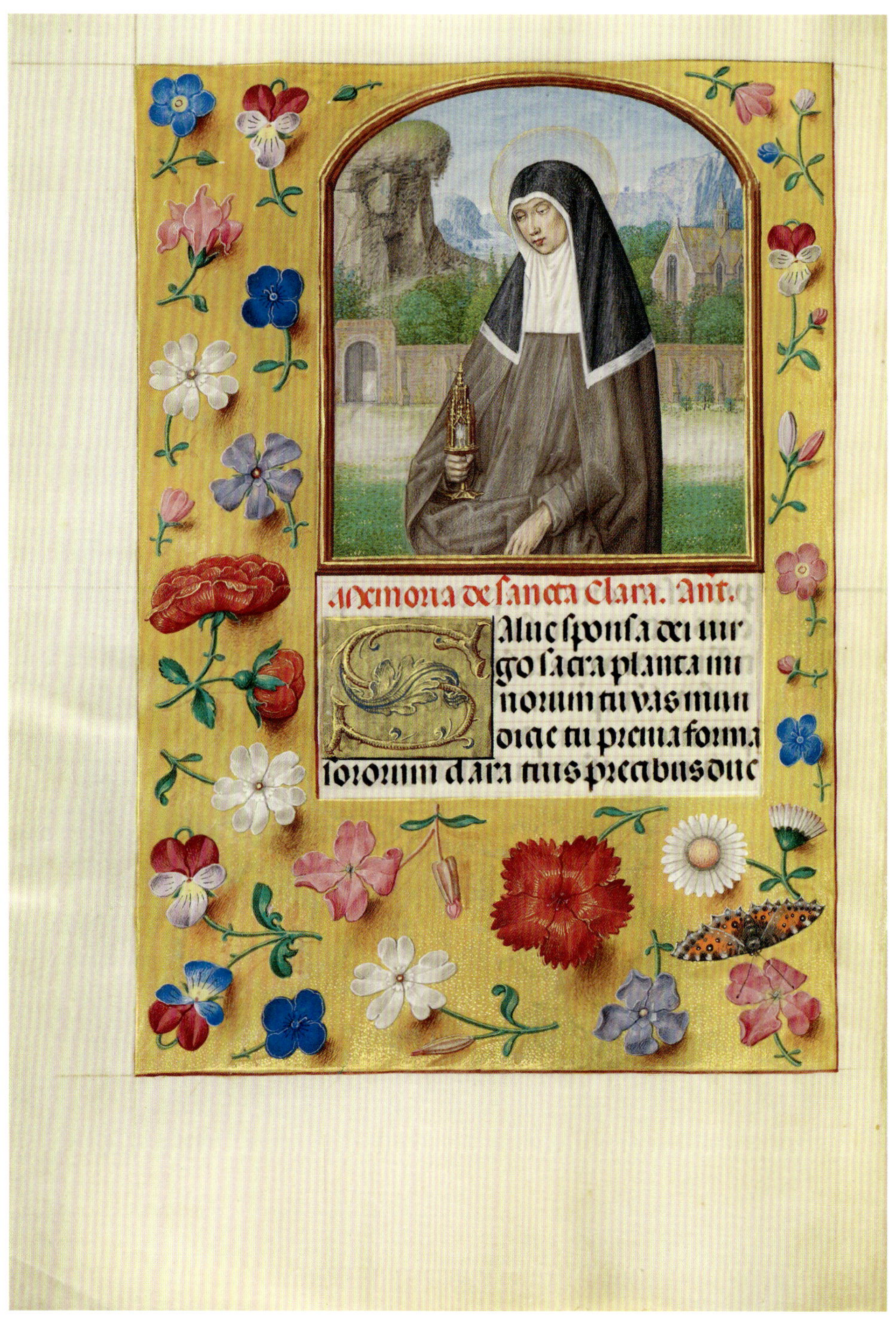

Charlotte de Latour's *Le Langage des Fleurs* (1819), the first formalized floral dictionary of its kind, is believed to have been influenced in part by Montagu's letters, though it primarily drew upon French and classical literature for its definitions.[20] Printed in Paris, *Le Langage des Fleurs* was swiftly translated into other languages, widely disseminating the concept of a coded floral language. An English translation first became available in 1834, and its influence, aided by legions of imitations, permeated Victorian art, literature, and material culture. The Victorian period also saw the introduction of an unprecedented number of plants to England, and the vogue for floral symbolism coincided with radical modern developments in botany and horticulture.[21]

The floral-dictionary format pioneered by De Latour usually lists flowers in alphabetical order, with each entry accompanied by a brief text about the flower's symbolic meanings. Occasionally, individual entries featured poetry, anecdotes, biblical verses, or botanical details, while some were paired with color chromolithographed plates. Texts also sometimes alluded to the much larger history of plant symbolism across diverse regions, mythologies, and systems of belief, reminding readers that, throughout human history, flowers have always been interwoven with our symbolic systems.[22] These dictionaries frequently included additional appendices that catalogued flowers according to the feelings or ideas they represented, allowing the reader to first consider the concept they aimed to convey and then easily identify the appropriate blossom that matched their sentiments. Readers could also design more precise messages by following guidance regarding the encoded status of a flower's particular color, its maturity, or its placement within a larger, cryptic arrangement known as a "tussie-mussie."

However, contrary to the ways in which floriography is often portrayed by contemporary Victorianists as something that was universally employed and understood, the codified language of flowers was neither standardized nor used widely beyond a particular social milieu. Today, many erroneously believe that the Victorian language of flowers was a socially agreed-upon symbolic language that men and women used broadly to exchange covert messages, allowing a woman to decipher complex emotional missives by effectively translating a bouquet.[23] In reality, the language of flowers functioned more as a hobby for the wealthy — a parlor game for the entertainment of an elite segment of the population, for whom precise definitions were not sacred. In fact, the literature that accounted for the nineteenth-century language of flowers was widely adapted, distorted, and plagiarized by writers and publishers at will.

By the mid-nineteenth century, flowers were a commodity and status symbol, as well as envoys of a semi-private language shared among these leisure-class hobbyists. While some middle-class women may have associated lavender with mistrust, bluebells with constancy, and oleander with warning, the language of flowers was largely an affectation of the wealthy.[24] Around 1865, board games inspired by the language of flowers were published in French, German, and English.[25] In Britain and the United States, floriography also became the subject of other amusements, including cigarette cards, chromolithograph postcards, and greeting cards.[26] The persistent nurturing of this floral language resulted in a surprisingly rich lexicon: in her 1993 book *Tussie-Mussies: The Victorian Art of Expressing Yourself in the Language of Flowers*, Geraldine Adamich Laufer compiles a comprehensive list totaling more than 850 varieties of plants, including flowers, trees, and vines, all with their own associations and meanings.[27] With every iteration, the language of flowers grew more comprehensive, incorporating new horticultural developments and discoveries.

Floriography took on new dimensions in the United States, where an even wider variety of plants provided opportunities for American writers to create their own definitions. While some American texts included "traditional" definitions largely plagiarized from earlier French and English publications, others featured arbitrary and idiosyncratic meanings, such as "rural happiness" for China asters (cat. no. 2) or "flattery" for chrysanthemums. Middle- and upper-class American women adopted the pastime, aided by parlor games, flower clocks and calendars, and popular magazines such as *Harper's Monthly Magazine* and *Godey's Lady's Book*, which frequently referenced floriography in volumes after 1860. Popular fiction, textbooks, articles, and poetry further disseminated the language of flowers — albeit with an American accent.[28]

Although floriography faded in popularity in the first half of the twentieth century, the Victorian revival of the 1960s and 1970s reintroduced the language of flowers to new audiences. Previously out of print for decades, once-popular titles began to be republished in facsimile, including *Mrs. Burke's Language of Flowers* (first published in 1920 and reissued in facsimile in 1963) and Kate Greenaway's *Language of Flowers* (first published in 1884 and reissued in facsimile in 1978).[29] The "flower power" aesthetics of the 1960s and 1970s were well suited to the drama and whimsy of the Victorian language of flowers, which complemented the larger milieu of counterculture fashion, art, and material culture.

Recent decades have again seen another revival of interest in floriography, with many new titles appearing on the subject within the past few years. Both S. Theresa Dietz's lavishly illustrated *The Complete Language of Flowers: A Definitive and Illustrated History* (2020) and Jessica Roux's *Floriography: An Illustrated Guide to the Victorian Language of Flowers* (2020) adapt the traditional Victorian format for twenty-first-century readers who may be discovering this symbolic language anew. Other contemporary audiences may have discovered the narrative power of floral symbolism for the first time upon reading about Kehinde Wiley's celebrated portrait of Barack Obama — its jasmine, chrysanthemums, and African blue lilies each alluding to an essential aspect of the president's complex biography.

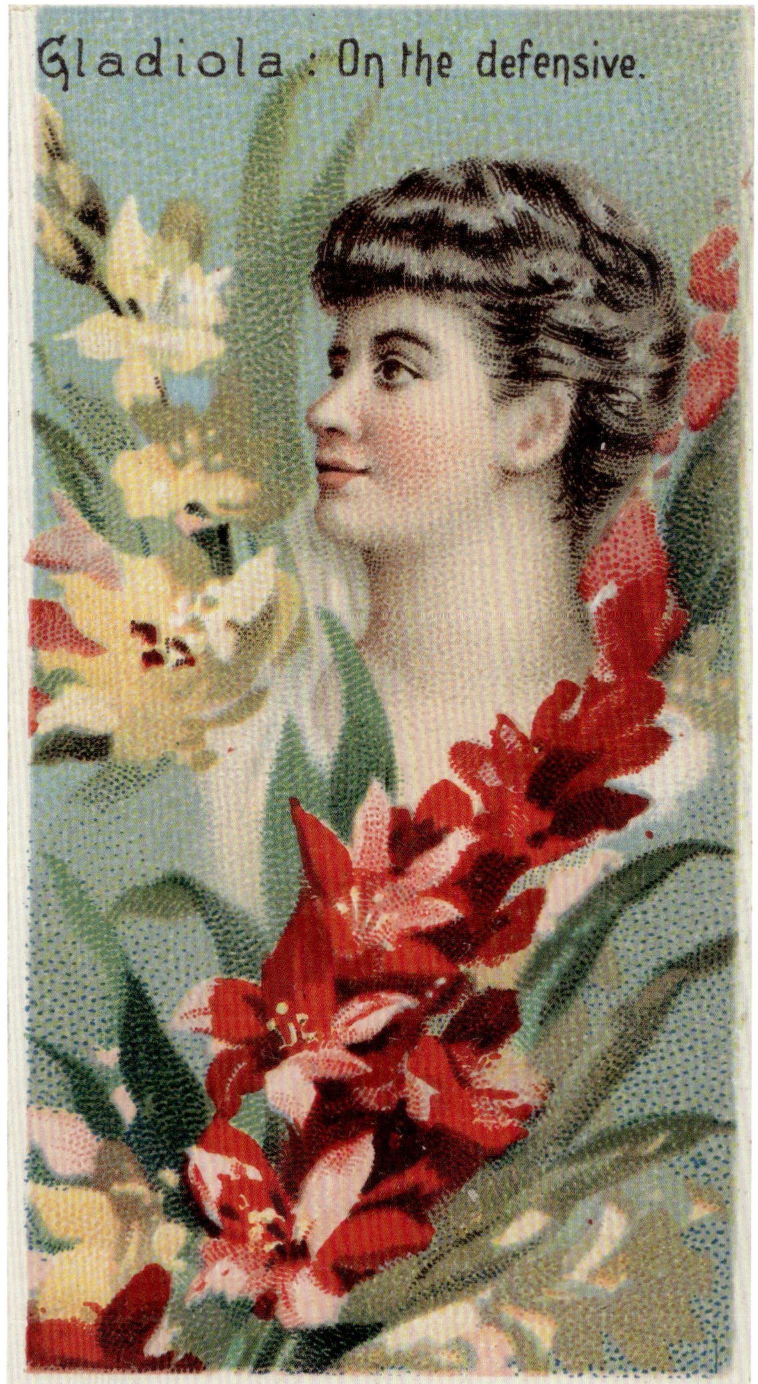

FIG. 5. "Gladiola: On the Defensive," from the series *Floral Beauties and Language of Flowers* (N75) for Duke brand cigarettes, 1892. Issued by Duke Cigarette branch of the American Tobacco Company. Lithograph by Donaldson Brothers (American, New York), 1892. Commercial color lithograph, 2¾ x 1½ in. (7 x 3.8 cm). The Metropolitan Museum of Art, New York, The Jefferson R. Burdick Collection, Gift of Jefferson R. Burdick, 63.350.204.75.16

The Language of Flowers in the Permanent Collection of the Fine Arts Museums of San Francisco

This volume aims to draw upon the rich history of the language of flowers in order to offer a new perspective on the permanent collection of the Fine Arts Museums of San Francisco. By examining well-known masterpieces through a cross-disciplinary floral lens, we open ourselves to the possibilities of seeing familiar artworks anew: a branch of azaleas recalls lines of poetry from the *Man'yōshū*, the oldest extant collection of Japanese verse first compiled in 759 CE (see cat. no. 3); the deep purple irises of a stained-glass window suggest the myth of Iris, the Greek goddess who carried messages of love from heaven to Earth (see cat. no. 22); and a lemon blossom atop a piece of French soft-paste porcelain evokes the lyrics of a 1960s pop song (see cat. no. 25). These connections reinforce an essential aspect of art appreciation: if approached with a keen eye, an open heart, and a curious mind, any artwork can be placed at the center of its own galaxy of associations.

The title *Bouquets of Art: A Flower Dictionary from the Fine Arts Museums of San Francisco* pays tribute to Bouquets to Art, the celebrated visual spectacle that has been held annually at the de Young museum since 1985 and inspired this volume. For the week-long event, talented floral artists from all over the Bay Area offer their interpretations of beloved museum objects in arrangements composed of fresh flowers. Each year, this event unifies the natural beauty of the de Young's setting in Golden Gate Park with a legion of original floral displays inside the museum, presented in conversation with the works that inspired them. Funds from Bouquets to Art help underwrite special exhibitions, conservation projects, and educational programs at the Legion of Honor and the de Young, and this publication honors this event's rich history and the visionary volunteers who make it possible. This floral dictionary is dedicated to all those who have helped truly make the Fine Arts Museums a place for flowers.

FIG. 6. Florine Stettheimer's *Still Life with Flowers* (1921, cat. no. 39) on view in Bouquets to Art at the de Young, 2019

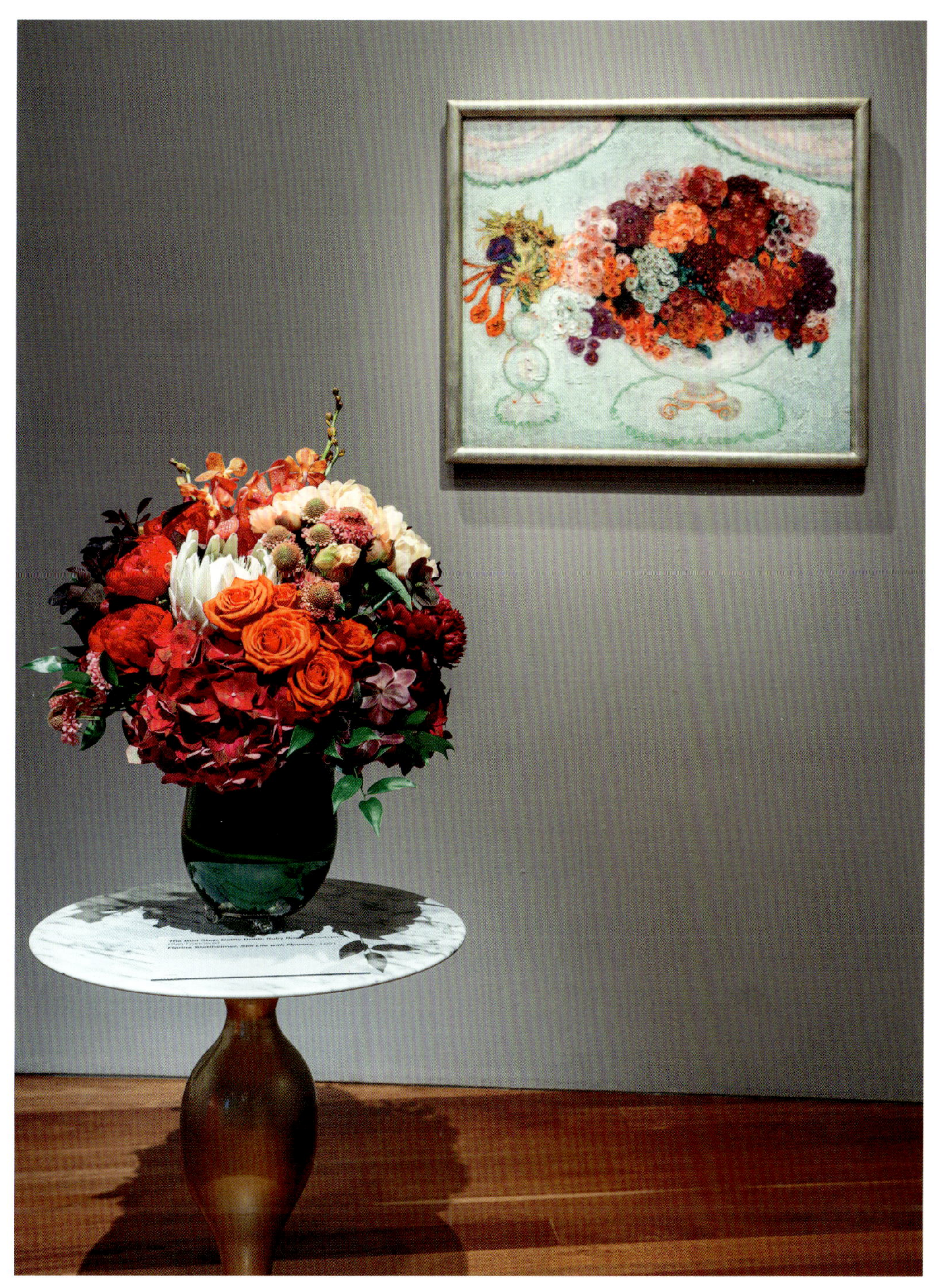

1 Ernst Lehner and Johanna Lehner, *Folklore and Symbolism of Flowers, Plants and Trees: With Over 200 Rare and Unusual Floral Designs and Illustrations* (Mineola, New York: Dover Publications, 2004), 11–12.

2 Kim Sajet, "In Obama's Official Portrait the Flowers Are Cultivated from the Past." *Smithsonian Magazine* (February 20, 2018). smithsonianmag.com/smithsonian-institution/obamas-official-portrait-flowers-cultivated-from-past-180968200, accessed January 27, 2021.

3 Dr. W.D. Spanton, "Water Lilies of Egypt," *Ancient Egypt, Part 1* (London: Macmillan and Co., 1917), 9.

4 For more on the rose of Sharon and lily of the valley, see the Song of Solomon 2:1, 2:2, 2:16, and 4:5.

5 Ernst Lehner and Johanna Lehner, *Folklore and Symbolism of Flowers, Plants and Trees: With Over 200 Rare and Unusual Floral Designs and Illustrations* (Mineola, New York: Dover Publications, 2004), 12.

6 "The earliest known grave that contains flowers is at a Natufian burial ground in Israel that is fourteen thousand years old." Sue Stuart-Smith, *The Well-Gardened Mind: The Restorative Power of Nature* (New York: Scribner, 2020), 143.

7 Luís Manuel Mendonça de Carvalho, "The Symbolic Uses of Plants." In *Ethnobiology,* edited by E.N. Anderson, Deborah M. Pearsall, Eugene S. Hunn, Nancy J. Turner, and Richard I. Ford (Hoboken, New Jersey: Wiley-Blackwell, 2011), 357–358.

8 For more on floral symbolism in the classical world, see Annette Giesecke, *The Mythology of Plants: Botanical Lore from Ancient Greece and Rome* (Los Angeles: J. Paul Getty Museum, 2014).

9 Elizabeth Haig, *The Floral Symbolism of the Great Masters* (London: Kegan Paul, Trench, Trübner & Co. Ltd., 1913), 9–10.

10 Elizabeth Haig, *The Floral Symbolism of the Great Masters* (London: Kegan Paul, Trench, Trübner & Co. Ltd., 1913), 28.

11 Paul Carus, "Poems of Confucius: Translated in Verse by Paul Carus." In *The Open Court,* vol. 27, no. 691 (December 1913), 734.

12 Merrily C. Baird, *Symbols of Japan: Thematic Motifs in Art and Design* (New York: Rizzoli, 2001), 10.

13 Amanda Luu, Ivanka Matsuba, and M.K. Sadler, *Ikebana Unbound: A Modern Approach to the Ancient Japanese Art of Flower Arranging* (New York: Artisan, 2020), 10.

14 Celia Fisher, *Flowers in Medieval Manuscripts* (Toronto: University of Toronto Press, 2004), 4–5.

15 Elizabeth Hyde, *Cultivated Power: Flowers, Culture, and Politics in the Reign of Louis XIV* (Philadelphia: University of Pennsylvania Press, 2005), 3.

16 Lady Montagu writes, "There is no colour, no flower, no weed, no fruit, herb, pebble, or feather that has not a verse belonging to it; and you may quarrel, reproach or send letters of passion, friendship or civility, or even of news, without ever inking your fingers." Lord Wharncliffe, ed. *The Letters and Works of Lady Wortley Montagu* (London: George Bell and Sons, 1898), 227.

17 Nancy Strow Sheley, "The 'Language of Flowers' as Coded Subtext: Conflicted Messages of Domesticity in Mary Wilkins Freeman's Short Fiction." *Working Papers on Design* 2 (2007), 5–14.

18 Edith Gülçin Ambros, "The 'Language of Flowers' and Ottoman Don Juans (*Zenpāres*)." *Wiener Zeitschrift für die Kunde des Morgenlandes,* vol. 95 (2005), 19.

19 Brent Elliott, "The Victorian Language of Flowers." *Occasional Papers from the RHS Lindley Library*, vol. 10 (December 2013), the Lindley Library, the Royal Horticultural Society, London, 10.

20 Brent Elliott, "The Victorian Language of Flowers." *Occasional Papers from the RHS Lindley Library*, vol. 10 (December 2013), the Lindley Library, the Royal Horticultural Society, London, 21. Elliott also notes that "Charlotte de Latour" was actually a pseudonym, identifying the book's author as Louise Cortambert.

21 Elizabeth A. Campbell, "Don't Say It with Nightshades: Sentimental Botany and the Natural History of 'Atropa Belladonna.'" *Victorian Literature and Culture* 35, no. 2 (2007), 607.

22 Luís Manuel Mendonça de Carvalho, "The Symbolic Uses of Plants." In *Ethnobiology*, edited by E.N. Anderson, Deborah M. Pearsall, Eugene S. Hunn, Nancy J. Turner, and Richard I. Ford (Hoboken, New Jersey: Wiley-Blackwell, 2011), 362.

23 Beverly Seaton, *The Language of Flowers: A History* (Charlottesville: University Press of Virginia, 1995), 1.

24 Tania O'Donnell, *A History of Courtship* (Barnsley, UK: Pen and Sword Books, 2017), 108.

25 The Lindley Libraries of the Royal Horticultural Society, London, holds a copy of a game, ca. 1865, with instructions and an accompanying floral dictionary in three languages (French, German, and English), titled "*Das Reich der Blumenkönigin. Sinnige Unterhaltung. / L'empire de la reine des fleurs. Récréation raisonnée.* / The realm of the queen of flowers. Rational entertainment."

26 Brent Elliott, "The Victorian Language of Flowers." *Occasional Papers from the RHS Lindley Library* 10 (December 2013), the Lindley Library, the Royal Horticultural Society, London, 48.

27 Geraldine Adamich Laufer, *Tussie-Mussies: The Victorian Art of Expressing Yourself in the Language of Flowers* (New York: Workman, 2000), 12.

28 Nancy Strow Sheley, "The 'Language of Flowers' as Coded Subtext: Conflicted Messages of Domesticity in Mary Wilkins Freeman's Short Fiction." *Working Papers on Design* 2 (2007), 5–14.

29 Brent Elliott, "The Victorian Language of Flowers." *Occasional Papers from the RHS Lindley Library* 10 (December 2013), the Lindley Library, the Royal Horticultural Society, London, 49.

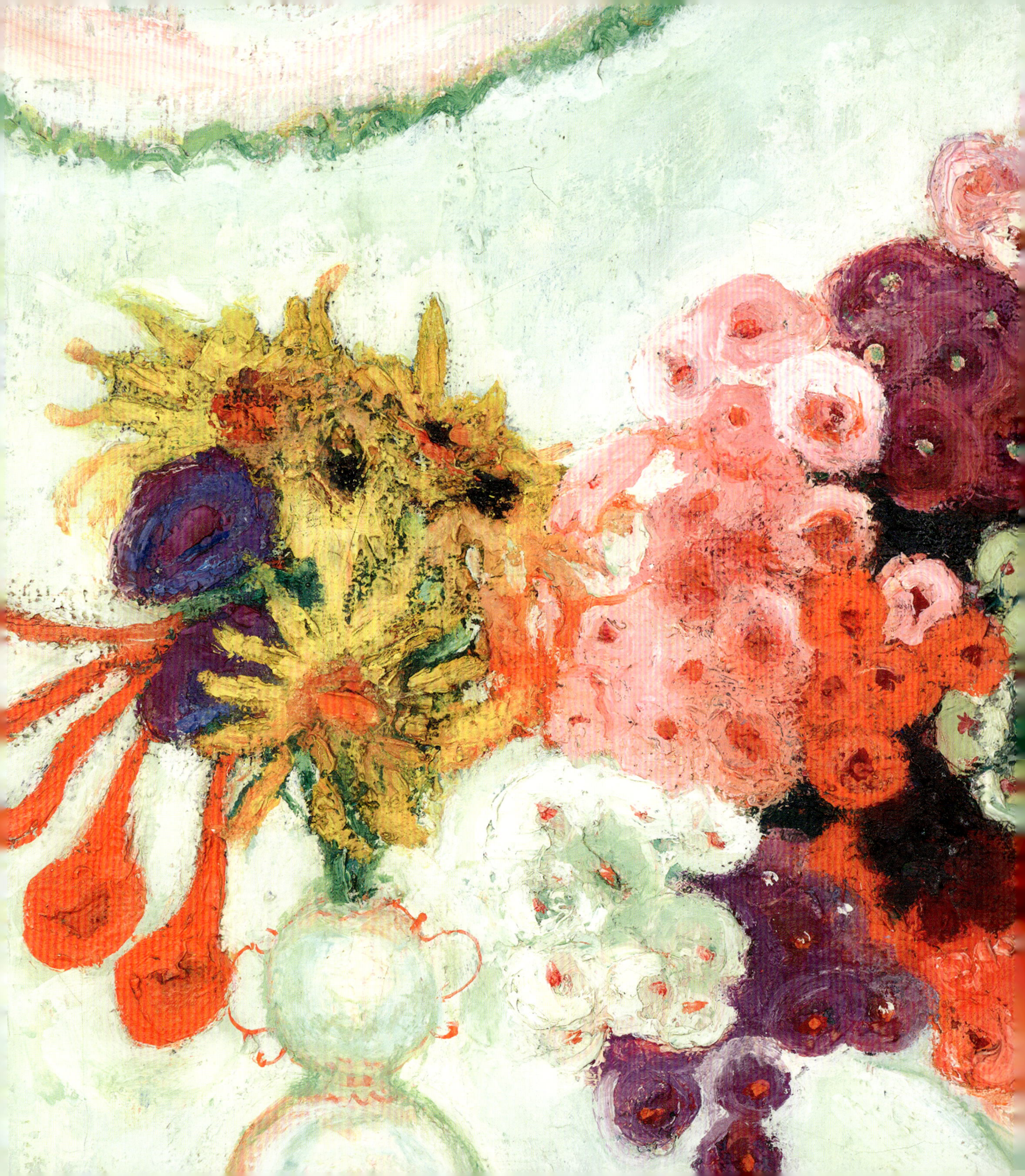

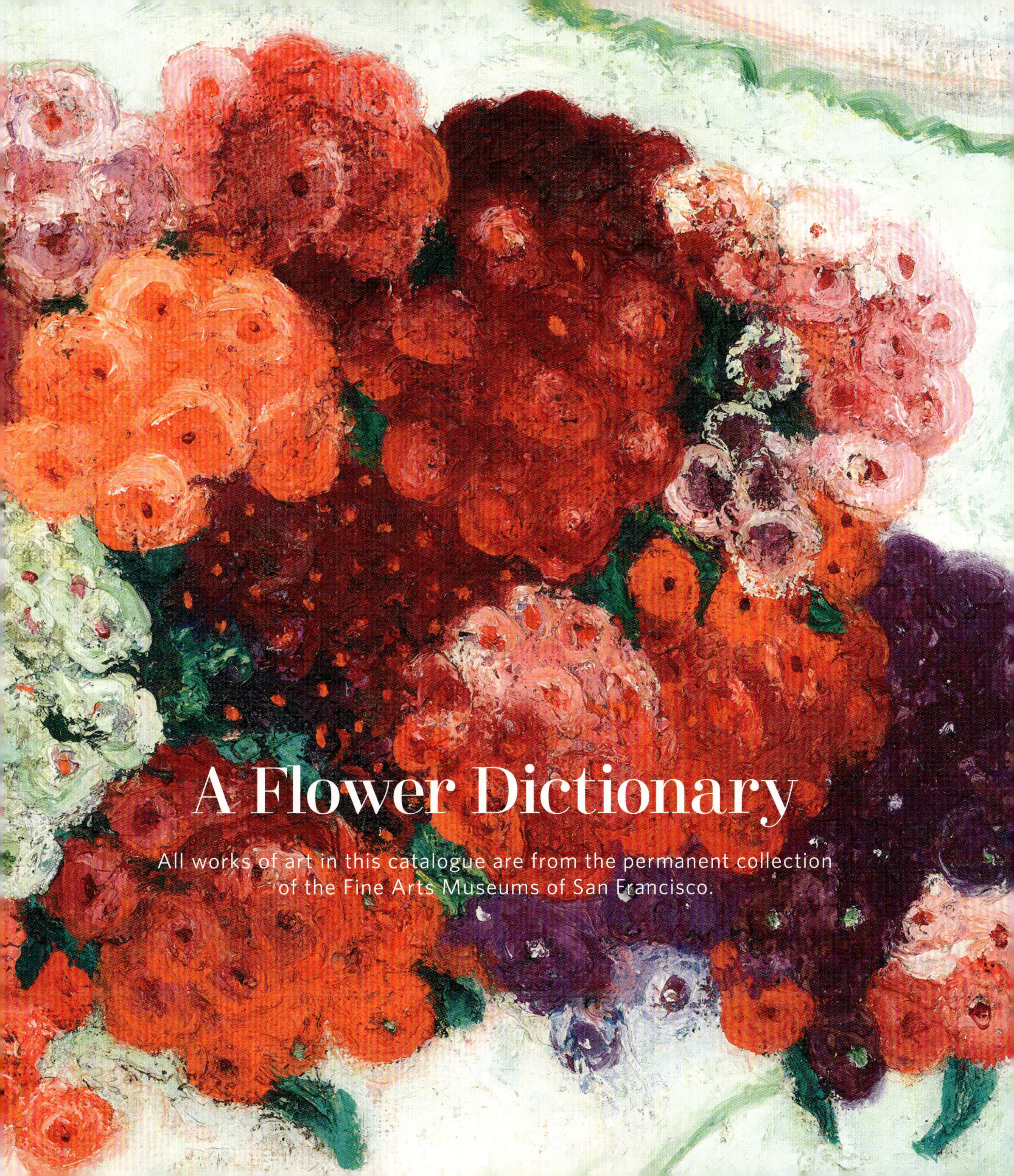

A Flower Dictionary

All works of art in this catalogue are from the permanent collection of the Fine Arts Museums of San Francisco.

Anemone

Expectation, anticipation

NATIVE TO THE MEDITERRANEAN, the anemone's name derives from *anemos*, the Greek word for wind. Also known as a windflower, the anemone can blossom in the earliest days of spring and thrive in exposed and windy environments. It is rich in associations: the mythological Greek goddess Aphrodite, grieving for Adonis after his death, cried as she held him in her arms, and the first anemone grew when her tears mixed with his blood. Another myth describes Anemone as a nymph beloved by the Greek wind god Zephyr. Jealous of her beauty, Chloris, wife of Zephyr and goddess of flowers, banished her and transformed her into the flower that now bears her name. In addition to its associations with heartbreak, the anemone possesses ominous connotations across cultures: in China it is closely affiliated with death. In ancient Egypt, the anemone was regarded as an emblem of sickness, while the Romans used these flowers to garland the deceased.

Painter and etcher Theodore Roussel captures the delicacy of the anemone in this simple still-life print — an example of the artist's contributions to the development of color printmaking. Roussel's anemones, banded by an elegiac black frame, appear to complement interpretations from contemporary floriography guides: the Victorian language of flowers often associates the wild anemone with brevity and anticipation, since they bloom for such a short time. The cultivated varieties are usually representative of expectation or being "forsaken"— a reference to the wretched myths of the flower's origin.

1 | Theodore Roussel (French, 1847–1926), *Anemones*, 1899
Color etching and drypoint, 11¾ x 10½ in. (29.8 x 26.7 cm)
Museum purchase, Achenbach Foundation for Graphic Arts Endowment Fund, 1981.1.84

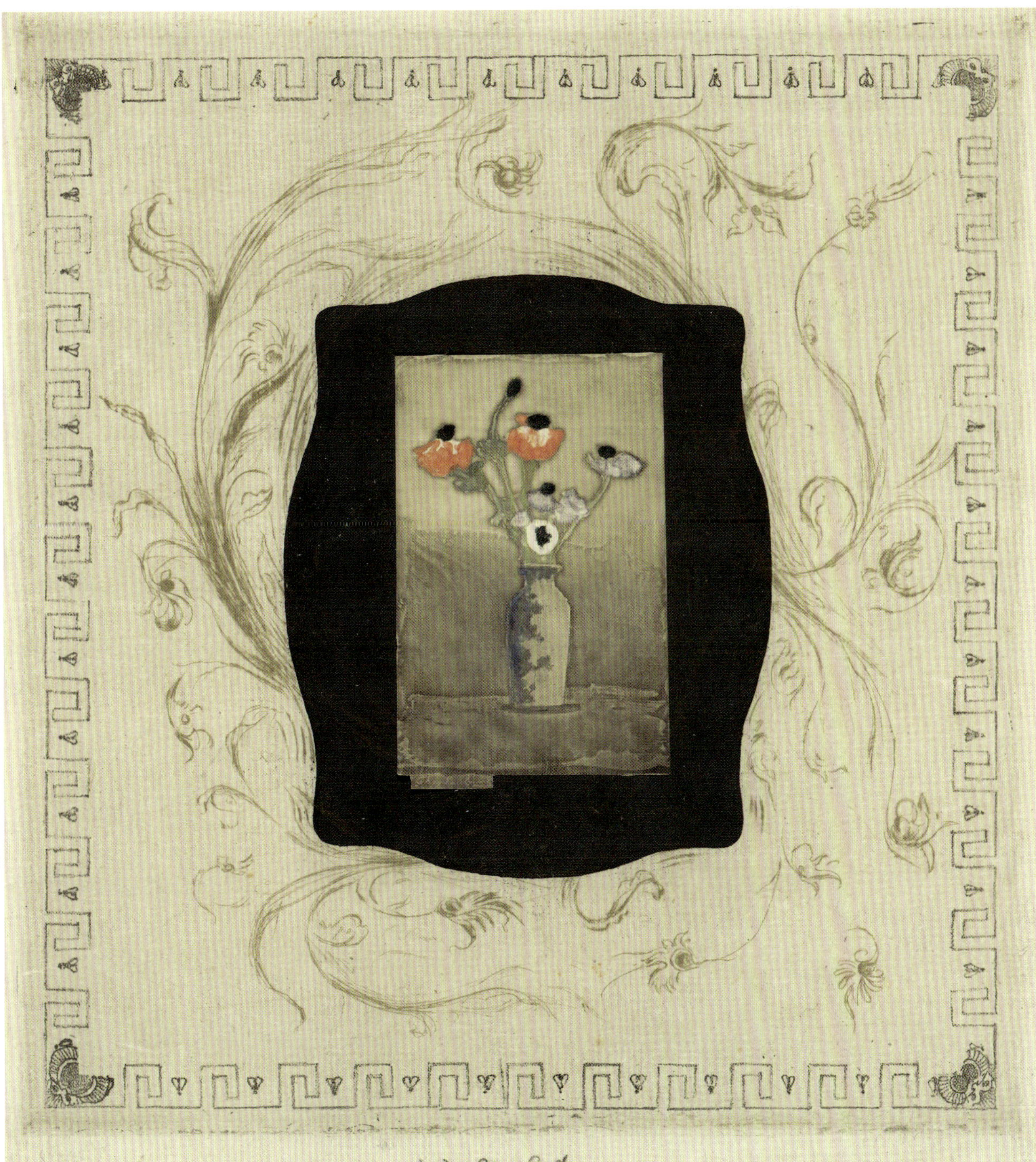
not counted

Aster

Afterthought, variety

ASTERS ARE ANCIENT wildflowers long believed to possess magical powers. It is believed that one can plant *Aster amellus* as a wish for love or carry it to win affection. The name comes from the Greek word *aster*, meaning "star," and may derive from the way in which the petals radiate from the center like rays of light. There is also a myth that the goddess Astrea, transformed into the constellation Virgo, scattered stardust on the earth and asters grew in the fields. Asters are said to symbolize afterthought because they blossom in late summer and early autumn after many other flowers have faded for the year. China asters, of the genus *Callistephus*, are particularly popular. Native to the temperate regions of China and Korea, this colorful species is synonymous with variety.

American artist Charles Burchfield explored the landscapes of upstate New York and closely studied what he called "the healthy glamour of everyday life." Wildflowers are particularly numerous among Burchfield's subjects, including this view of a wild, impassable field in full autumnal bloom. In a notebook believed to be from around 1912 or 1913, he recorded a list of 125 "Flowers I Know." Later, in the same volume, he expanded his "List of Flowers" to include 304 varieties. In 1953, he wrote in his journal upon viewing a field of asters in Gardenville, New York: "The full glory of September — warm and gentle S.W. wind. Asters and goldenrod in such great profusion — I cannot get my fill of looking at them."

2 | Charles E. Burchfield (American, 1893–1967), *September*, 1949–1956
Watercolor over graphite, sheet: 21 13/16 x 48 1/16 in. (55.4 x 122 cm)
Gift of Mr. and Mrs. John D. Rockefeller 3rd, 1993.35.2

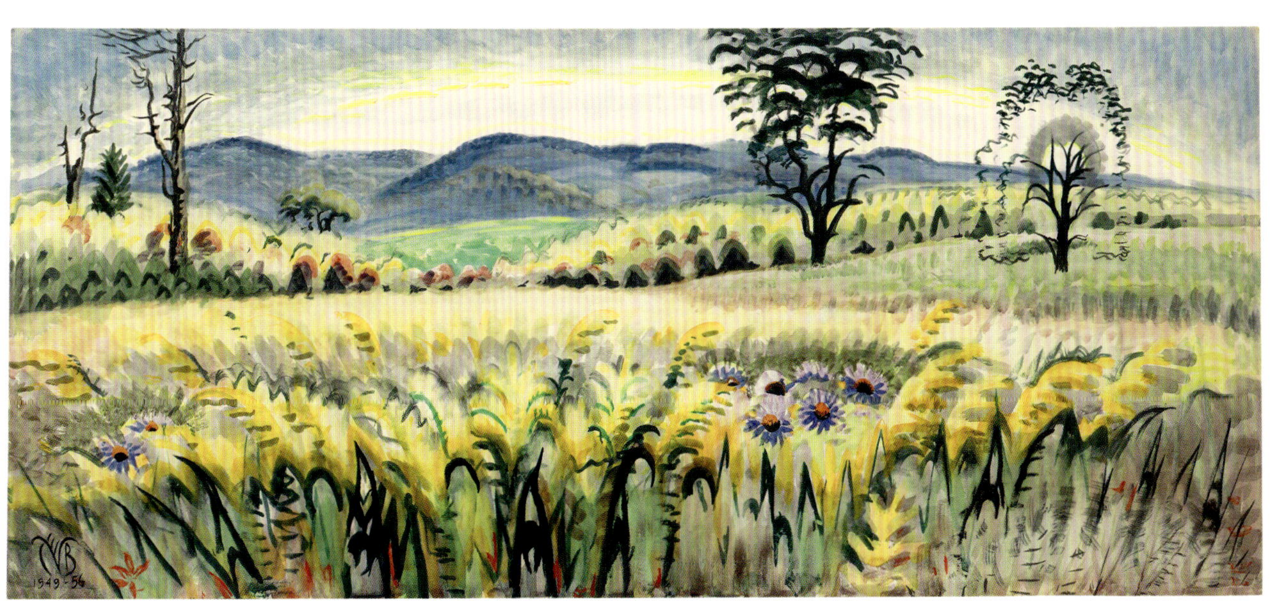

Azalea

Temperance

MANY AZALEAS ARE BELIEVED to be native to Japan, where they were mentioned in the *Man'ōshū*, or "Collection of Ten Thousand Leaves," the oldest extant collection of Japanese verse first compiled in 759 CE: "That path through the azaleas / Blooming thick on the rocky margin / Of the meandering stream / Shall I ever see it again?" In 1692, the famed gardener Ito-Ihei III wrote *Kinshumakura*, an illustrated guide to azaleas that included more than three hundred varieties he had developed. Azaleas may have traveled with Buddhist monks from Japan to China, where they developed symbolic associations with womanhood. The English name comes from the Greek word *azaleos*, meaning "dry." Azaleas are more likely to thrive in challenging environments than in nutrient-rich soil, which led to this flower's association with temperance.

Charles Caryl Coleman was an American expatriate artist who lived in Rome after the US Civil War. This painting belongs to Coleman's larger series of about fourteen works featuring various depictions of elegant flowers arranged in harmony with decorative objects drawn from the artist's eclectic personal collection. With an elongated format resembling a Chinese or Japanese scroll painting and featuring lavish, attenuated azalea branches placed in a Japanese jardinière, or ornamental pot, *Azaleas and Apple Blossoms* demonstrates how artists and writers affiliated with the Aesthetic Movement inventively combined elements of design from the East and West, past and present. One contemporary review praised Coleman's still lifes for their "thousand charms which the ordinary spectator would never discover."

3 | Charles Caryl Coleman (American, 1840–1928), *Azaleas and Apple Blossoms*, 1879
Oil on canvas, 71¼ x 25 in. (181 x 63.5 cm)
Museum purchase, Roscoe and Margaret Oakes Income Fund, gift of Barbro and Bernard Osher, J. Burgess & Elizabeth Jamieson Endowment Fund, and bequest of William A. Stimson, 2008.9

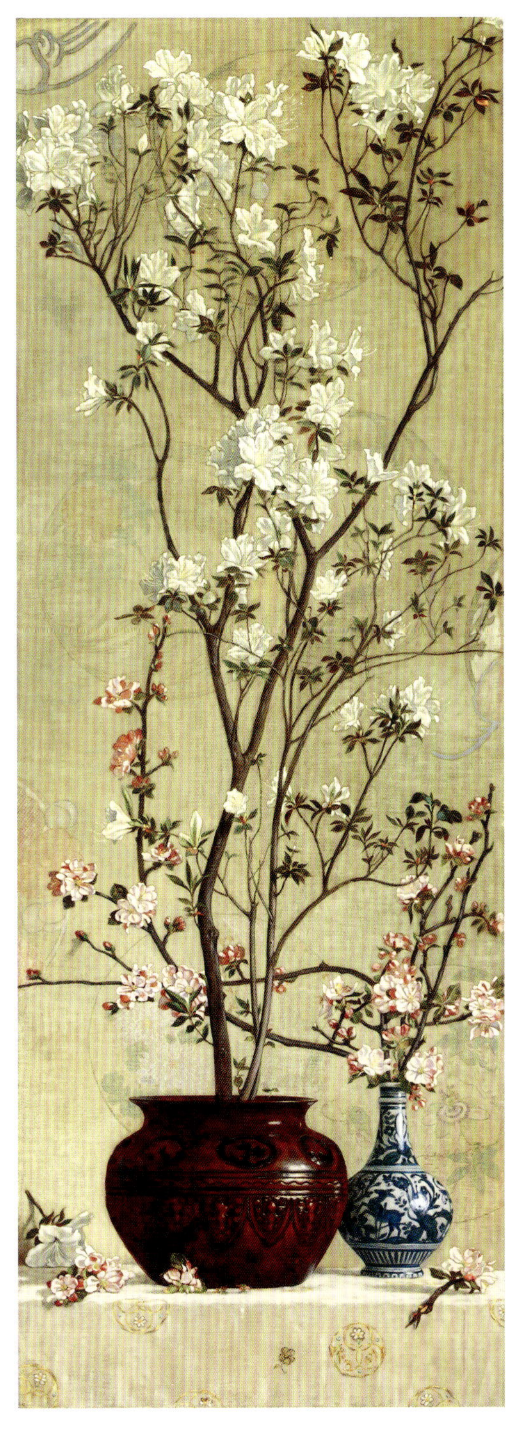

Bluebell

Constancy, sorrowful regret

"The Bluebell is the sweetest flower / That waves in summer air: /
Its blossoms have the mightiest power / To soothe my spirit's care."
— Emily Brontë, "The Bluebell," 1846

THIS SIMPLE FLOWER is particularly prevalent in the United Kingdom, which is home to about half of the world's bluebell population. A symbol of constancy in the Victorian language of flowers, the bluebell is associated with St. George, and in much of England, it was once customary to wear bluebells on St. George's Day (April 23). In parts of Scotland, the bluebell was called "The aul' man's bell" (devil's bell) and left untouched in the field. Others believed bluebells were fairies' flowers and that disturbing them was unlucky. British folklore also held that wearing a garland of bluebells would compel you to tell the truth.

Bluebells are featured among the intricate floral patterns of this tapestry designed by Edward Burne-Jones and woven by Morris and Company. Burne-Jones and William Morris were affiliated with the influential Pre-Raphaelite Brotherhood, a group of English painters, poets, and art critics who rebelled against the tastes of the Royal Academy and shared a devotion to the "simple chastity of nature." Morris promoted a medieval-inflected tapestry weaving revival, and he tasked Burne-Jones with designing the central figural composition for *Flora*, which Morris and his weavers surrounded with stylized flowers. Burne-Jones also played with the conventional language of flowers in his watercolor album *The Flower Book* (1882–1898), which features interpretive illustrations of the poetic names of some floral varieties.

4 | Edward Burne-Jones (English, 1833–1898), designer
Morris and Company (1861–1940), manufacturer
Flora, 1886–1920
Cotton warp, wool, and silk weft; slit- and double interlocking-tapestry weave
69 5/16 x 40 3/16 in. (176 x 102 cm)
Museum purchase, Dorothy Spreckels Munn Bequest Fund, 2001.120.1

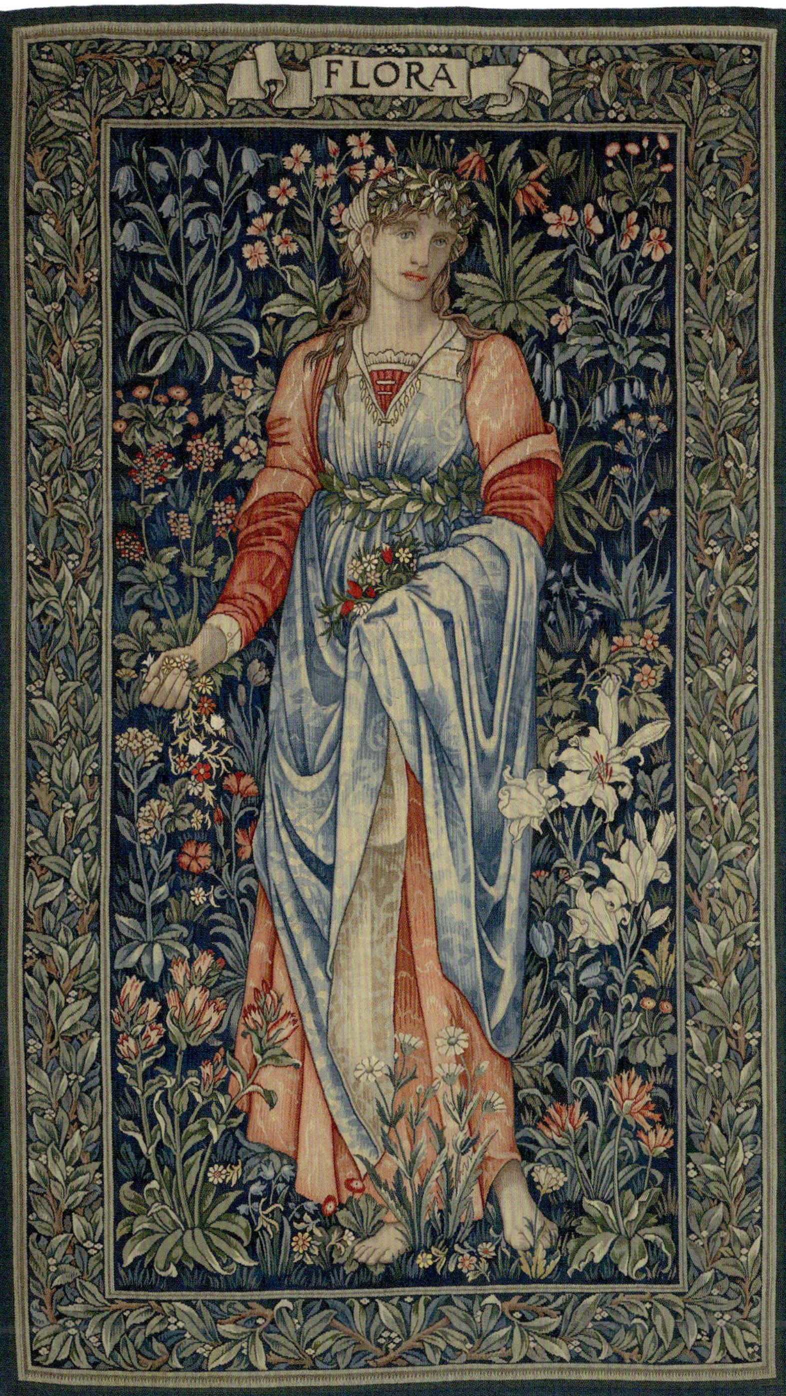
FLORA
MERTON ABBEY 1920

Bleeding Heart

Love

THE POPULAR NAME for the arching displays of small pink-and-white *Lamprocapnos spectabilis* refers to its resemblance to a heart and its pendant "drops." Native to Japan, Korea, and China, the common bleeding heart was introduced to Western gardens by Scottish botanist and plant hunter Robert Fortune, who was hired by the Horticultural Society of London to collect plants from foreign countries. In 1846, he collected bleeding heart specimens from a grotto garden in China's Zhoushan archipelago, and the flower proliferated in Europe and the United States, where it came to represent true love. It is believed that bleeding hearts can also prophesy one's romantic fate: if you crush the flower and the juice runs red, your love is reciprocated. If the juice is white, your intended does not share your sentiments.

San Francisco artist Clare Rojas works across media, including painting, printmaking, installation, and video. Affiliated with the "San Francisco Mission School," her work straddles high art and popular culture. The silhouette-like *Bleeding Hearts*, with its network of stems recalling arms outstretched, belongs to a series of floral prints inspired by imagery found in traditional American arts. Rojas explains, "I grew up in a house with Mom's quilts everywhere — across from the cow field with green and blue and red barns. My dad is Peruvian, so he had all this South American folk art . . . All that was just part of my background. Quilts are full of icons . . . that people have used forever. It's there for the taking."

5 | Clare Rojas (American, b. 1976), *Bleeding Hearts*, 2009
Color sugar-lift aquatint, printed chine collé, 14 x 11 in. (35.6 x 27.9 cm)
Published by Paulson Press
Berkeley Foundation purchase, Phyllis C. Wattis Fund for Major Accessions, 2015.37.395

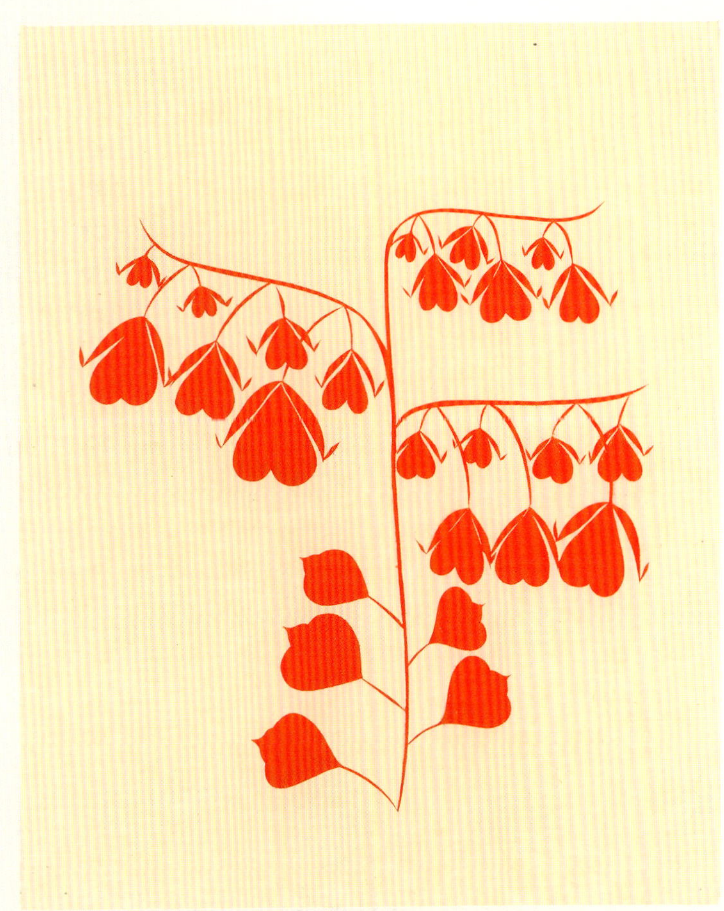

Calla Lily

Feminine beauty, modesty

THE STRIKING *Zantedeschia aethiopica*, native to South Africa, derives its common name from the Greek word *kalos*, meaning "beautiful." Believed to be one of the oldest-known flowers, calla lilies are said to grow wherever Eve's tears of regret and penitence fell upon the earth as she and Adam were expelled from the Garden of Eden. Popularized in Great Britain and the United States during the Victorian period, calla lilies became a common feature of both bridal bouquets and funeral decorations. Documentary photographs show that Queen Victoria was crowned by a halo of calla lilies on her deathbed, in 1901. For those who associated these flowers with mourning, the calla lily became an unlucky plant, not to be brought indoors.

Calla lilies are recognized as a signature element in the work of Mexican artist Diego Rivera, who painted many heroic depictions of local flower vendors. In a career that spanned diverse media, Rivera frequently portrayed the daily lives of working people, and his images of women selling calla lilies are among his most iconic. In this drawing of a strong woman carrying a heavy basket overflowing with these flowers, Rivera offers a testament to the beauty of the calla lilies and the dignity of labor. With its distinctive, elegant shape, the calla lily became an appealing subject for many modernists and enjoyed heightened popularity as an artistic subject in the 1920s and 1930s.

6 | Diego Rivera (Mexican, 1886–1957), *A Good Load*, 1925
Brush and black ink over graphite, sheet: 12⅝ x 8¹⁵⁄₁₆ in. (32 x 22.7 cm)
Gift of Albert M. Bender, 1926.73

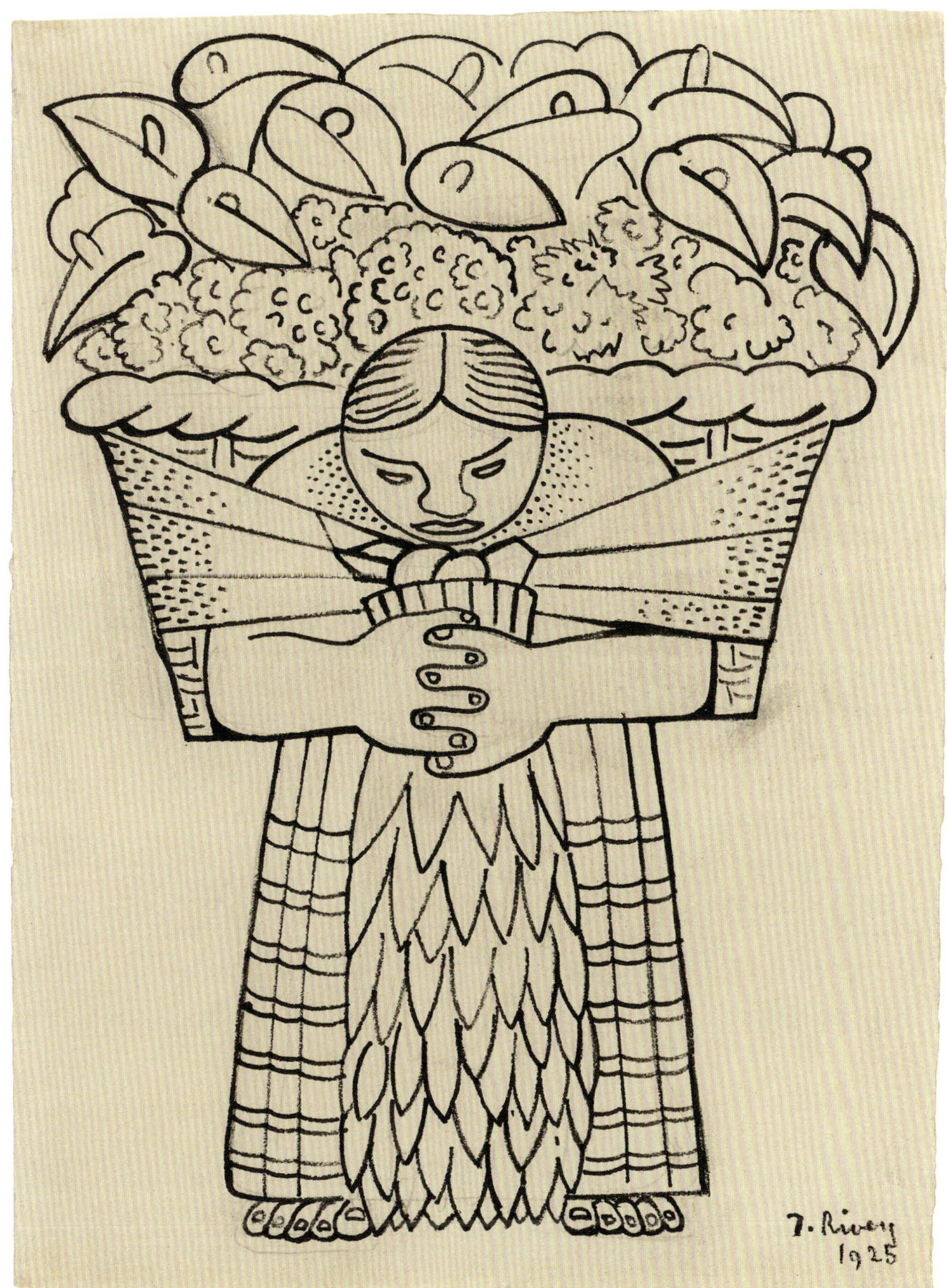
1925

Camellia

Unpretending excellence, perfect loveliness

"The chaste camellia's pure and spotless bloom / That boasts no fragrance, and conceals no thorn."
— William Roscoe, "Sonnet. — The Camellia," 1830

IN THE WEST, the camellia blossom has long been associated with excellence, loveliness, and perfection. Endemic to southeastern Asia, it has been associated there with longevity. Chinese legend tells of Emperor Shen Nong (2737–2697 BCE), credited as the originator of tea culture. It is said that one day, the emperor was about to drink boiled water when a gust of wind blew *Camellia sinensis* ("tea plant") leaves into his cup. He was pleased by the flavor and invigorated by the beverage. The camellia was popularized in France by Empress Joséphine Bonaparte (1763–1814), who cultivated her gardens at the Château de Malmaison with rare flowers from all over the world. Camellias would later become the signature flower of French fashion designer Gabrielle "Coco" Chanel.

Nakayama Sugakudo's print *No. 38 Shrike, Withered Oak, Water Camellia* (*Mozu karegashiwa fuyutsubaki*) illustrates the historical Japanese interest in camellia blossoms. Known in Japan as *tsubaki*, or "tree with shining leaves," camellias hold a special place in shrine and temple gardens, and songs describing events of the fourth and fifth centuries refer to the sacredness and beauty of this flower and its leaves. Camellias are not only a popular subject in Japanese prints but also a component of Japanese printmaking practices, as the oil from *C. sinensis* was traditionally used to help the baren (the rubbing-pad tool used in Japanese woodblock printing) slide smoothly during the printmaking process.

7 | Nakayama Sugakudo (Japanese, active 1850–1860)
No. 38 Shrike, Withered Oak, Water Camellia (*Mozu karegashiwa fuyutsubaki*)
from the series *Forty-Eight Birds Drawn from Life* (*Ikiutsushi yonjuhachiyo*), 1860
Color woodcut, 14½ x 9⅞ in. (36.9 x 25.1 cm). Published by Koeido (Tsutaya Kichizo), Edo (Tokyo)
Achenbach Foundation for Graphic Arts, 1963.30.5552

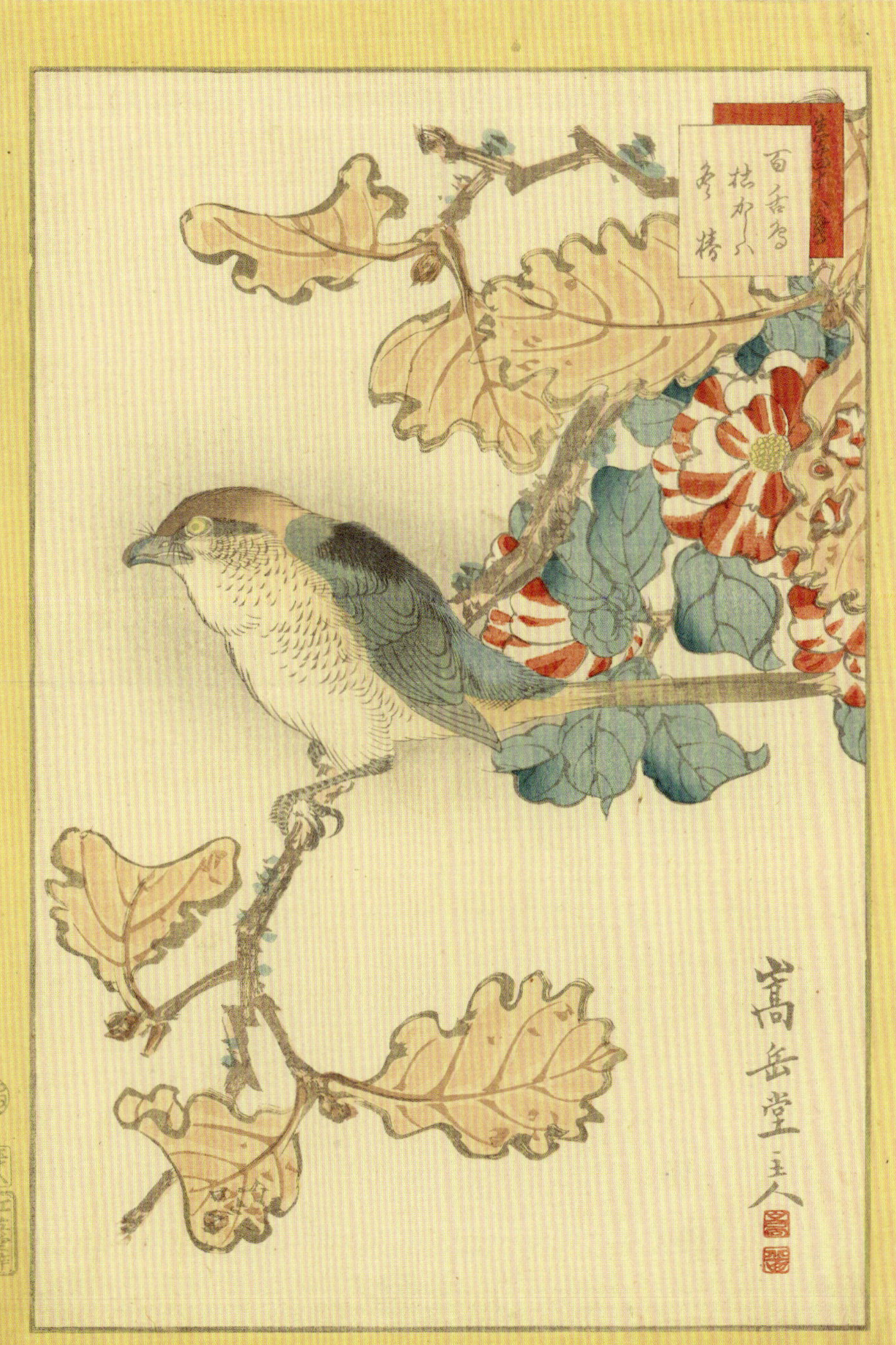
百舌鳥
枯かしハ
冬椿
嵩岳堂主人
三十八
紅英堂梓

Carnation

Disdain, antipathy, admiration

THE ATTRACTIVE APPEARANCE and sweet, spicy scent of carnations have made them popular across cultures for centuries. In Old Norse legend, carnations grew from the graves of young lovers. During the Renaissance, a carnation represented faithfulness. In the Victorian language of flowers, yellow carnations mean disdain and rejection, the striped variety signifies refusal, purple stands for antipathy, and red signals admiration. Pink carnations are associated with the Virgin Mary at the crucifixion and have become a symbol of a mother's love — in 1907 they were chosen as the official emblem for Mother's Day in the United States. In 1974, the Carnation Revolution overthrew the forty-eight-year dictatorship in Portugal. There, carnations became associated with liberty and political freedom, demonstrating how the language of flowers is constantly being rewritten.

In Japan, carnations are associated with love and good luck. Sumio Kawakami's *Carnations and Spoon on a Tray* depicts two stylized carnations in profile. In the corners of the print, Japanese characters appear to refer to wild mulberry or a boxwood tree (upper right), pomegranate (lower right), and flowers (upper left). A schoolteacher and self-taught artist, Kawakami is recognized for a distinctive printmaking style that he forged independently. He later recalled, "I was never much in the swim of things as far as prints were concerned. Since I didn't live in Tokyo, I never knew many of the print artists and never was much influenced by them. I've just gone my own way, doing what interested me, and hoping it would interest somebody else. If it has, I'm happy."

8 | Sumio Kawakami (Japanese, 1895–1972), *Carnations and Spoon on a Tray*, late 20th century
Color woodcut, 8¼ x 11½ in. (21 x 29.2 cm)
Museum purchase, Achenbach Foundation for Graphic Arts Endowment Fund, 1966.80.94

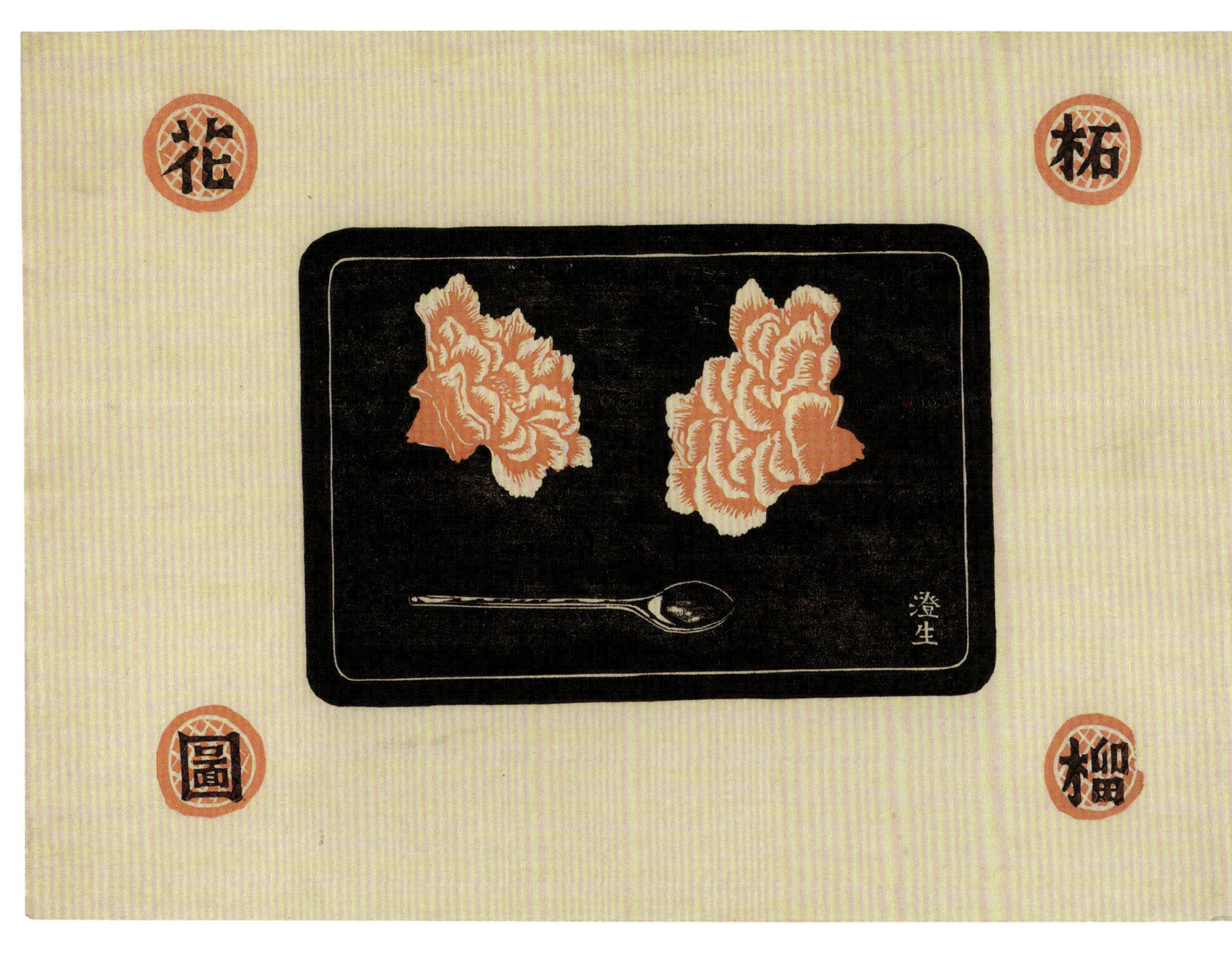
柘
榴
花
圖
澄生

Chrysanthemum

Love, truth, slighted affection

THE WORD "CHRYSANTHEMUM" is derived from the Greek *chrysos*, golden, and *anthemon*, a flower. Native to North Africa and Asia, the chrysanthemum carries powerful associations. In China, the flower came to represent the virtues of endurance and integrity, and the dictates of feng shui suggest that chrysanthemums will bring luck into the home. During the Heian period in Japan (794–1185 CE), chrysanthemums rose to prominence as a theme in poetry and became affiliated with autumn imagery. In the thirteenth century, the chrysanthemum became a symbol of the Japanese imperial family, and the flower persists as a symbol of Japan. The Order of the Chrysanthemum, Japan's highest and most exclusive chivalric order, was established in 1877. In the Victorian language of flowers, chrysanthemum's meaning varies by color: red signals love; white, truth; and yellow, slighted affection.

This naturalistic arrangement of four varieties of chrysanthemums against a light-dappled wall represents George Cochran Lambdin's distinctive approach to flower painting. After successfully establishing himself as a genre painter, Lambdin turned to the floral subjects for which he is best remembered. He began to focus on these still lifes after 1870, when he settled in Germantown, Pennsylvania, then the epicenter of the gardening activities for the greater Philadelphia area. There, Lambdin planted an impressive flower garden and served as a founding member of the Germantown Horticultural Society. Painted seven years after his trip to France in 1870, this work also demonstrates Lambdin's debt to contemporary French still-life masters such as Henri Fantin-Latour (cat. nos. 26 and 33).

9 | George Cochran Lambdin (American, 1830–1896), *Flower Study*, 1877
Oil on canvas, 27⅛ x 20 in. (68.9 x 50.8 cm)
Gift of Mr. and Mrs. John D. Rockefeller 3rd, 1979.7.72

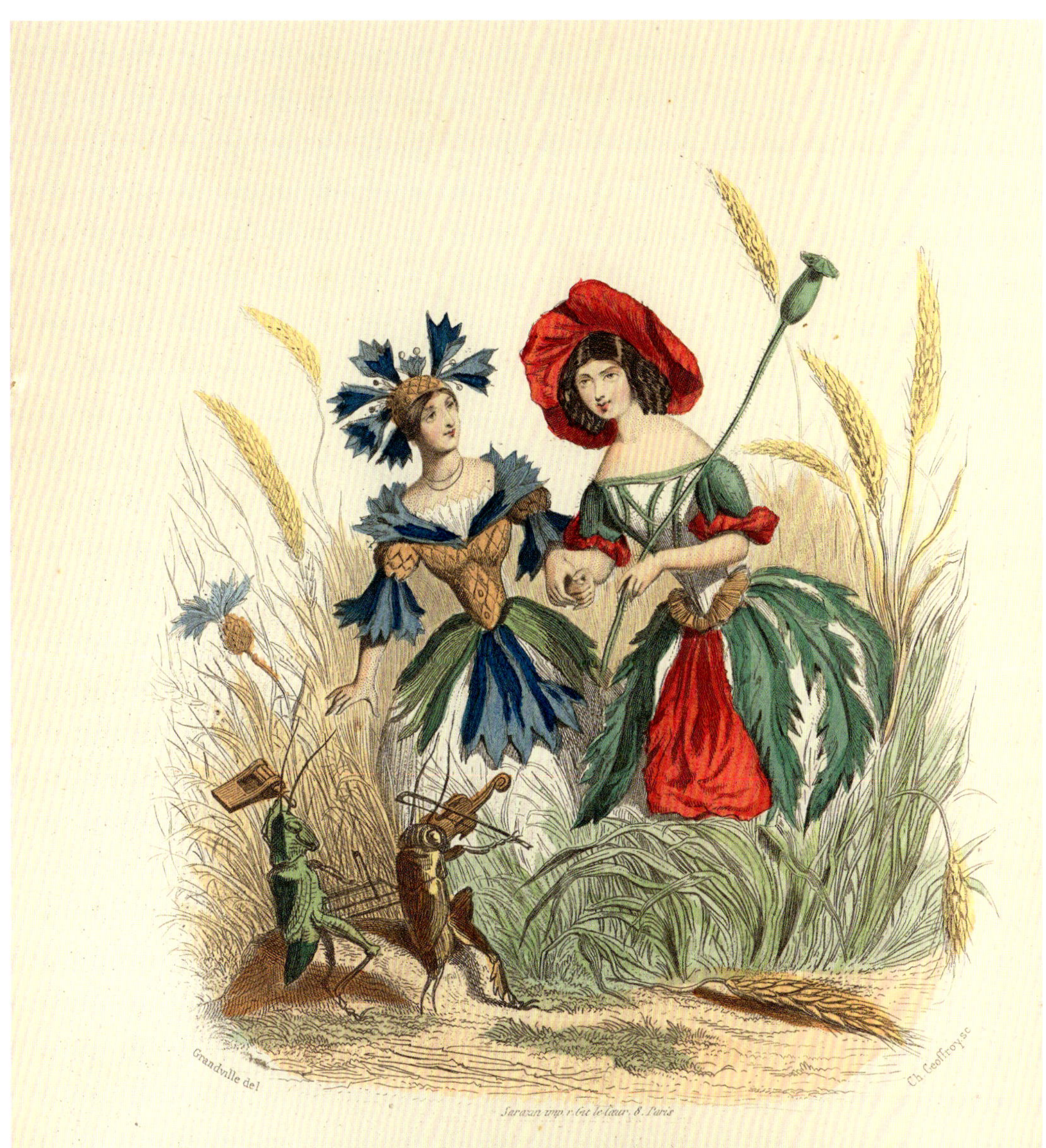

Grandville del

Ch. Geoffroy sc

Sarazan imp. r. Git le Cœur, 8. Paris

BLEUET ET COQUELICOT

Garnier frères Editeurs

Crocus

Cheerfulness, mirth

SAFFRON CROCUSES produce the treasured saffron derived from the flower's dried stigmas. One of the most precious substances in world history, saffron has been used as a spice, dye, fragrance, and medicine. "Crocus" derives from the Greek word *krokos*, or "thread," a reference to the flower's pollinated pistils. Ancient Greeks often used crocus petals to decorate their marriage beds after the Greek poet Homer wrote that crocus flowers adorned the marriage bed of the mythical Zeus and Hera. When it was discovered that saffron threads could be used to create a beautiful golden-colored dye, this tint was used for royal garments in many cultures around the world. In England, the crocus was historically associated with Saint Valentine, since the flowers appear near his saint's day on February 14.

According to the Victorian language of flowers, the crocus is associated with mirth and cheerfulness, which can be sensed in this animated still life by Grand Duchess Kyril (Victoria Melita Romanov). A woman of many names, the grand duchess was also known as Princess Victoria Melita of Edinburgh and Saxe-Coburg and Gotha, Grand Duchess of Hesse and by Rhine, Grand Duchess Victoria Feodorovna of Russia, and "Ducky" to her family. A granddaughter of Queen Victoria, "Ducky" had diverse artistic interests. In addition to nurturing her own talents in oils and watercolors, she supported the work of others. One contemporary publication noted: "Victoria Melita [is] naturally endowed with fine artistic tastes . . . offering cordial encouragement to painters, sculptors, and architects."

11 | Grand Duchess Kyril (Victoria Melita Romanov) (German-Russian, 1876–1936)
Still Life - Flowers, late 19th century. Oil on canvas, 11 x 21¾ in. (27.9 x 55.2 cm)
Gift of Victoria Melita, Grand Duchess Kyril of Russia, through Alma de Bretteville Spreckels, 1925.576

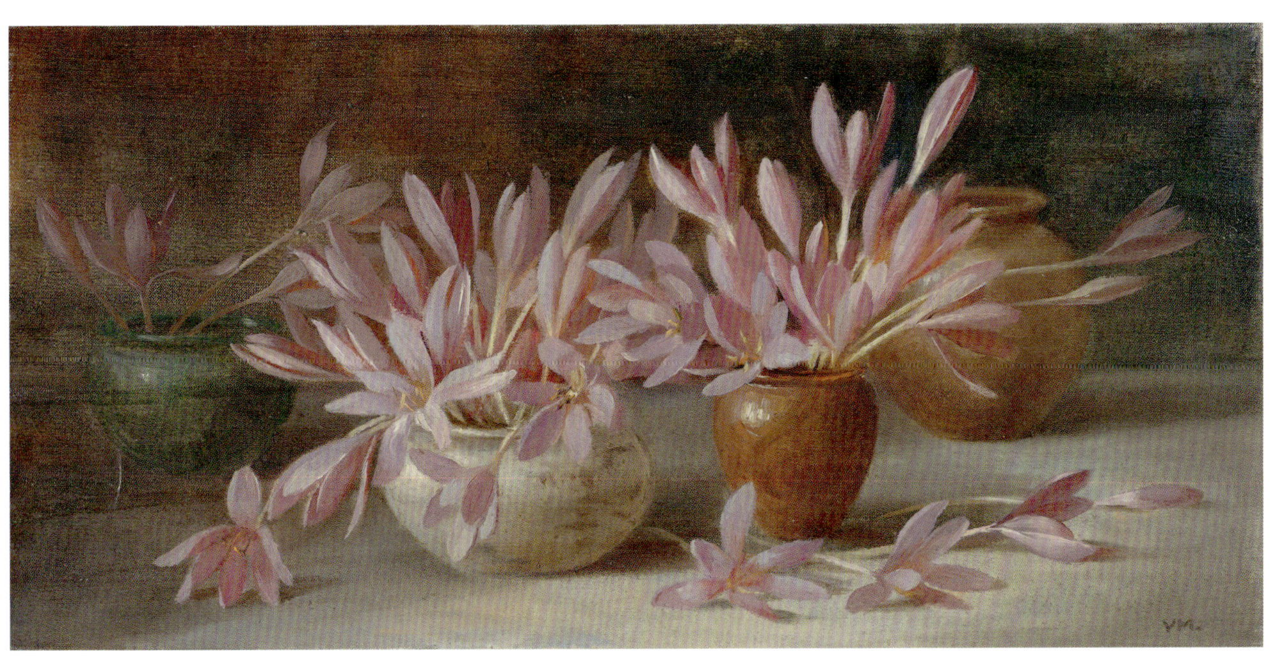

Daffodil

Regard, unrequited love

"I wandered lonely as a cloud / That floats on high o'er vales and hills, / When all at once I saw a crowd, / A host of golden daffodils . . ."
— William Wordsworth, 1807

THIS YELLOW-COLORED narcissus, generally known as the daffodil, is widely associated with rebirth and new life. Since the related paperwhite daffodil blooms around lunar January, it is one of the flowers most associated with Chinese New Year. The daffodil is the national flower of Wales and traditionally worn on March 1, the day of the country's patron saint David ("Dewi sant" in Welsh). In the Victorian language of flowers, daffodils are linked to regard and unrequited love due to their association with the myth of Narcissus, who fell in love with his own reflection and wasted away with unrequited yearning.

Beloved California artist Wayne Thiebaud is well known for his distinctive, candy-hued still lifes depicting everyday objects such as gumball machines, lipsticks, ice-cream cones, and slices of cake. His painting practice is intertwined with his work across various other media, including printmaking. The artist explains that printmaking "has its own unique powers of expression . . . I don't see myself so much as a printmaker, but a painter who likes to make prints. And those are the people in printmaking that I admire the most." In this image, the break in the daffodil's stem at the water line serves as a reminder of transience: this lovely blossom heralding spring will ultimately perish.

12 | Wayne Thiebaud (American, b. 1920), *Daffodil*, pl. 4, from the portfolio *Recent Etchings II*, 1979
Color aquatint and soft-ground etching, 23 ⅛ x 16 1⁄16 in. (58.7 x 40.8 cm)
Published by Parasol Press, Ltd., New York
Crown Point Press Archive, Gift of Kathan Brown, 1991.28.267

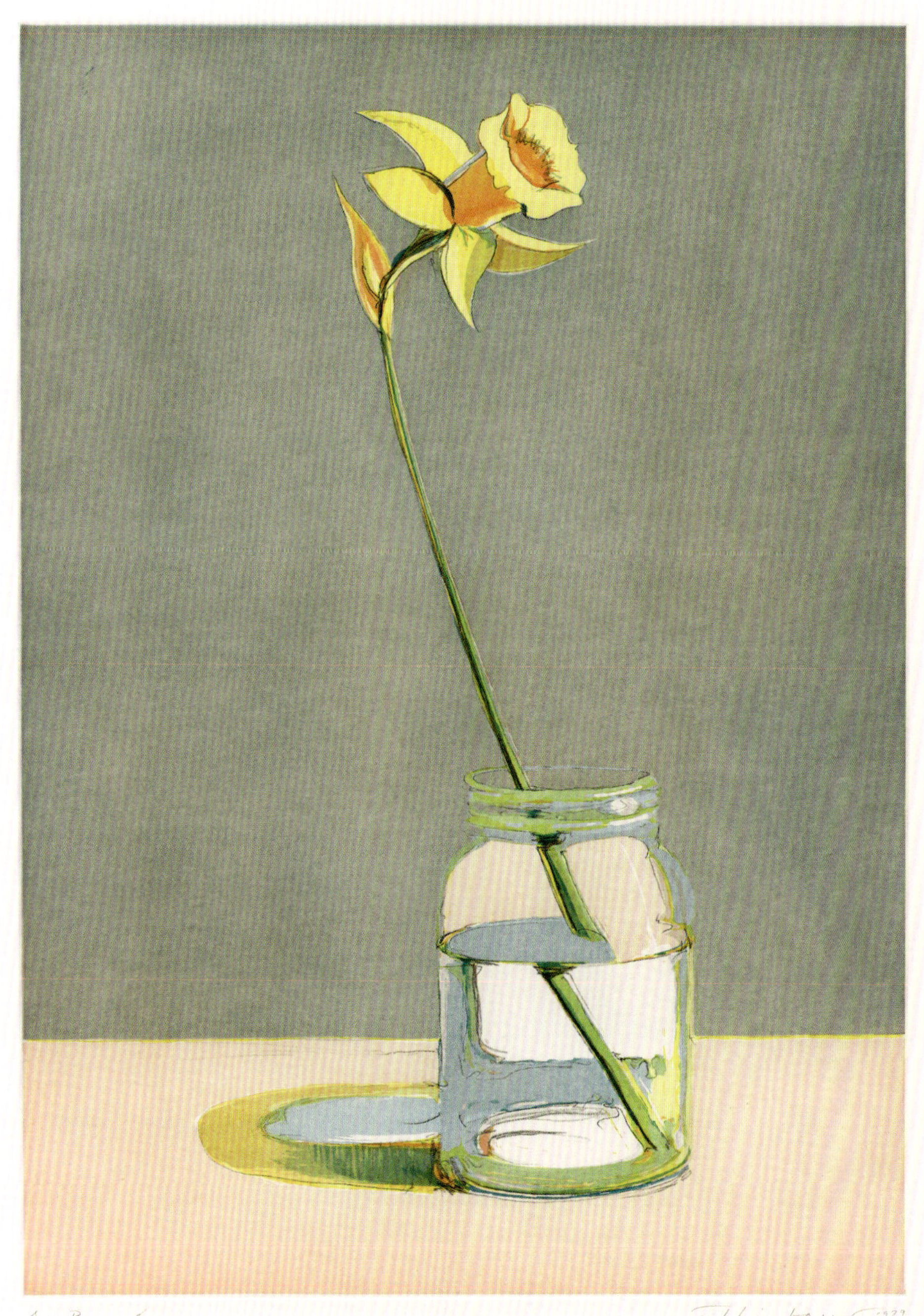

Dahlia

Heartless beauty, dignity, instability, pomp

Cocoxochitl, the flower we know as a dahlia, was cultivated by the Aztecs and is said to have flourished in the gardens of Montezuma, the Aztec king. Europeans reportedly first encountered dahlias when Spanish conquistador Hernán Cortés saw them growing in Tenochtitlán in 1521. With European colonization and conquest, the *cocoxochitl* made its way back to Spain, where it was eventually renamed "Dahlia" in honor of the Swedish botanist, Anders Dahl, effectively rewriting the flower's history. The writer Jamaica Kincaid reflects, "The naming of things is so crucial to possession — a spiritual padlock with the key thrown irretrievably away. . . . I love the dahlia, but can also see its tarnished history." In the Victorian language of flowers, the dahlia is associated with heartless beauty, since its blossoms disappoint with their lack of fragrance. Perhaps in response to the flower's physical attributes, other Victorian writers endowed it with the qualities of dignity, instability, and pomp.

William Seltzer Rice was an American woodblock print artist associated with the Arts and Crafts movement in Northern California. He took an illustrative approach to subjects selected from California landscapes, and *Dahlias*, included in his book *Block Printing in the School*, is a work by his student Charlotte Spalteholtz. Dahlias flourish across the state, though they bloom with special distinction in San Francisco: on October 4, 1926, the San Francisco Board of Supervisors adopted a resolution making the dahlia the city's official flower, describing the city as the dahlia's "favorite home . . . where it thrives in the cool summers and the moist air of our fog-swept, sandy gardens by the sea."

13 | Charlotte Spalteholtz (American, born Germany, 1899–1972), *Dahlias*, illustration 14 in the book *Block Printing in the School* by William Seltzer Rice (Milwaukee: Bruce Publishing Company, 1930), 1930
Woodblock print, 10 x 7 ⅜ in. (25.4 x 18.7 cm)
Gift of Rozell Overmire, 2000.106.3.14

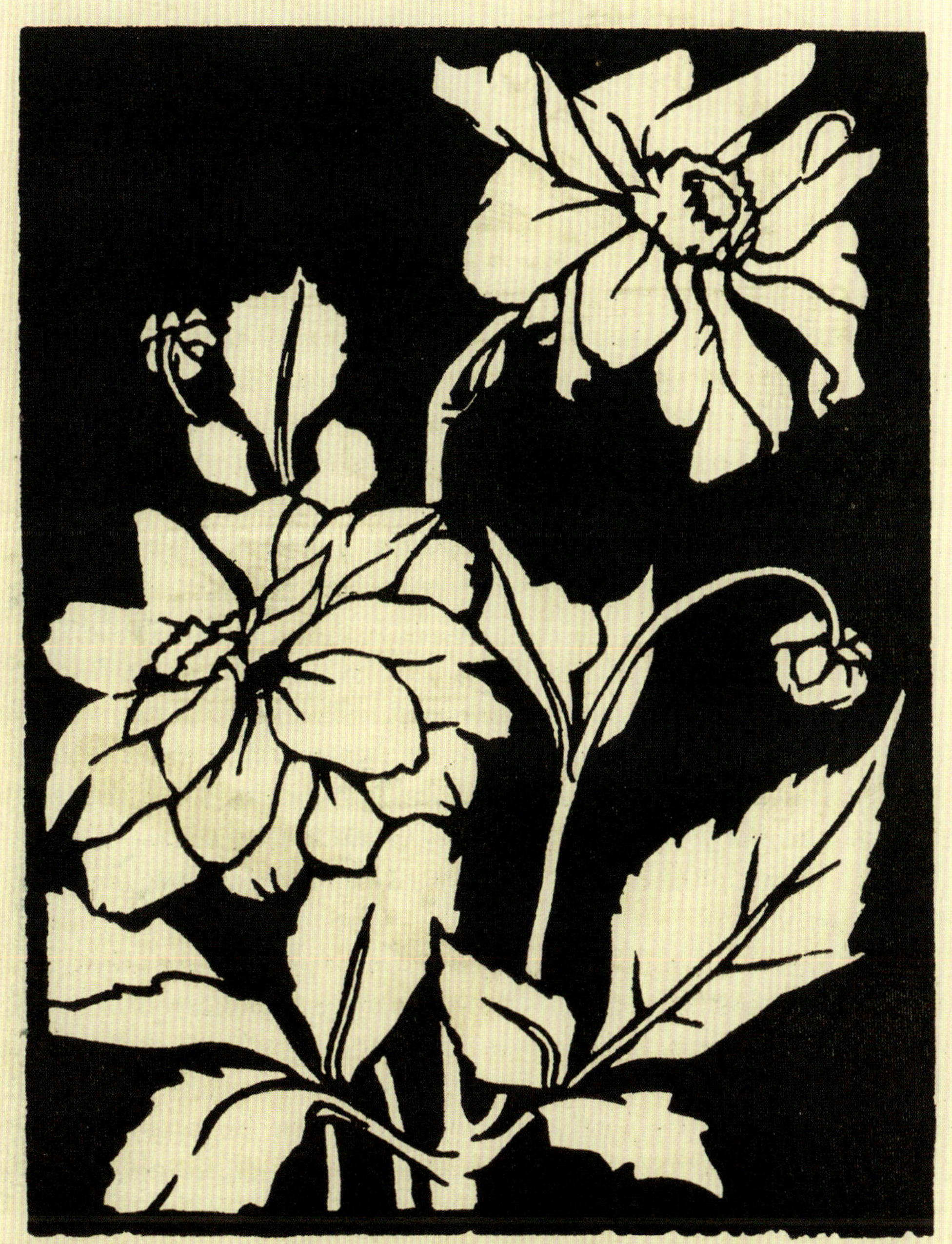

DAHLIAS, BY C. SPALTEHOLTZ

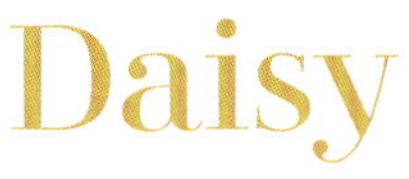

Daisy

Innocence

THE NAME "DAISY" comes from the Anglo-Saxon *daeges eage*, meaning "day's eye," describing the way that the flower's petals close at nightfall and open at daylight. The botanical name *Bellis* is derived from the Latin *bellus*, meaning "pretty." In the Victorian language of flowers, the daisy represents innocence. The British poet James Montgomery explained the daisy's appeal in his 1803 poem "A Field Flower": "The rose has but a summer reign; The daisy never dies!" In many cultures, daisies were used to foretell one's romantic future, as one would pull petals one by one and alternate reciting "They love me" or "They love me not," with the final petal revealing the answer.

This stylized image of a vase of daisies by the artist Blanche Lazzell is a white-line woodcut, wherein a line drawing is cut into the block and translated into white lines surrounding each colored section of the final print. Born in West Virginia, Lazzell studied art in Paris in the early 1920s. There she began developing her own approach to Cubism, inspired by "the organization of flat planes of color, with an interplay of space, instead of perspective." She established a studio in the Cape Cod art community of Provincetown, Massachusetts, where she displayed her white-line prints and offered lessons on woodblock printing techniques. Lazzell was also a devoted gardener who incorporated many flowers into her work, and contemporary photographs capture the profusion of flowers growing around her Provincetown studio.

14 | Blanche Lazzell (American, 1878–1956), *Daisies*, 1932
Color woodcut, 14 x 11 7/8 in. (35.6 x 30.1 cm)
Museum purchase, Robert Ray Schmidt Bequest Fund and Gift of the Graphic Arts Council, 1993.42

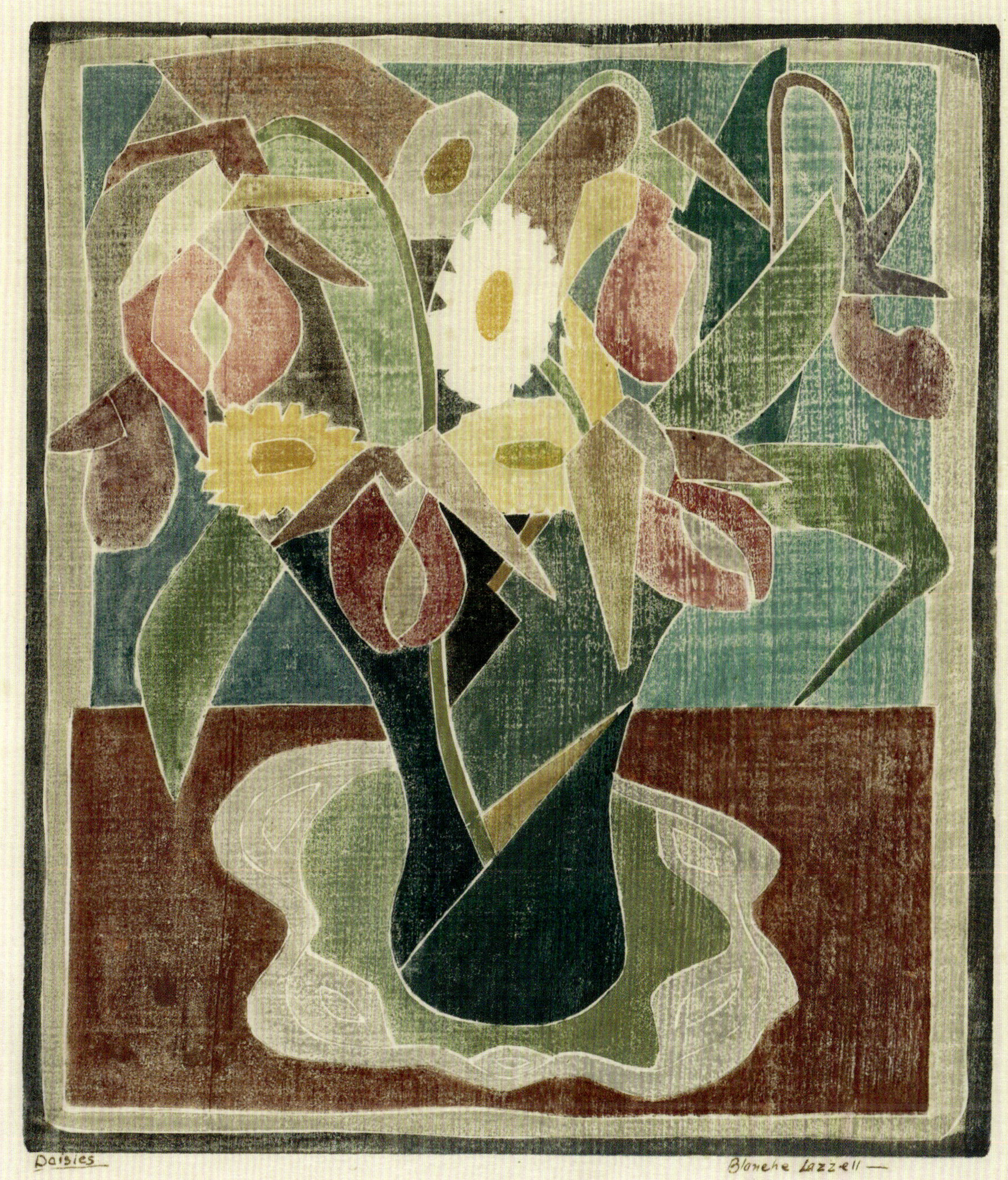
Daisies
Blanche Lazzell —

Dandelion

Oracle

THE AMERICAN MINISTER and social reformer Henry Ward Beecher referred to yellow dandelion blossoms as "those golden kisses all over the cheeks of the meadow." Sometimes dismissed as a weed, this little flower possesses many qualities: its leaves are enjoyed as salad greens and its roots are sometimes roasted and used as a coffee substitute. In the Victorian language of flowers, the dandelion represents oracles, an association based on how its feathery seeds are used to make wishes and prophecies. For example, some believe that a message can be sent to a loved one by visualizing the sentiment and blowing the seeds in that person's direction. The word "dandelion" is derived from the notched shape of the plant's leaves, which resemble the teeth of a lion, or "*dent de lion*" in French.

This dramatic rendering of dandelions features one yellow flower beside two seed balls, one of which has already partially blown away. Painted by the artist Barbara Regina Dietzsch, this watercolor demonstrates the skill of a botanical artist immersed in illustrious artistic and scientific traditions. Working under the patronage of the royal court at Nuremberg, Dietzsch specialized in compositions featuring insects and flowers set against dark, velvety textures. In works such as this depiction of three heads of a dandelion surrounded by a tiger moth, butterfly, snail, and beetle, she seems to understand the mutualism between plants and insects, her microcosm of nature reflecting a scientific understanding of the natural world.

15 | Barbara Regina Dietzsch (German, 1706–1783), *A Dandelion with a Tiger Moth, a Butterfly, a Snail, and a Beetle*, 18th century. Opaque watercolor on parchment, sheet: 11¼ x 8¼ in. (28.6 x 21 cm) Museum purchase, Gift of the Museum Society Auxiliary, 1984.2.8

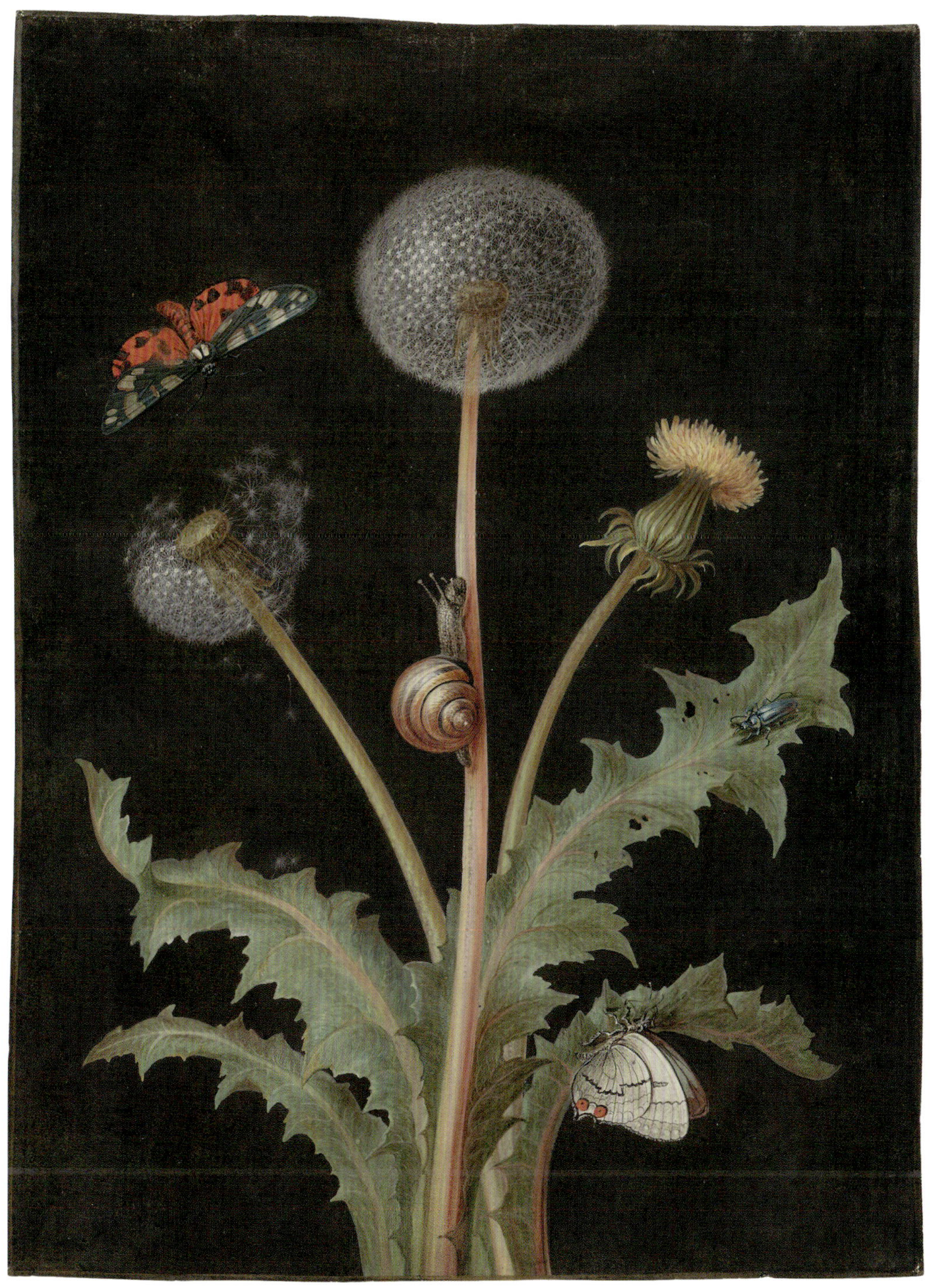

Fuchsia

Taste

NUMBERING MORE THAN one hundred species, the fuchsia is native to South America, Mexico, the Caribbean, New Zealand, and some Pacific islands. After Europeans first encountered them in the eighteenth century, these flowers were named "fuchsia" in honor of the German botanist Leonhart Fuchs (1501–1566). With a bright color and dramatic shape resembling elegant earrings, the fuchsia became representative of good taste, and it was particularly prized in England and France. In the almanac of symbols associated with China's feng shui traditions, fuchsia flowers resemble lanterns and symbolize good luck.

This small piece of English porcelain with its unusual faux-stem handle illustrates the appeal of the fuchsia as a theme in the decorative arts. In addition to serving as a subject for porcelainware, the fuchsia also became a popular motif in Victorian jewelry design, particularly after 1830. For instance, in 1864, Queen Victoria had a pendant made in the shape of a fuchsia bloom featuring a stamen fashioned from the baby teeth of her daughter Princess Beatrice. With its distinctive petals, the fuchsia also became prized as an ornamental plant of particular renown during the Victorian era, when as many as ten thousand were sold each day at Covent Garden Market in London. Huge quantities of fuchsias were used to decorate the famed exhibition halls of London's Crystal Palace, where, in 1858, one writer admired "the splendid specimens" that "towered up to immense heights in order to crown the lofty pillars with their classic wreaths of weeping stems and brilliantly colored flowers."

16 | Pitcher (white with red fuchsias), ca. 1885
Possibly Ott and Brewer (American, Trenton, New Jersey, 1871–1893)
Porcelain, 4 ½ x 3 ¼ in. (11.4 x 8.3 cm)
Museum collection, Z1982.19

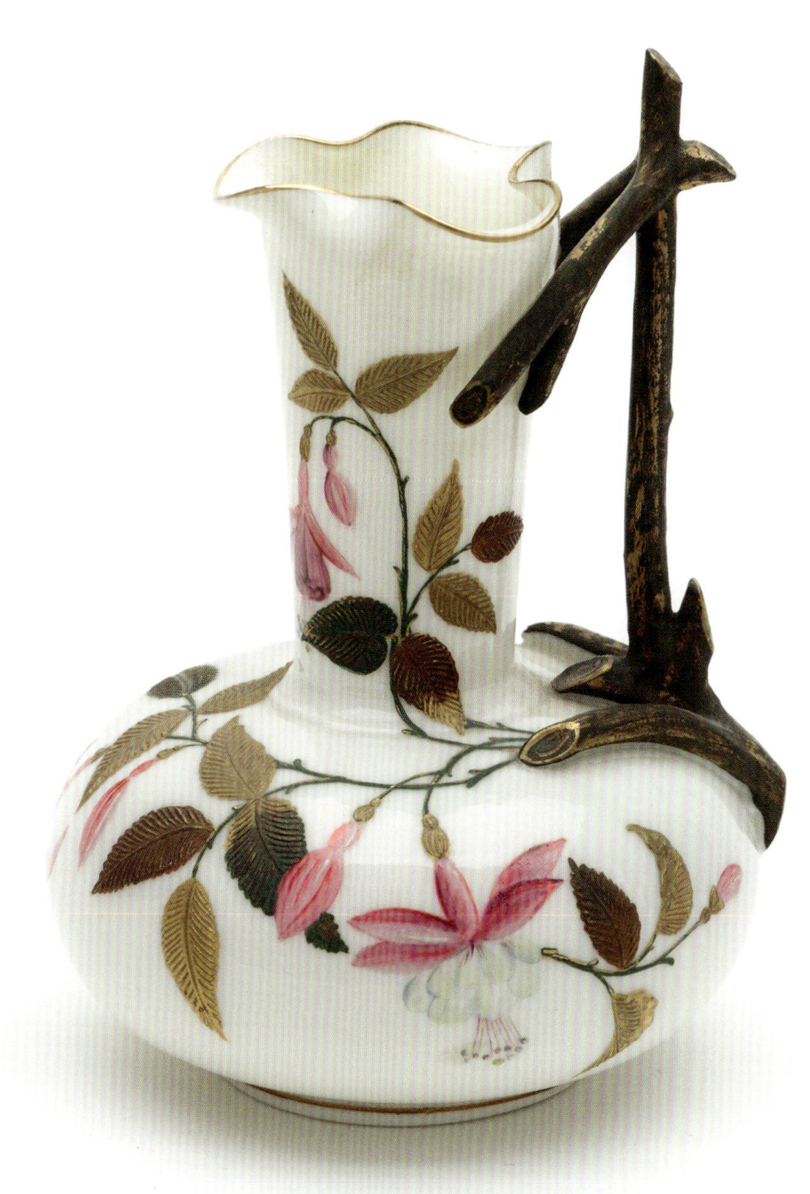

Geranium

Preference, folly, deceit

THE VICTORIAN LANGUAGE OF FLOWERS is inconsistent on the ultimate meaning of the geranium. With its velvet-soft leaves and distinctive perfume, it has been considered an emblem of "preference," though some varieties symbolize folly, deceit, friendship, ingenuity, piety, and stupidity. The name "geranium" is derived from the Greek word *geranos*, meaning "crane"; the seeds possess a long spur that resembles a crane's bill. Brought to England from South Africa in the seventeenth century, geranium seeds eventually reached the famed American botanist John Bartram in 1760. These flowers became popular in the American colonies, where they were associated with hospitality and home and were later carried among the household goods of pioneers heading west.

Grant Wood is best known for his stylized depictions of everyday life in the American Midwest. Such imagery extended to still lifes, such as this print featuring a bright, "tamed" potted geranium with two fallen petals on the ground, suggesting a traditional *memento mori*. Wood's work across media reflected an interest in American mythmaking, and *Tame Flowers* is one of a series of four lithographs that partially emulate the work of influential printing firm Currier and Ives, whose imagery helped establish a shared visual American mythology. The series was originally marketed by Associated American Artists in New York City for ten dollars each. Although the prints were advertised as being hand-colored by Wood himself, tinting was actually done by the artist's sister, Nan, and her husband, Edward Graham, who worked at their kitchen table following Wood's instructions.

17 | Grant Wood (American, 1891–1942), *Tame Flowers*, 1938
Lithograph with hand coloring, 10 9/16 x 13 1/8 in. (26.9 x 33.4 cm)
Published by Associated America Artists, Inc., New York
Museum purchase, Achenbach Foundation for Graphic Arts Endowment Fund, 1976.1.164

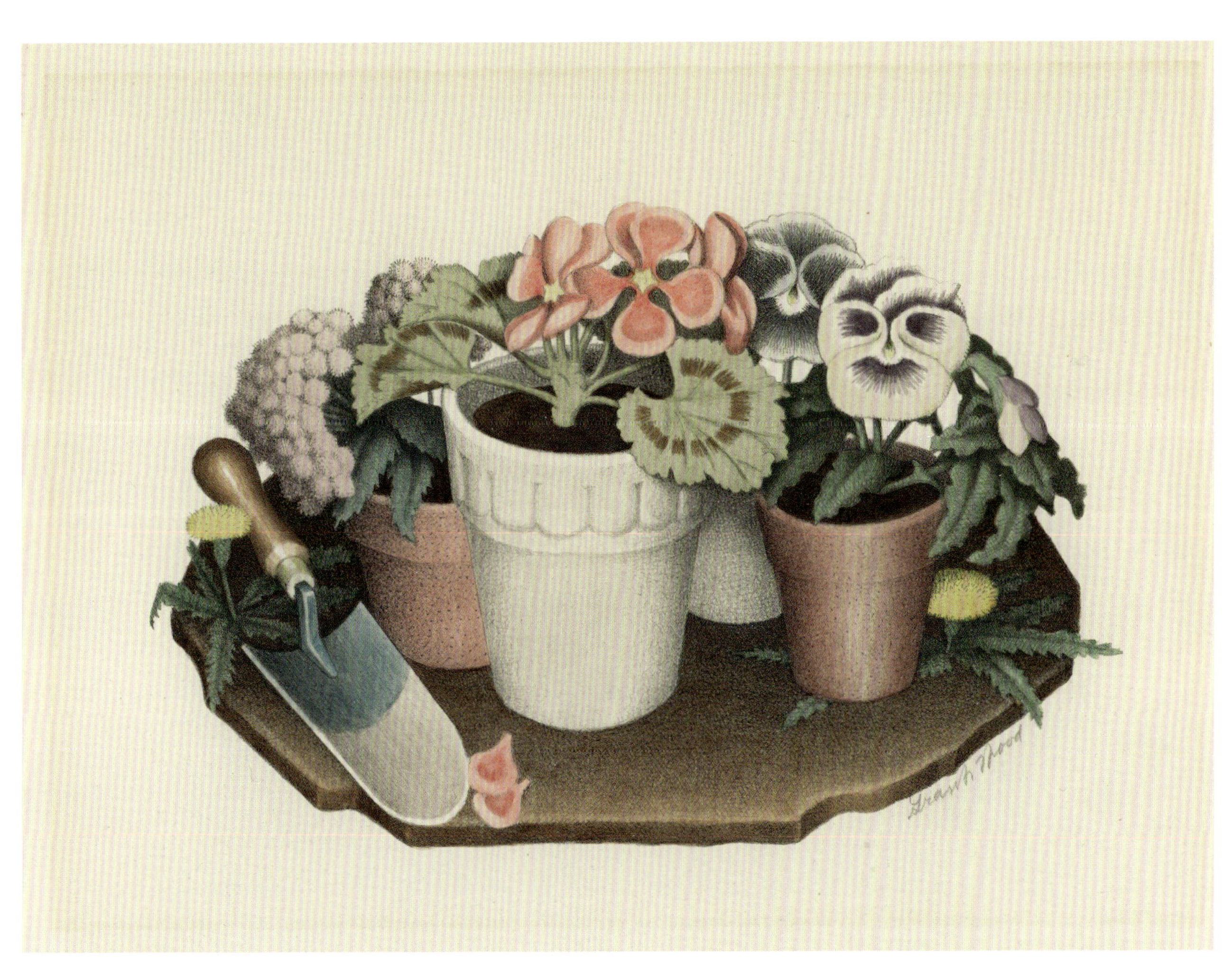
Grant Wood

Hibiscus

Delicate beauty

THE BRIGHT, TRUMPET-SHAPED hibiscus signifies "delicate beauty" in the Victorian language of flowers. Found throughout the world, various species of hibiscus are endowed with particular significance around the Pacific Rim, and the rare yellow hibiscus (*Hibiscus brackenridgei*), also known as *Pua Aloalo* or *Maʻo-hau-hele*, is the state flower of Hawaiʻi. Hibiscus flowers vary in size and color, ranging from red and pink to white, orange, purple, and yellow. These flowers can also be used to make a sweet and soothing tea that is used in many folk remedies around the world and is associated with many health benefits.

Best known for his iconic Pop art portrayals of celebrities and consumer products, Andy Warhol constantly straddled the boundary between fine art and popular culture. He often began his work by looking at advertisements and photographs culled from magazines, and his *Flowers* (1964) was based on an image published in a 1964 issue of *Modern Photography*. Originally photographed by Patricia Caulfield, the source image depicted a tabletop arrangement of hibiscus flowers at a Barbados restaurant. Warhol cropped and magnified this picture, infusing the flowers with shocking, high-keyed, and unnatural colors. The resulting print seems to stridently reiterate the artist's declaration, "I always notice flowers."

18 | Andy Warhol (American, 1928–1987), artist
Leo Castelli Gallery (American, b. 1957), publisher
Total Color (American, active 20th century), printer
Flowers, 1964
Color offset lithograph, 23 x 23 in. (58.4 x 58.4 cm)
Museum purchase, Achenbach Foundation for Graphic Arts Endowment Fund, 2001.53

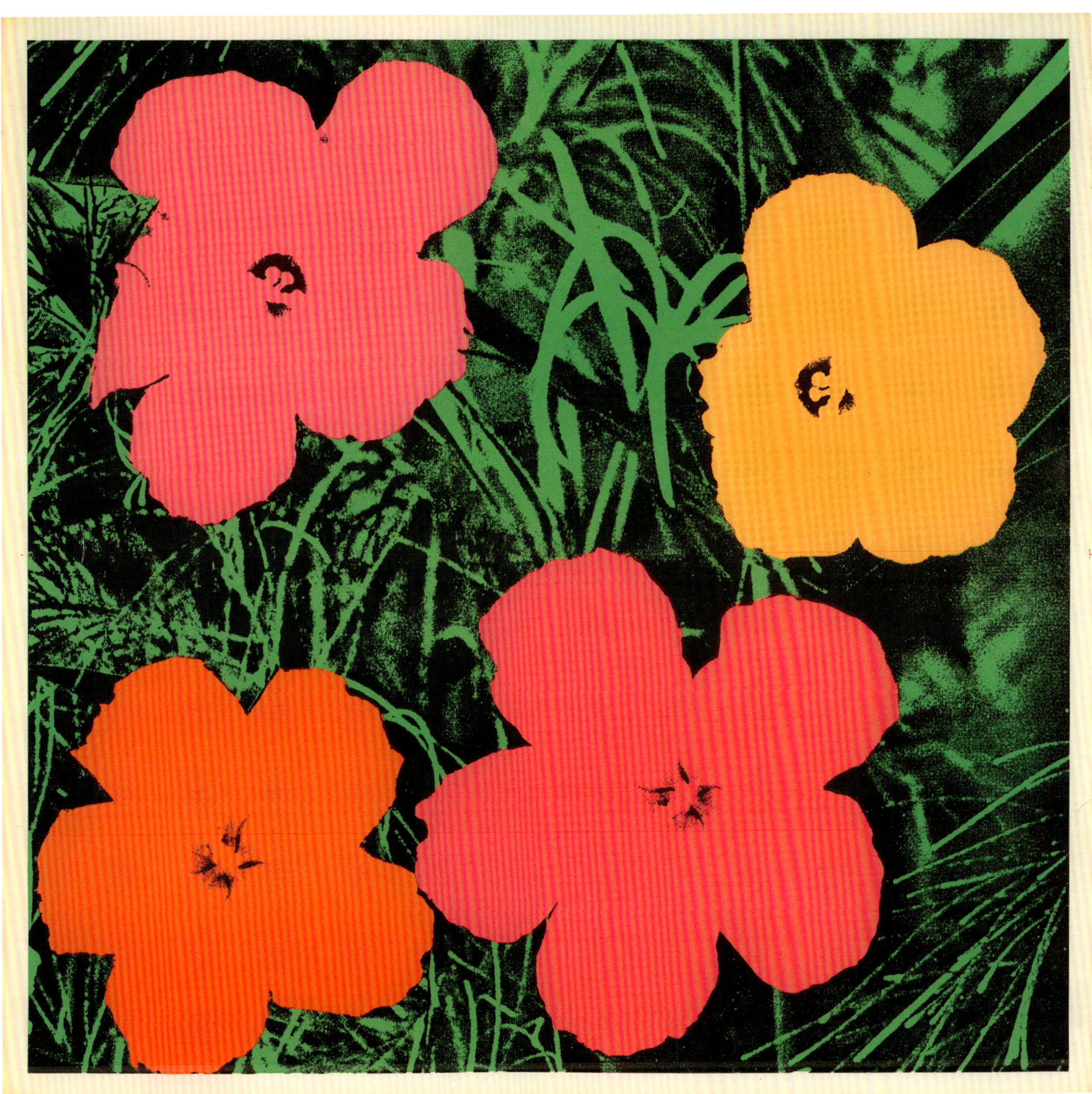

Honeysuckle

Devoted affection

"Good lord, how sweetly smells the honeysuckle / In the hushed night, as if the world were one / Of utter peace, and love, and gentleness!"
— Alfred, Lord Tennyson, "Gareth and Lynette" from *Idylls of the King*, 1859–1885

DELICATE HONEYSUCKLE flowers are admired for their sweet, eponymous nectar, and in the Victorian language of flowers, they represent devoted affection. One Victorian writer effused, "All the glories of East and West cannot rival its blossoms in our estimation." The name "honeysuckle" was traditionally used for a variety of fragrant flowers, and because this plant entwines itself around others, Shakespeare used it as a metaphor for embrace. Japanese honeysuckle (*nindo* or *suikazura*) can grow wild, and in ancient times, its roots were presented at some Shinto shrines to appease the gods and stave off illness.

In her image of sinuous *Honeysuckle,* artist Mabel Allington Royds captures the distinctive shapes of these sweet-smelling flowers from several winding angles. Royds is best known for her color woodcuts, which she executed in a distinctive technique derived from traditional Japanese printmaking practices. In 1919, the contemporary English critic Malcolm Charles Salaman noted, "She achieves both rich and delicate harmonies with flat tints." Royds studied at London's progressive Slade Art School and later absorbed the influence of Japanese-style carving and printing. She adopted the habit of carving her designs into inexpensive breadboards from Woolworth's (instead of more traditional and expensive wood blocks), and the resulting stylized designs often feel modern and vivacious.

19 | Mabel Allington Royds (English, 1874–1941), *Honeysuckle,* 1933–1938
Color woodcut, 8 x 6½ in. (20.3 x 16.4 cm)
Gift of Misses H. Dorothy and Margaret Tilly, 1966.78.4

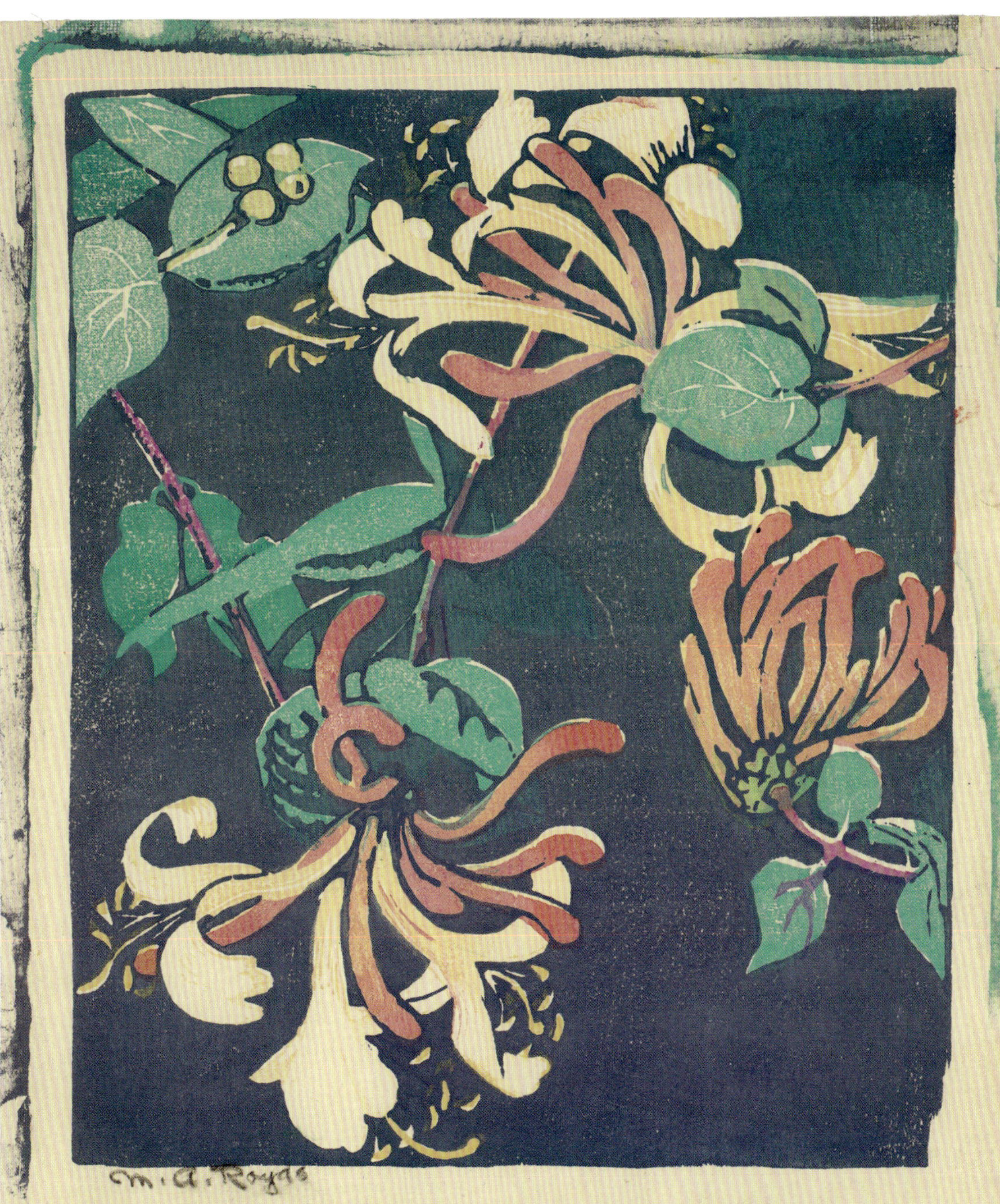
M.A. Royds
MABEL ROYDS.
8

Hyacinth

Sport, play

THE HYACINTH'S NAME is linked to various myths of Hyacinthus, an athletic young man from Sparta who was beloved by both the god Apollo and Zephyr, the god of the west wind. One day, as Hyacinthus and Apollo were throwing a discus or a quoit, Zephyr flew into a jealous rage and accidentally killed Hyacinthus by lifting the discus and delivering a fatal blow. Apollo, stricken with grief, made hyacinth flowers spring from his lover's blood. In the Victorian language of flowers, the hyacinth's association with sport and play seems a fitting tribute to the mythical Hyacinthus. Some floral dictionaries also depict purple hyacinths as flowers of sorrow — emblems of Apollo's lament.

The stylized purple hyacinth in Kōshirō Onchi's color woodcut *Avril* (*April*) captures the allure of this distinctive blossom: its flower spike, composed of deep blue-violet trumpet-shaped flowers, dominates the left side of the composition. Their rich color and full shape contrast with the patterned yellow ground and elegant simplicity of the woman's smiling face. Onchi was one of the key figures associated with *sōsaku hanga*, the creative print movement in Japan. In addition to Onchi's respected work as a print artist, he was also influential as a poet, print scholar, founder and editor of magazines, and leader and organizer of arts organizations. Often looking beyond histories of Japanese art, he absorbed international influences and counted Edvard Munch and Wassily Kandinsky among the artists he admired.

20 | Kōshirō Onchi (Japanese, 1891–1955), *Avril* (*April*), 1925
Color woodcut, 7 x 7½ in. (17.8 x 19.1 cm)
Museum purchase, Achenbach Foundation for Graphic Arts Endowment Fund, 2004.43

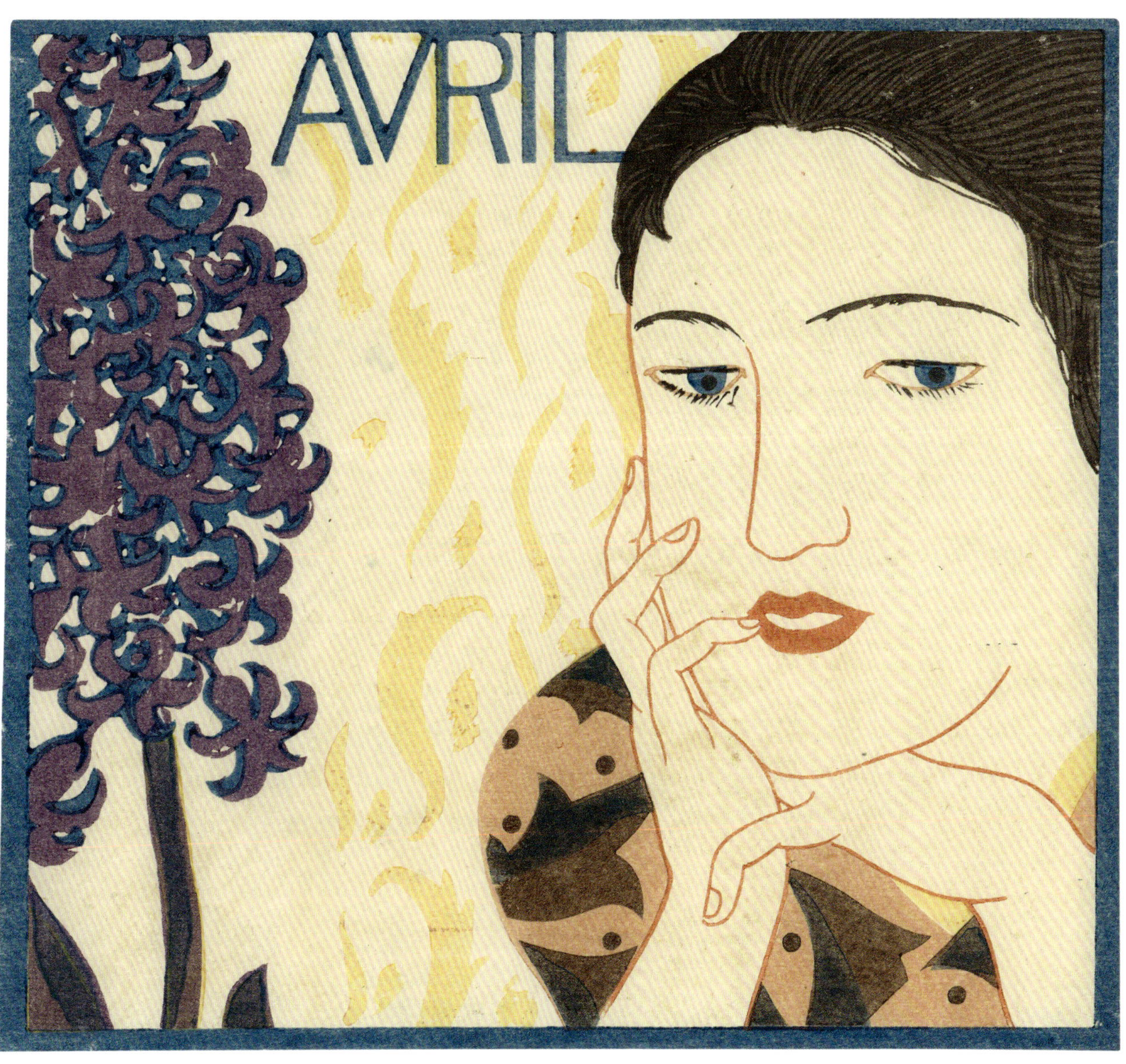
AVRIL

Impatiens

Impatience

"With fierce distracted eye Impatiens stands, / swells her pale cheeks and brandishes her hands; / With rage and hate the astonished groves alarms / And hurls her infants from her frantic arms."
— Erasmus Darwin, "The Loves of the Plants, Canto III"
from *The Botanic Garden, a Poem, Etc.* 1791

THE NAME "IMPATIENS" comes from the Latin word meaning "impatient"— a reference to this plant's fragile seedpods. When the impatiens matures, the seed capsules become sensitive to the lightest touch, releasing forcefully and instantaneously when disturbed. This characteristic led to some of the plant's other names, including snapweed and *Noli me tangere* ("touch me not"). Its cheerful blossoms and long growing season make impatiens popular for summer gardens.

Paul Wonner's *Still Life with Fruit and Flowers* features the distinctive impatiens on the right side of the composition: its bright pink flowers stand out against the dark background. Associated with the Bay Area Figurative movement, Wonner worked parallel to other giants of Bay Area painting, including David Park, Elmer Bischoff, and Richard Diebenkorn. Expressive brushwork characterized his figurative paintings before the late 1970s, giving way in the 1980s and 1990s to his realistic "Dutch" still lifes featuring precisely rendered flowers and everyday objects arranged with the meticulousness of Dutch Baroque still-life painting. Art critic Juan Rodriguez noted, "Wonner [is] not looking back in nostalgic repose to the codes of classical canons as if [he] had come to a reconciliation with the uncertainty and brutality of modern life, and yes, postmodern art. Through [his] artistic efforts, [he is] continuing to deepen the pleasures one can find in representational painting."

21 | Paul Wonner (American, 1920–2008), *Still Life with Fruit and Flowers*, 1992
Color lithograph and screenprint with opaque watercolor and colored pencil,
29¾ x 21⅞ in. (75.5 x 55.5 cm)
Museum purchase, Gift of the Richard and Rhoda Goldman Fund,
Bernard A. Osher, Alfred S. Wilsey, and Aristides Demetrios, 1993.126.1

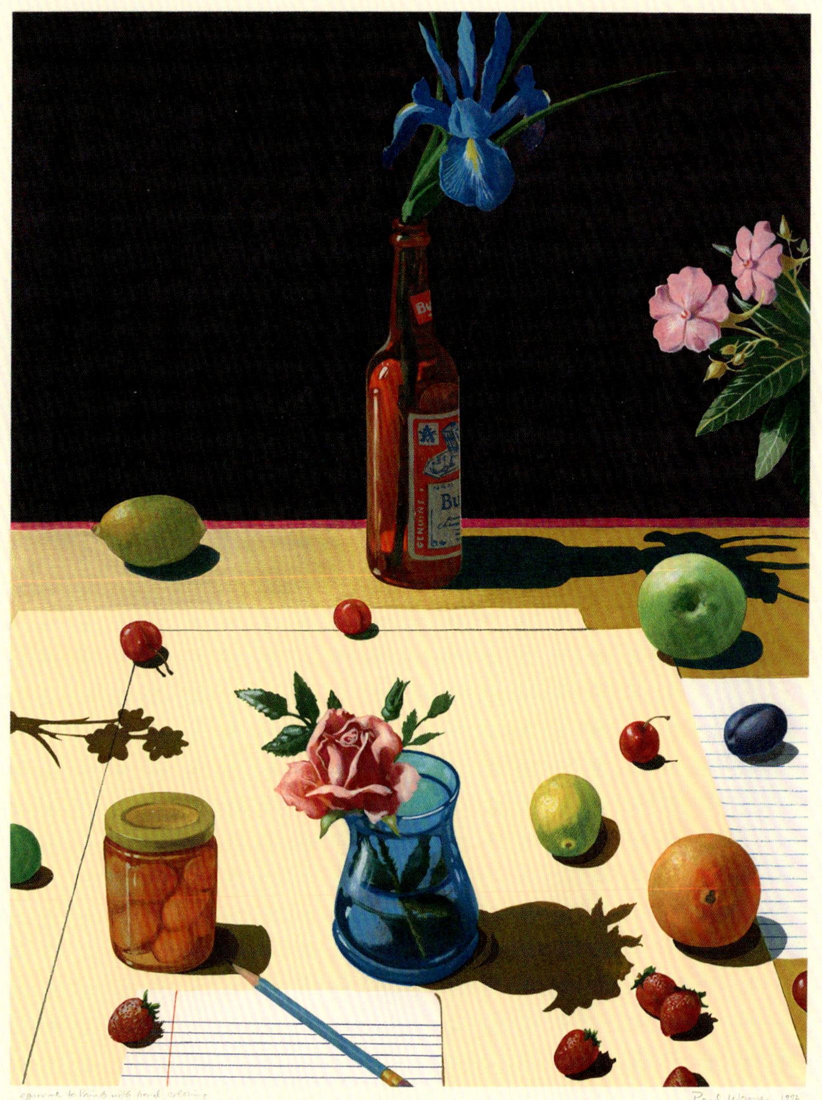
approval to Print with hand coloring
Paul Wonner 1992

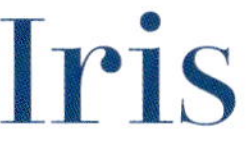

Iris

Message

THE IRIS IS NAMED for Iris, the Greek goddess of the rainbow, who carried messages of love from heaven to earth using the rainbow as a bridge between the two realms. Because of its association with this goddess, the iris is widely accepted as the symbol of messages and communication. The three petals of the iris flower are said to represent faith, wisdom, and valor. Irises were historically associated with royalty, power, and divine protection: ancient Egyptians placed irises on the scepters of the pharaohs and on the brows of the Sphinx. King Charles IV of France is believed to be the first ruler to include the iris on French banners, where it served as the basis for the iconic fleur-de-lis design still in use today. The Japanese iris, *kakitsubata*, grows wild near bodies of fresh water and is widely celebrated in Japanese poetry and art.

This exceptional example of American stained glass features an array of irises in various rich blue and purple colors. Situated in a lush marshland, the bright irises stand out against the abundant greenery, white lilies, and brown cattails surrounding them. This large window, attributed to Rudolph Geissler and former Tiffany artist Louis Lederle, captures the love of nature that influenced the development of both the Aesthetic and Arts and Crafts Movements in Europe and the United States. It was originally installed in the Ansonia apartment building in New York City, where it likely replaced a view of the urban cityscape with a peaceful vision of an Edenic wetland.

22 | Attributed to Lederle and Geissler, New York, *Iris, Lily and Cattail Window*, ca. 1904
Stained, leaded, and plated glass with wood frame, 57 15/16 x 51 3/8 x 2 in. (147.2 x 130.5 x 5.1 cm)
Museum purchase, Calvin L. Malone American Arts and Crafts Fund, 2017.18

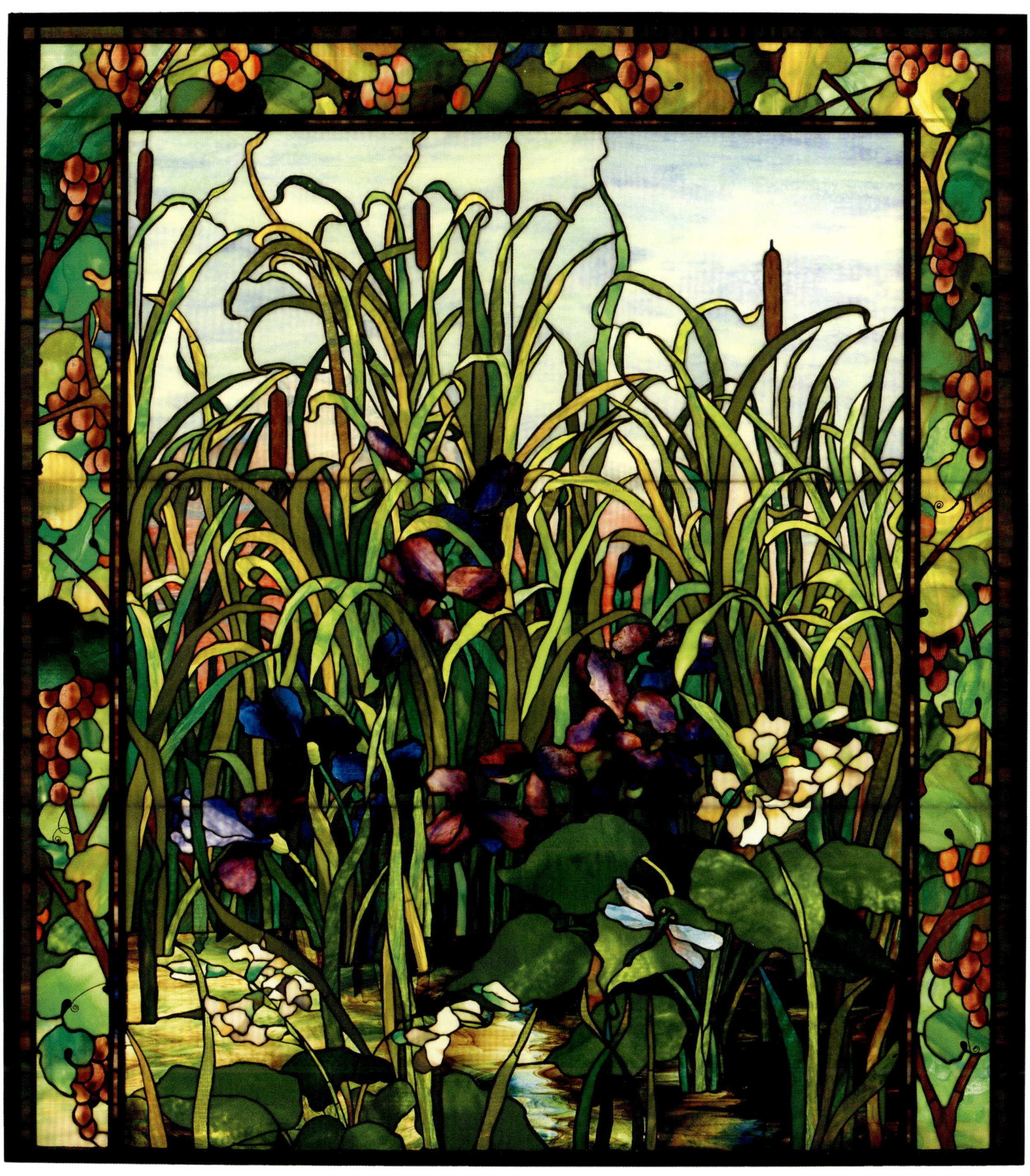

Larkspur

Levity, lightness

PRETTY YET POISONOUS, the larkspur possesses numerous symbolic meanings, with levity and lightness being the most common. This plant's name is derived from the long spur of the individual flowers resembling the claw of a lark (most lark species have long hind claws). In French, the colorful annual is known as *pied-d'alouette*, or "lark's foot." The larkspur's association with levity is suggested by the lark's bright, joyful song, which it sings in early morning during breeding season. The popular idiom "Happy as a lark," in use since the early nineteenth century, further suggests the lightheartedness of this flower and the song of its avian eponym.

Childe Hassam's *Larkspur and Lilies* depicts a field of flowers including tall, purple larkspur. This print is based on a watercolor Hassam produced for Celia Thaxter's book *An Island Garden* (1894) — an ode to the author's flower garden on Appledore, the largest of the Isles of Shoals, in the Atlantic waters between Maine and New Hampshire. Thaxter, a poet who helped manage her family's hotel on the island, hosted lively gatherings of musicians, writers, and artists at her private cottage adjacent to the hotel. Hassam loomed large among those who found inspiration there, eventually becoming the painter most closely associated with Appledore and Thaxter's famous garden. Thaxter herself described the view of the larkspur there: "*And tall blue larkspur waved its spikes / Against the sea's deep violet, / That every breeze makes deeper yet / With splendid azure where it strikes.*"

23 | Childe Hassam (American, 1859–1935), *Larkspur and Lilies*, ca. 1894
Color electrotype, 5 7/16 x 3 11/16 in. (13.8 x 9.3 cm)
Gift of Dr. and Mrs. Robert A. Johnson, 1984.1.79

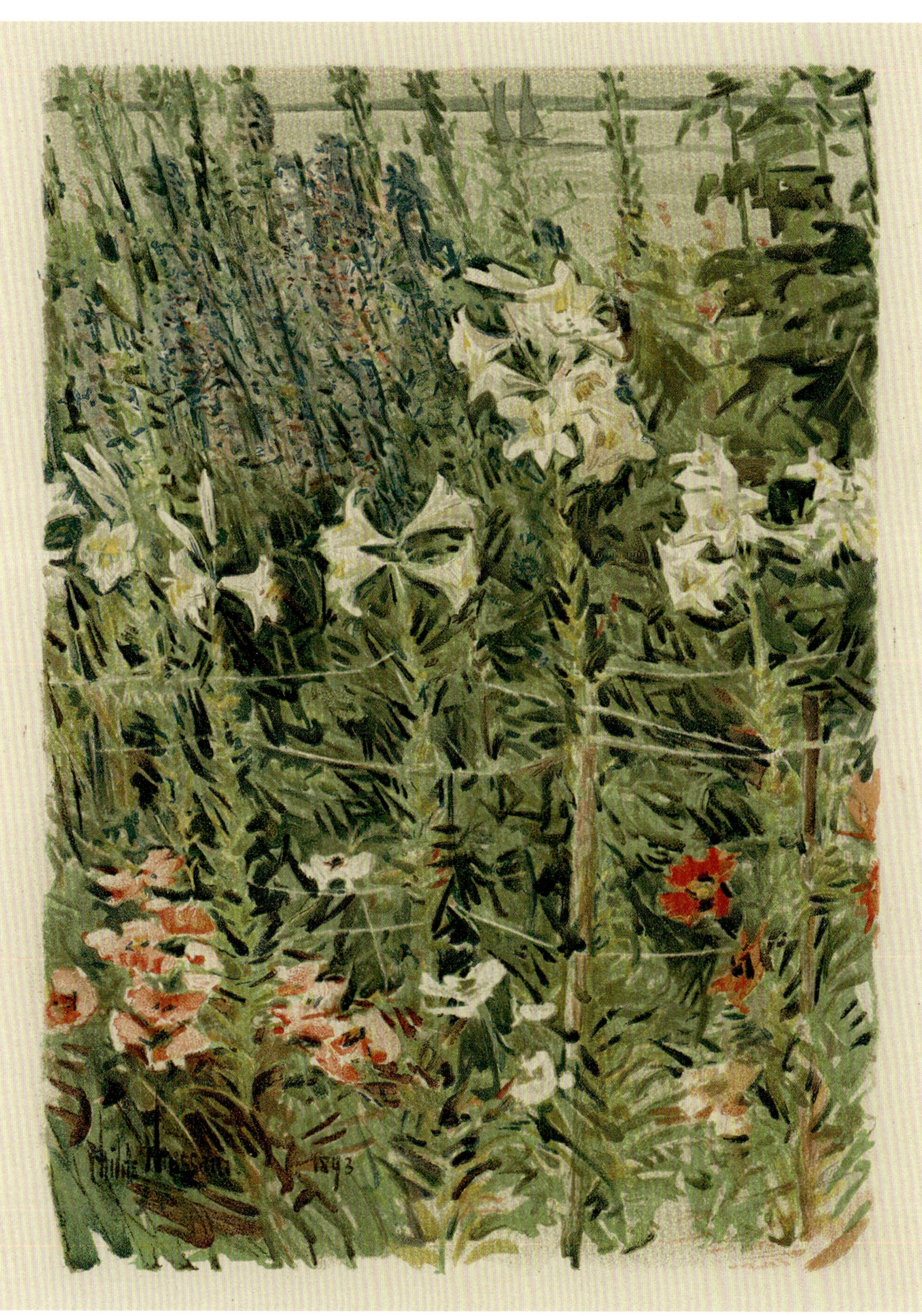
1893

Lavender

Mistrust, calmness

PEOPLE ONCE THOUGHT that asps, or small vipers, lurked beneath lavender plants, a belief that endowed this fragrant flower with its symbolic association with mistrust. The name "lavender" is derived from the Latin *lavare,* "to wash," reflecting the ancient Roman custom of adding lavender fragrance to bath water and to freshen rooms and linens — practices still common today. The scent of lavender is associated with rest and relaxation and has long been used in many medicinal applications: historically, women in labor were given sprigs of lavender to squeeze, releasing a calming fragrance during childbirth. Some believed that lavender could bring peacefulness into the home and that lavender-scented clothing would attract true love, while others perpetuated a superstition that people who carried lavender would be able to see ghosts.

This stylistic depiction of lavender was designed to accompany the popular Victorian nursery rhyme "Lavender's Blue," based on the Elizabethan love song "Diddle Diddle, or the Kind Country Lovers." In this version of the song, the lyrics read: "Lavender's blue, diddle, diddle! Lavender's green; When I am king, diddle, diddle! You shall be queen." This page of music was illustrated by Walter Crane, a prolific artist and creator of books for children. Crane is credited with transforming children's books into a serious art form and vehicle for mass communication, blurring the boundaries between high art and popular culture. Generously illustrated and widely celebrated, Crane's books set the stage for future generations of artists who made work for younger audiences.

24 | Walter Crane (English, 1845–1915), *Lavender's Blue* in *The Baby's Opera,* page 29 in the book *Walter Crane's Picture Book* (London: Frederick Warne & Company, 1900)
Color wood engraving, sheet: 11 7⁄16 x 12 in. (29.1 x 30.5 cm)
Achenbach Foundation for Graphic Arts, 1963.30.39119.19

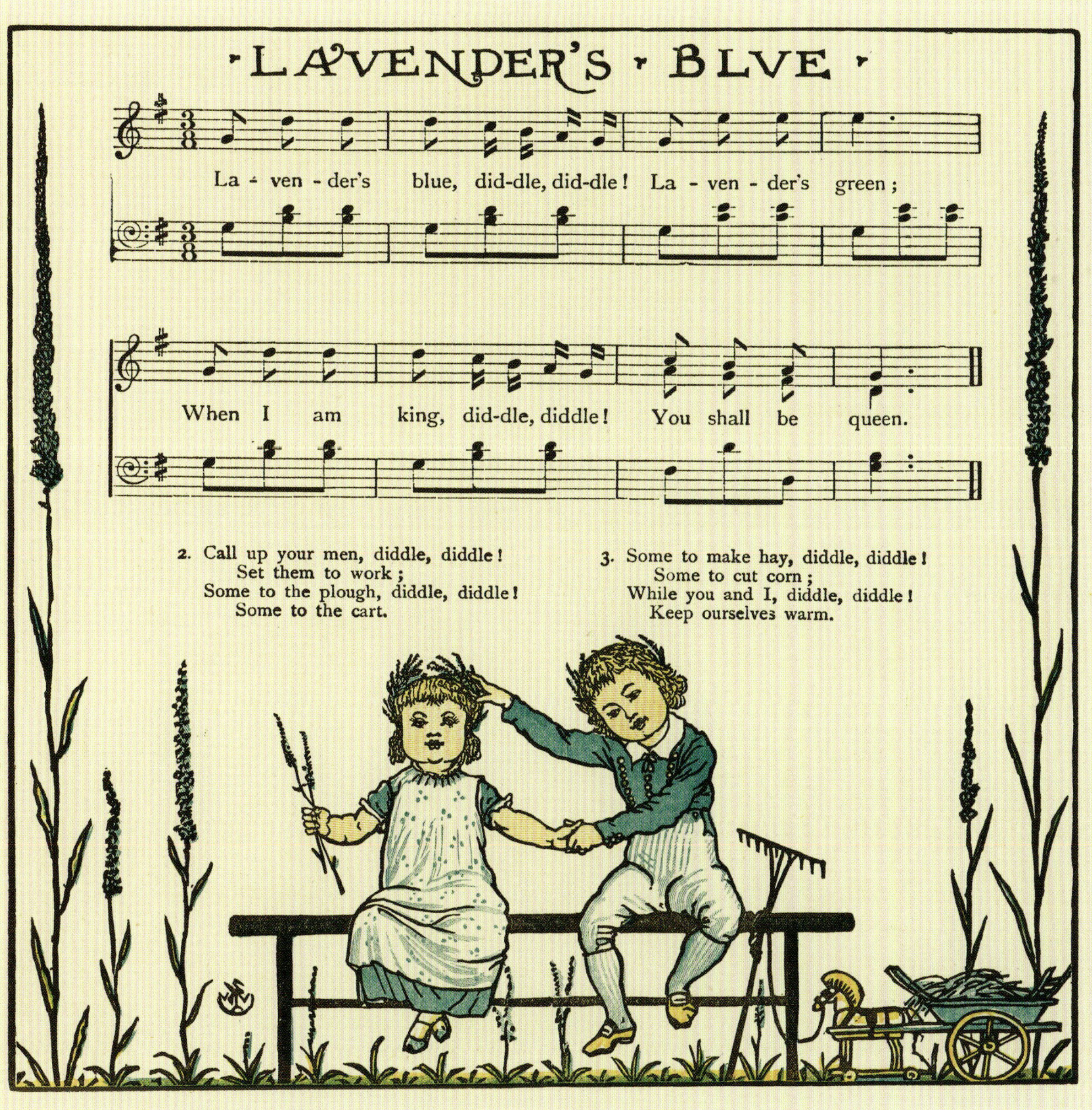
LAVENDER'S BLUE
La - ven - der's blue, did-dle, did-dle! La - ven - der's green;
When I am king, did-dle, diddle! You shall be queen.
2. Call up your men, diddle, diddle!
Set them to work;
Some to the plough, diddle, diddle!
Some to the cart.
3. Some to make hay, diddle, diddle!
Some to cut corn;
While you and I, diddle, diddle!
Keep ourselves warm.

Lemon Blossom

Fidelity in love

IN THE MODERN American folk song "Lemon Tree" made famous by Peter, Paul, and Mary in 1962 and Trini López in 1965, a father explains to his young son that a lemon tree can be interpreted as a metaphor for the complexities of love: "Lemon tree, very pretty, and the lemon flower is sweet, But the fruit of the poor lemon is impossible to eat." Lemon trees, fruits, and flowers have historically been linked to themes of love and romance, and in the Victorian language of flowers, the small, fragrant blossoms of the lemon tree are an emblem of fidelity in love. Lemon blossom honey, with its golden color and citrus essence, is highly prized and often sourced near Mediterranean lemon groves.

This rare, porcelain *pot à oille*, topped by a lustrous, yellow lemon and punctuated by a small lemon blossom, attests to the enduring appeal of lemons and lemon blossoms in the decorative arts. This service was produced by the famed Vincennes Manufactory (later Sèvres), which was established in the Château de Vincennes southeast of Paris in 1740. The company received support from the French king Louis XV, who assumed complete ownership of the firm in 1759. Tureens, or *pots à oille,* were a particularly valuable part of a lavish dinner service. The word "*oille*" is derived from the Spanish "*olla*," which described a Spanish-style meat stew that was popularized in France following the marriage of Louis XIV to Marie-Thérèse of Austria, daughter of Philip IV of Spain, in 1660.

25 | Tureen and stand (*pot à oille*), 1754–1755, Vincennes Factory, maker
Jean-Claude Duplessis père, designer
Soft paste porcelain, enamels, and gilding, 9 7/16 x 10 5/8 in. (24 x 27 cm)
European Decorative Arts Trust Fund, 2016.4a–c

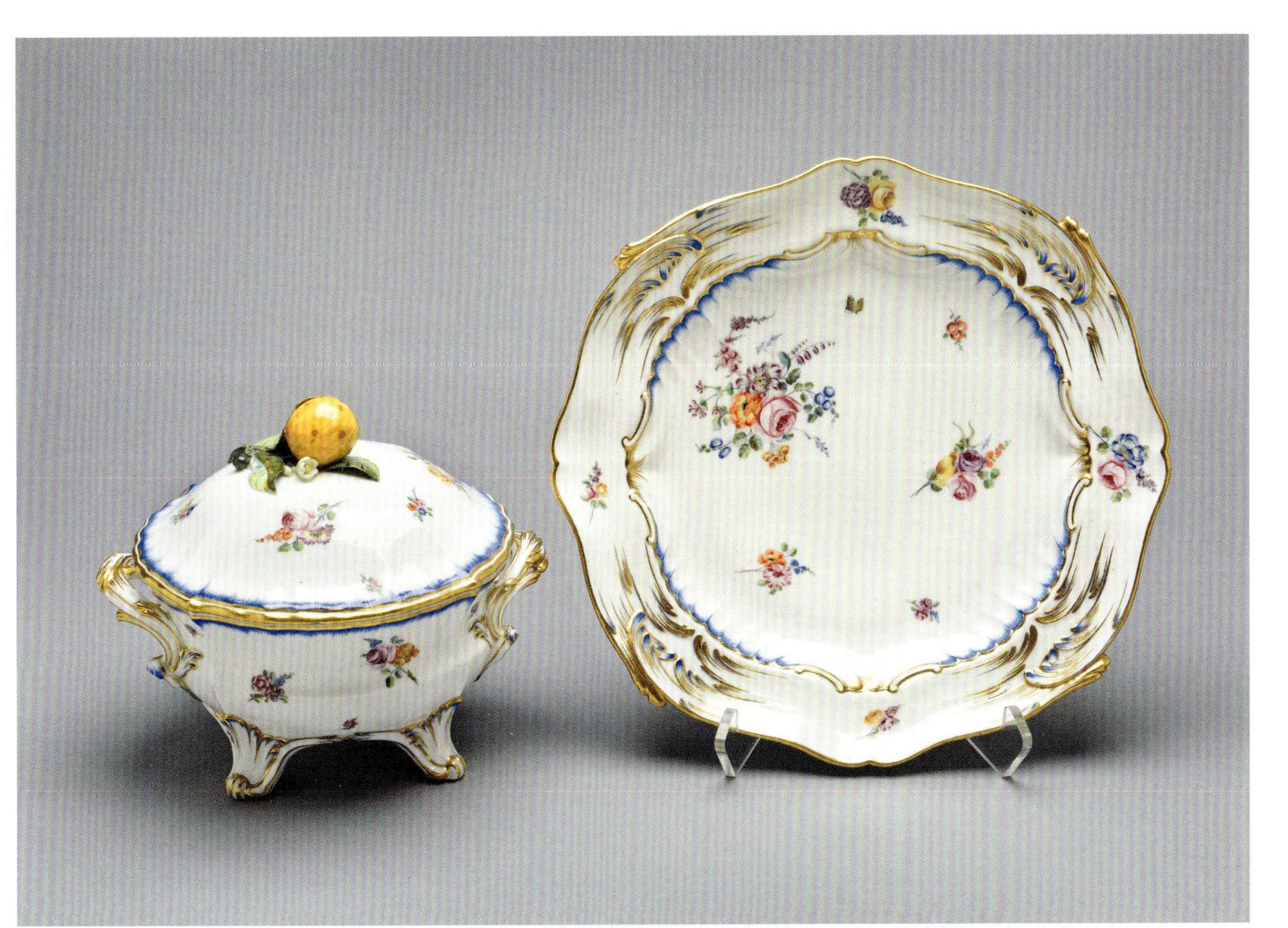

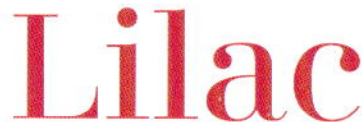

Lilac

First emotions of love

THE LILAC, or *lilag* — Persian for "flower" — was traced to Europe from Persia in the early sixteenth century. According to the Victorian language of flowers, the lilac symbolizes the first emotions of love. The nineteenth-century American writer Frances Sargent Osgood explained, "Nothing is more delightful than the sensations [the lilac] produces on its first appearance on the return of spring. The freshness of its verdure, the pliancy of its tender branches, the abundance of its flowers — their beauty, though brief and transient — their delicate and varied colors, all their qualities summon up those sweet emotions." Old New England superstition recommended planting lilac in the garden to ward off evil from the home; antique lilac bushes found in the region can now sometimes indicate the site of an old farmstead, and purple lilac was designated the state flower of New Hampshire in 1919.

This work is characteristic of the flower paintings of Henri Fantin-Latour, who socialized and exhibited with the French Impressionists but did not share their devotion to plein air painting. Unlike the Impressionists who painted flowers in natural settings, Fantin-Latour painted cut flowers artfully arranged against neutral backdrops (see cat. no. 33). In *Spray of Purple Lilac*, the eponymous flowers sparkle before a simple ocher-colored wall. Numerous international collectors coveted Fantin-Latour's flower works, and in the course of his career he produced more than eight hundred flower paintings to satisfy demand. In 1872, he wrote, "*Ma vie se passe dans les fleurs* (My life passes in flowers)."

26 | Henri Fantin-Latour (French, 1836–1904), *Spray of Purple Lilac*, 1880
Oil on canvas, 14 x 11½ in. (35.6 x 29.2 cm)
Gift of Osgood Hooker, 1963.22

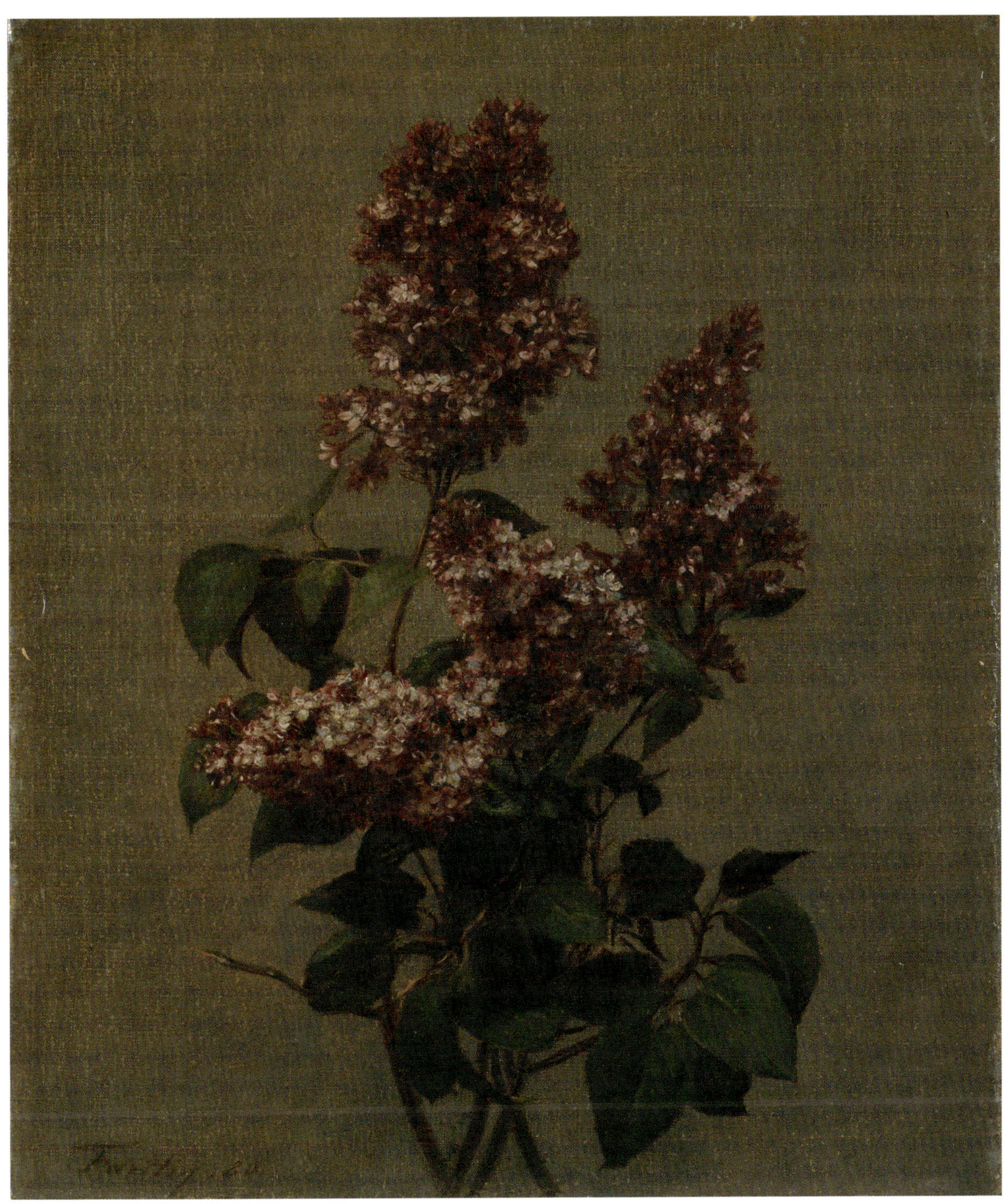

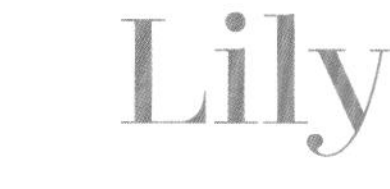

Lily

Purity, majesty, sweetness

LILIES HAVE BEEN actively cultivated for over 5,000 years, ever since Sumerian culture flourished in ancient Mesopotamia. The lily was a divine attribute of the Bronze Age Minoan goddess Britomartis, "Great Mother" and patron of hunters, fishermen, and sailors. In time, it became associated with the Roman goddess Juno and her Greek equivalent, Hera, and later with the Virgin Mary. By the fourteenth century, lilies were common in images of the Annunciation. Lilies decorated the columns of the Holy Temple built by King Solomon and were nurtured in the gardens of Charlemagne. They hold significance in Asian cultures too, as Japan adopted the ancient Chinese belief that the lily (*yuri*) can dispel the sorrow brought on by the departure of one's beloved.

The lily was a popular emblem of the international Aesthetic Movement, which embraced "art for art's sake" and sought harmony between art, nature, and the home. In this drawing of a young woman in artistic dress admiring a potted lily, James McNeill Whistler models the reverence that nineteenth-century Aesthetes such as the provocateur Oscar Wilde paid to the beauty of flowers. Whistler, an expatriate American artist and perhaps the most lauded figure of the Aesthetic Movement, enjoyed working in pastels, which he often deployed on inexpensive brown wrapping paper. He wrote to a friend, "I picture to myself the joy I shall have in showing you my pastels . . . you can form no idea of their bright beauty — their merry lightness and daintiness."

27 | James McNeill Whistler (American, 1834–1903), *The Lily*, ca. 1870–1872
Black chalk and pastel on brown paper, sheet: 10 3/16 x 7 in. (25.8 x 17.8 cm)
Bequest of Whitney Warren Jr. in memory of Mrs. Adolph B. Spreckels, 1988.10.31

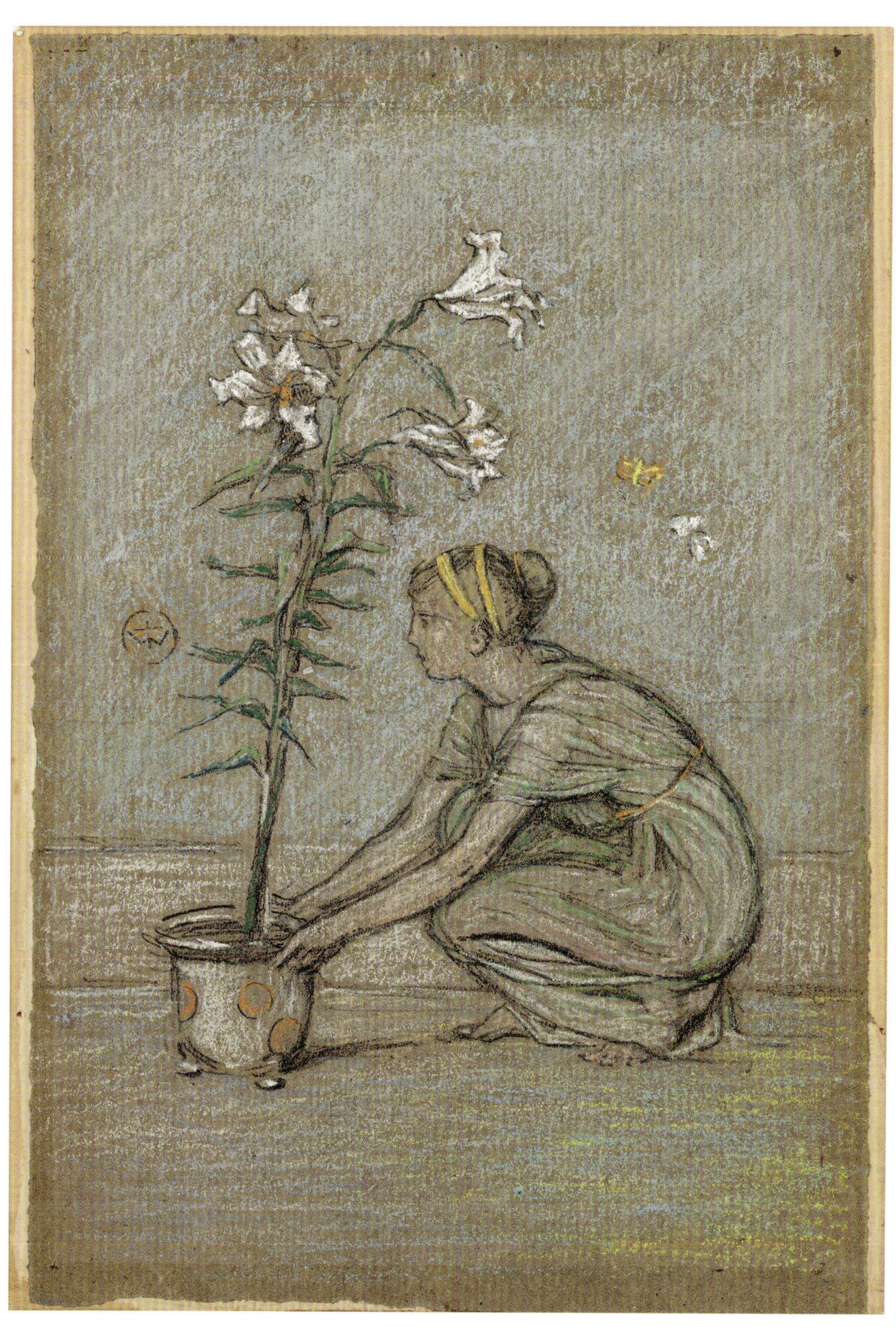

Lotus Flower

Purity, rebirth, estranged love

THE LOTUS is an aquatic flower that grows from mud — it rises above the surface of still, shallow waters, held in place by a stem extending into the mire below. Revered by many cultures, the lotus is a powerful emblem in Buddhism, which regards it as sacred and metaphorical for purity. The Buddha is sometimes depicted sitting on a lotus flower. Because the beautiful bloom grows in muddy waters, it often represents the act of overcoming pain and materiality in order to find enlightenment. As the Zen spiritual leader and peace activist Thích Nhất Hạnh teaches, "No mud, no lotus." In secular Chinese art, the lotus holds auspicious associations, including harmony, love, sympathy, and prosperity.

In Mark Adams's tapestry *Lotus, Sumatra*, a pink lotus blossom opens fully, displaying brilliant colors shimmering across its petals. This image was derived from a specific flower that grew in North Sumatra, Indonesia, on the shores of Lake Toba, in a village of the Batak people. Behind the lotus, two orange pillars suggest the Batak Toba's distinctive, raised architecture. Adams originally trained as a painter and studied with the artist Hans Hofmann in New York City, where he was also influenced by medieval tapestries in the Met Cloisters. In the 1950s Adams apprenticed with the significant French tapestry designer Jean Lurçat, who greatly influenced the development of his own work in tapestry. Adams helped spark a California-based tapestry renaissance and played a critical role in the development of San Francisco Bay Area fiber art.

28 | Mark Adams (American, 1925–2005), designer
Phoebe McAfee (American, b. 1944), weaver; Rudi Richardson (American, b. 1952), weaver
Lotus, Sumatra, 1989. Wool, cotton; slit- and interlocked-tapestry weave, 80 x 92 in. (203.2 x 233.7 cm)
Gift of Mark Adams and Beth van Hoesen honoring Anna Bennett, her husband, Ralph, and the volunteers who saved the Museums' tapestry collection, 1992.34

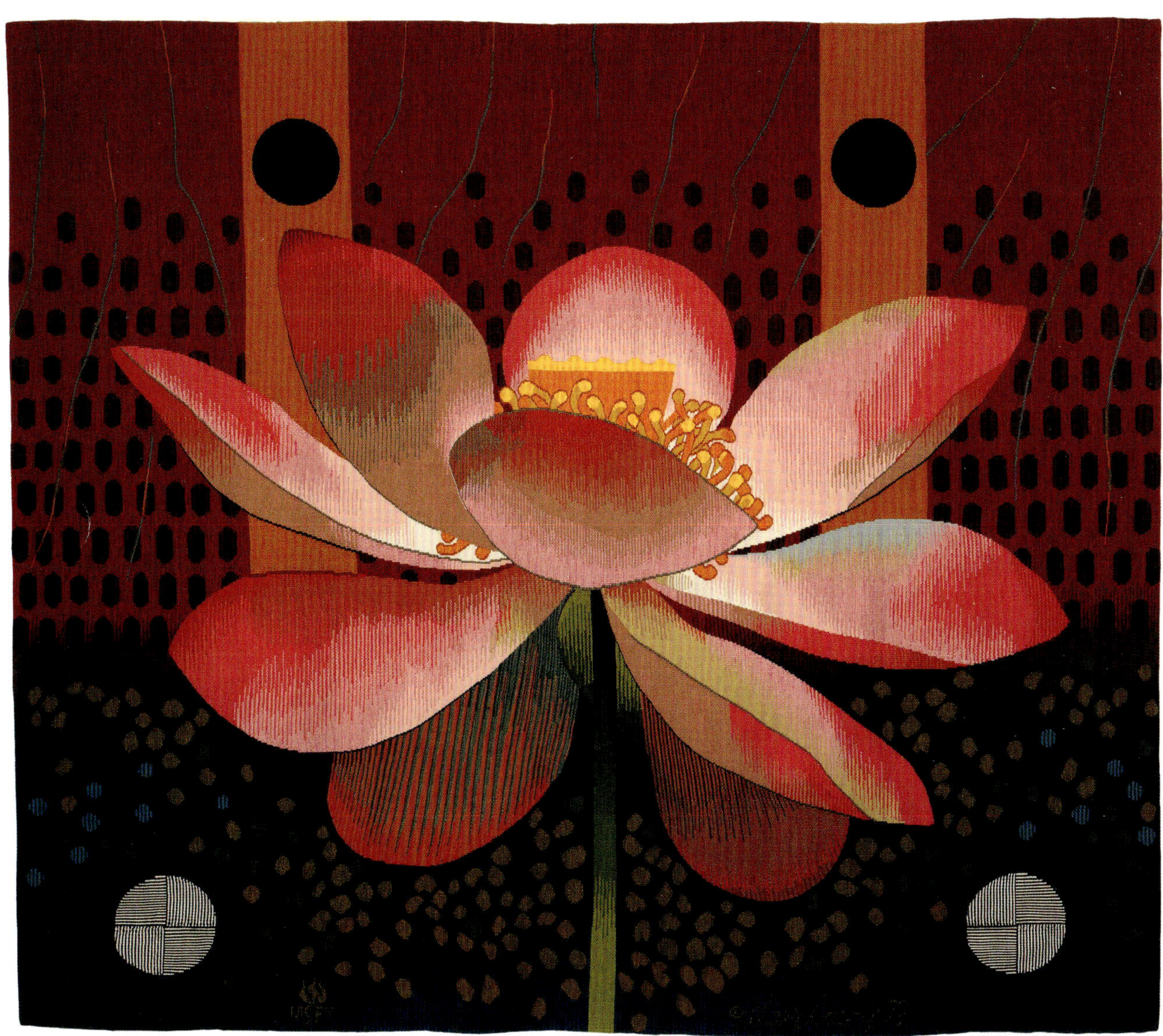

Magnolia

Love of nature, magnificence

FOSSILS INDICATE that the magnolia has flourished since the time of the dinosaurs, making it one of the oldest-known flowering plants. Today, this fragrant bloom, with soft white petals reminiscent of porcelain, is closely associated with the American South. In the Victorian language of flowers, the magnolia represents love of nature and magnificence, suggested by the plant's refined appearance and sweet perfume. Some species are endemic to China, including the *Magnolia fuscata*, known as *Han hsiao hua*, or "Secretly Smiling Flower." The *Magnolia yulan* is called *Ying Ch'un Hua*, or "Flower that Welcomes the Spring." The magnolia has inspired many artists and writers including the American poet Sylvia Plath, who mused in her 1963 poem "Paralytic": "*The claw / Of the magnolia, / Drunk on its own scents, / Asks nothing of life.*"

Modernist California photographer Imogen Cunningham photographed *Magnolia Blossom* with a botanist's eye. Filling the frame, the magnolia offers a performance of light, shadow, and shape, embodying nature's majesty. This was a landmark image for Cunningham, whose botanical works formed a major contribution to the development of modern photography. A cofounder of the influential Group *f.64*, Cunningham conveyed the medium's artistic value with her succinct, direct images of nature. Many of her botanical works were based on subjects cultivated in her Oakland hillside garden: "The reason I really turned to plants was because I couldn't get out of my own backyard when my children were small. I photographed the plants in my garden and steered my children around at the same time."

29 | Imogen Cunningham (American, 1883–1976), *Magnolia Blossom*, ca. 1925 (printed 1930)
Gelatin silver print, 9 5/16 x 11 5/8 in. (23.6 x 29.5 cm)
Museum purchase, M.H. de Young Memorial Museum, 54042

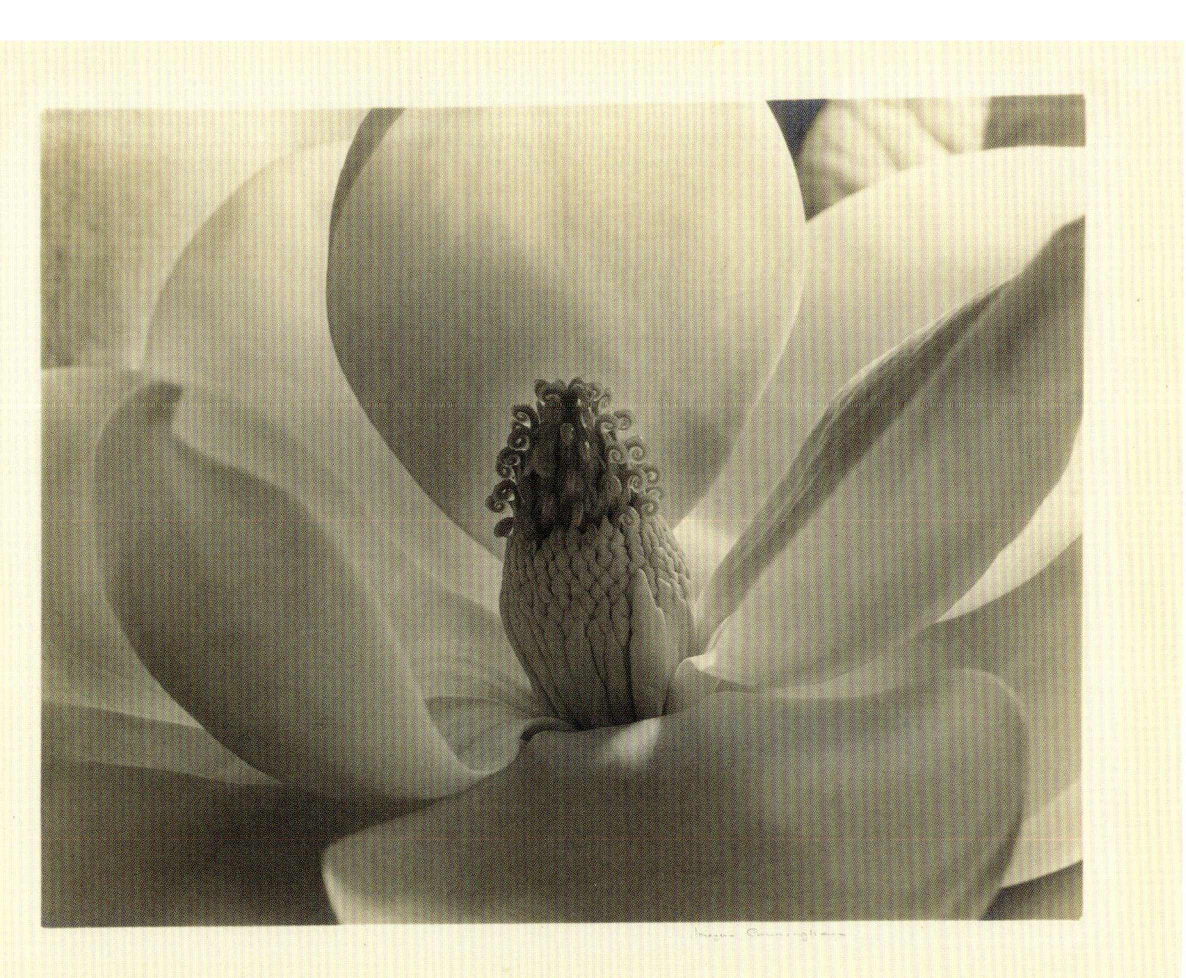

Moonflower

Dreaming of love, night

Ipomoea alba, also known as the moonflower, is the nocturnal sister of the morning glory (cat. no. 31). Moonflower blossoms stay tightly shut during the daytime, but when night falls, these white trumpet-shaped flowers unfurl within moments. Used throughout many cultures as a medicinal plant, moonflowers are honored for their healing and visionary powers. Because they bloom only at night, the language of flowers associates them with dreams of love. Others interpret the moonflower as an emblem of the creativity that can blossom in the darkest of times. In Japan, it is called *yugao*, or "evening faces," and is featured on family crests, usually beside an image of the moon.

The moonflower's sweet perfume is known to attract moths, a phenomenon captured in this color woodcut by the South Carolina artist Alice Ravenel Huger Smith. A leader of the Charleston arts community, Smith was largely self-taught. After encountering Japanese ukiyo-e prints through her cousin, collector Motte Alston Read, she began working in her own Japonism-inflected printmaking style from 1917 to 1919. A talented watercolorist, Smith dedicated herself to combining Japanese compositional strategies and traditional subjects with her own passionate interests in the flora and fauna of her native South Carolina. Many of her prints, including *Moonflower and Hawkmoth,* feature a stylized red double "S" emblem that refers to her surname as well as the geography of her beloved Charleston, which is sited between the sinuous Cooper and Ashley Rivers.

30 | Alice Ravenel Huger Smith (American, 1876–1958), *Moonflower and Hawkmoth*, 1917–1918
Color woodcut, 8 15/16 x 7 15/16 in. (22.7 x 20.1 cm)
California State Library long loan, L467.1966

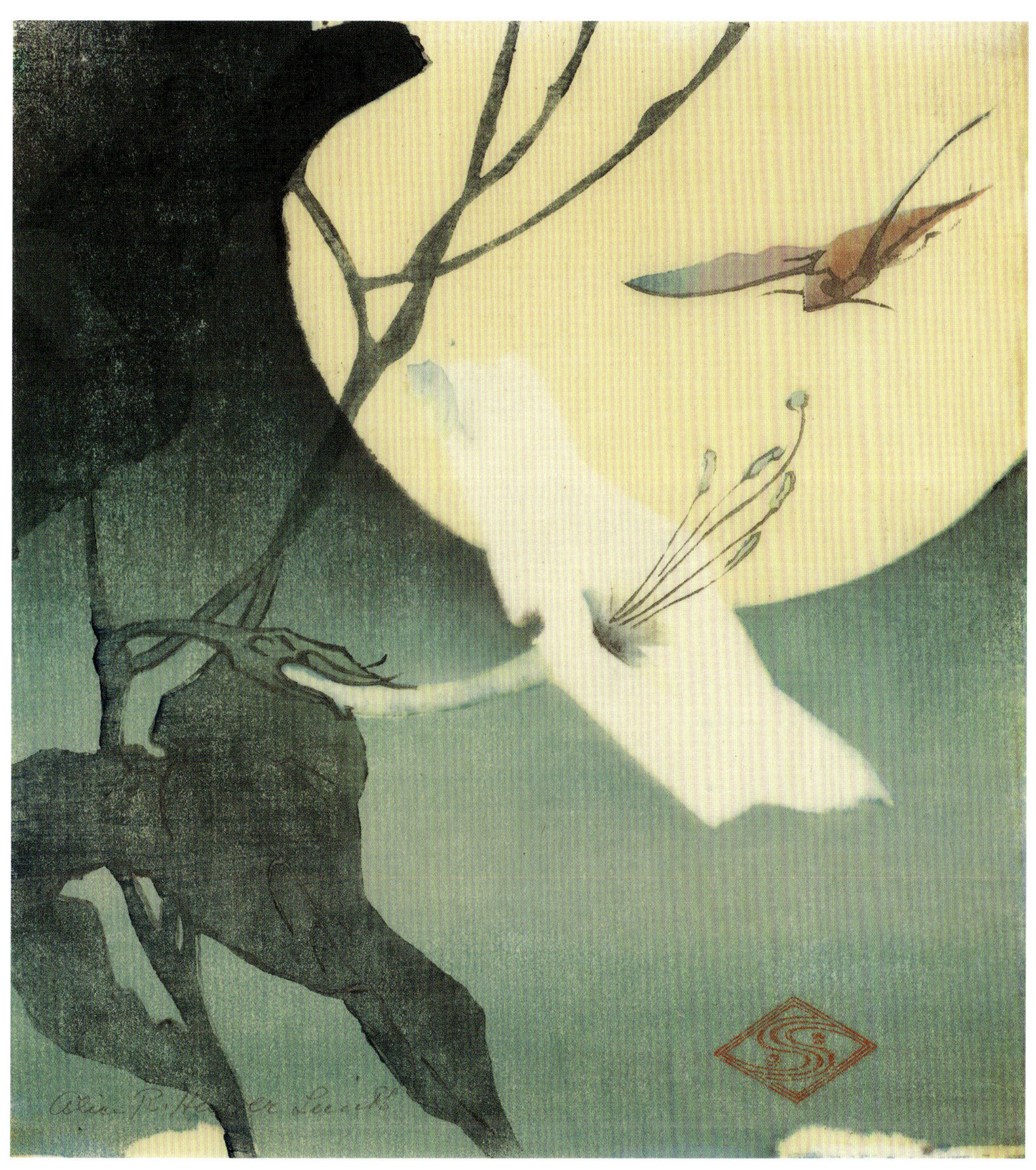

Morning Glory

Affectation, repose

"A morning-glory at my window satisfies me more than the metaphysics of books . . ."
— Walt Whitman, "Song of Myself," 1855

CONTRASTING WITH their nocturnal sibling the moonflower (cat. no. 30), most morning glories unfurl their trumpet-shaped flowers in the early morning. "Morning glory" refers to more than one thousand species of flowers in the family *Convolvulaceae*, from the Latin word *convolvere,* meaning "to entwine," describing the robust spread of their vines. Many morning glories are bright blue, violet, or pink, and these vivid colors, combined with the prodigious spread of their climbing vines, may account for the flower's Victorian association with affectation. However, their cultivation dramatically predates the popularization of floral dictionaries: ancient Mesoamerican civilizations used morning glory seeds to produce rubber, and they prized these flowers for their medicinal psychoactive properties.

In *Morning Glories*, the Japanese artist Kobayashi Kiyochika depicts agile vines of blue and pink morning glories climbing bamboo supports set against a dark background. Often referred to as "the last ukiyo-e artist," the eclectic autodidact Kiyochika continued working with woodblock prints long after the Western influences of photography, etching, and lithography were popularized in Japan. Although he was not trained as a traditional ukiyo-e artist, he endeavored to modernize these traditions, which helped secure the future of woodblock printmaking in Japan in the twentieth century. Here, Kiyochika's representation of morning glory (*asagao*) blossoms alludes to the flower's significance in Japanese culture: after Japan imported the morning glory for medicinal purposes about a thousand years ago, it became a popular motif in art and design.

31 | Kobayashi Kiyochika (Japanese, 1847–1915), *Morning Glories*, 1877
Color woodcut, 9 9/16 x 14 1/4 in. (24.3 x 36.2 cm), Published by Matsuki Heikichi, Tokyo
Museum purchase, Achenbach Foundation for Graphic Arts Endowment Fund, 1968.13.17

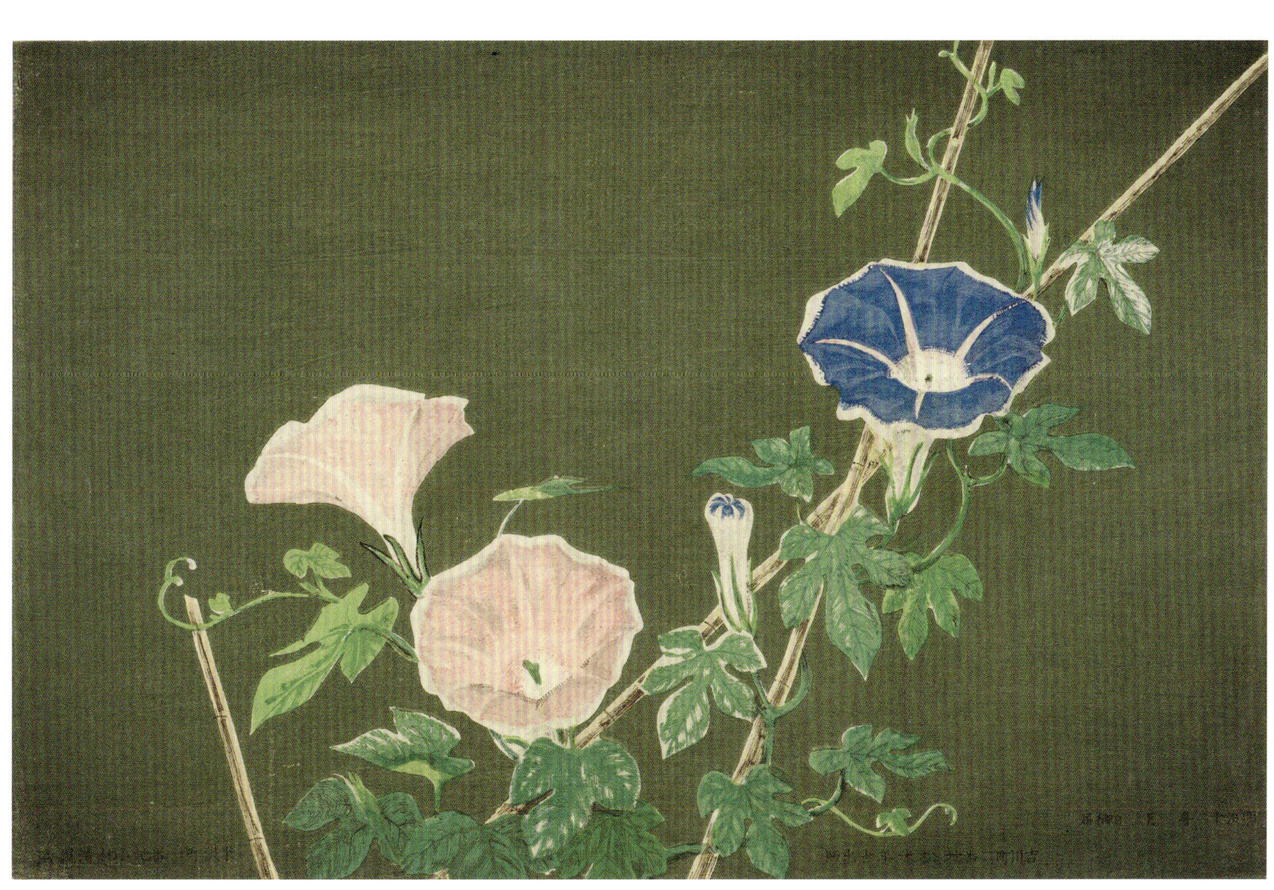

Nasturtium

Patriotism, heroism

"Nasturtiums, who colored you, you wonderful, glowing things? You must have been fashioned out of summer sunsets."
— Lucy Maud Montgomery, *Emily Climbs*, 1925

NASTURTIUMS BELONG to the genus *Tropaeolum*, a word that may derive from *tropaion*, the Greek word for trophy, perhaps because these flowers resemble a helmet, and their leaves, a shield. First discovered in Mexico and Peru, they were brought to Europe in the sixteenth century, where they became an emblem of conquest and victory. In time, their meaning slightly shifted toward notions of patriotism, a quality still associated with nasturtiums today. Thomas Jefferson is known to have admired the edible, peppery nasturtium flower, which he planted in his ornamental and vegetable gardens at Monticello in the late eighteenth century.

Nasturtiums flourish in the San Francisco Bay Area, where they proliferate wildly. This print captures the sensation of encountering an abundant patch of these bright red, orange, and yellow flowers. California artist Ruth Asawa created *Nasturtiums* during her 1965 fellowship at the Tamarind Lithography Workshop in Los Angeles. Although the artist is best known as a sculptor, her time at Tamarind resulted in a notable body of prints. Working with accomplished printers, she created more than fifty lithographs, many of which reflect a curiosity about the natural world. *Nasturtiums* demonstrates Asawa's sensitivities to patterning and texture, as well as an interest in abstracting nature. Throughout her fellowship, she experimented with compositions and revised her prints, as evidenced by the number of second-, third-, and even fourth-state impressions she made there.

32 | Ruth Asawa (American, 1926–2013), *Nasturtiums*, 1965
Color lithograph, sheet: 22 ¼ x 30 in. (56.5 x 76.2 cm)
Printed at Tamarind Lithography Workshop, Los Angeles
Gift of Ruth Asawa and Family, 2007.28.40

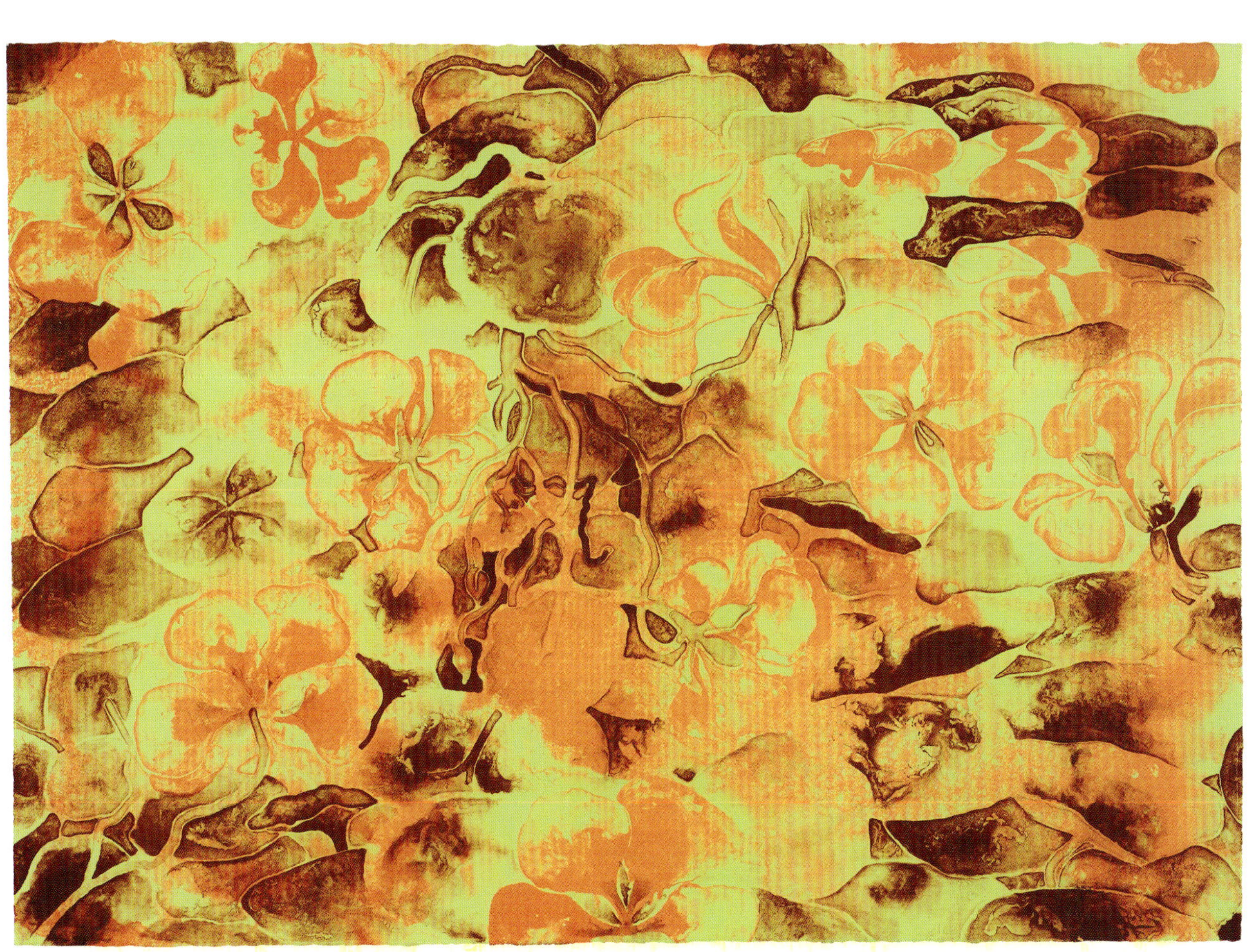

Nigella

Perplexity

THE DISTINCTIVE NIGELLA, consisting of about twenty species of annuals native to the Mediterranean region, belongs to the buttercup family *Ranunculaceae*. The name nigella, from the Latin word for black, describes the flower's dark, shiny seeds, though its unusual appearance has inspired a legion of quirky alternate names, including "love-in-a-mist," "bird's nest," "blue spiderflower," "devil-in-the-bush," "Jack-in-prison," and "kiss-me-twice-before-I-rise," an English nickname from the seventeenth century. Some species, such as *Nigella damascena*, feature a frill of green bracts hovering above the flower — thence the mist of the "love-in-a-mist" name. Popular in Victorian times, nigella became symbolic of perplexity, likely due to its curious shape.

In this tabletop still life, small, sky-blue nigella flowers crown an arrangement of large, colorful roses. Delicate and distinguished, the nigellas are shown at different angles, providing a full view of their distinctive anatomy. Representing Henri Fantin-Latour's achievements as a still-life painter, *Flowers in a Vase* demonstrates his ability to create serious, naturalistic works that celebrate flowers. With his wife, the artist Victoria Dubourg, Fantin-Latour planted a cutting garden to cultivate subjects for the couple's still-life paintings. They tended a wide variety of flowers to satisfy their interest in painting many kinds of arrangements in different vessels. After selecting, cutting, and arranging his flowers, Fantin-Latour painted them as quickly as possible before they began wilting. According to the artist's friend and British agent, Mrs. Edwin Edwards (née Elizabeth Ruth Escombe), one woman had asked her if Fantin-Latour could provide lessons — not in painting, but in flower arranging.

33 | Henri Fantin-Latour (French, 1836–1904), *Flowers in a Vase*, 1882
Oil on canvas, 13 ⅝ x 10 ⅞ in. (34.6 x 27.6 cm)
Gift of Mrs. Thomas Carr Howe, Jr. in memory of Sidney H. Ehrman, 1954.58

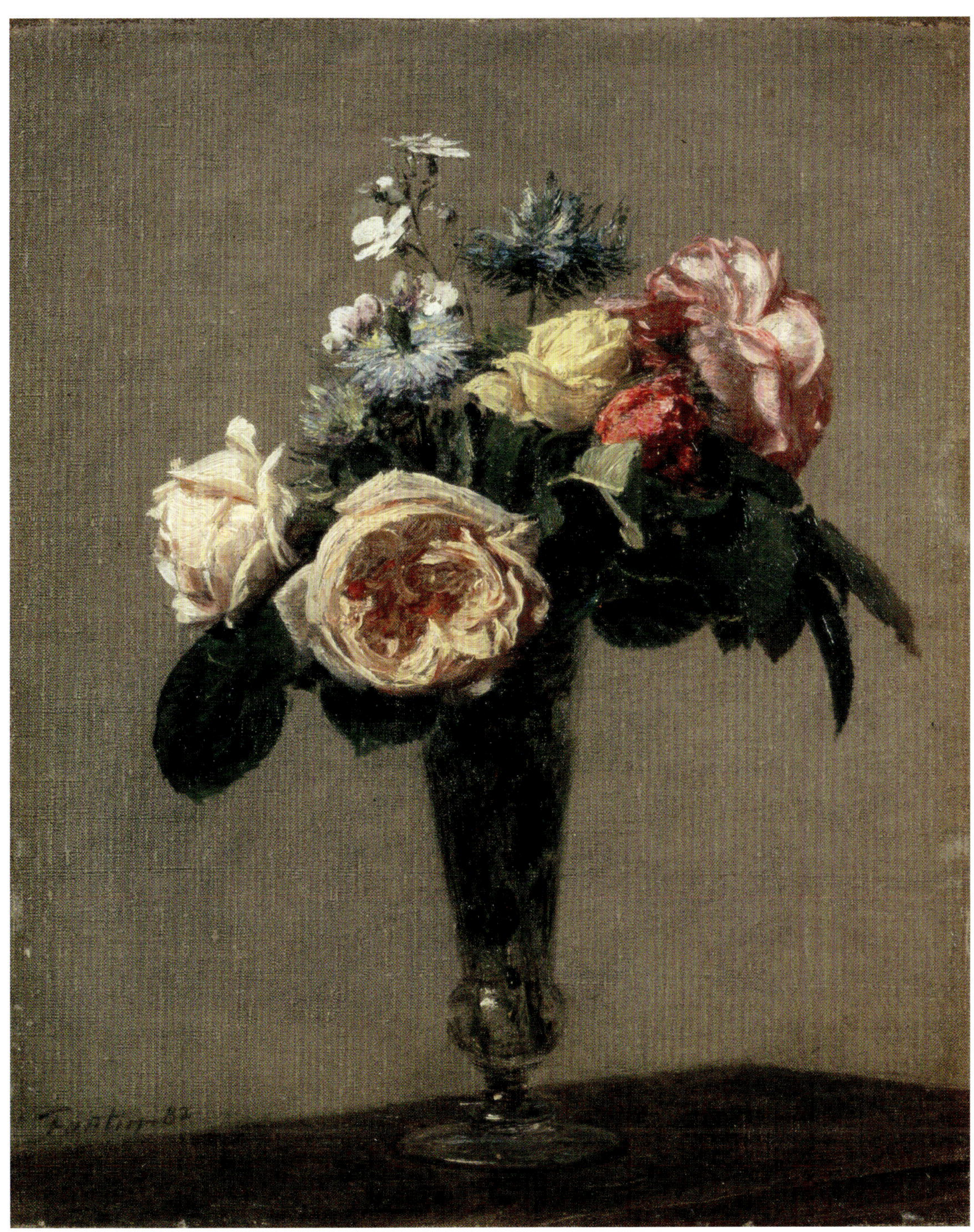

Oleander

Caution, beware!

OLEANDER IS BELIEVED to be native to the Mediterranean region and the Middle East. This evergreen, branching shrub often produces pink flowers, though its pleasing appearance masks the plant's fatal toxicity. In the Victorian language of flowers, oleanders warn of danger — many nineteenth-century guides simply say that this flower means "Beware!" However, the oleander also possesses positive associations: in China, the plant represents beauty and grace, while in Italy's Tuscany region, it is known as the *mazza di San Giuseppe*, or Saint Joseph's staff, which is said to have blossomed when Joseph announced his betrothal to the Virgin Mary. In parts of the world, including India, Greece, and Italy, the beautiful (but deadly) oleander is used as a funeral flower.

In this scene, Cupid, the god of love, approaches a maiden who reclines in a grove of trees and flowers. Surprise and apprehension are apparent on the young woman's face: her nervous gestures telegraph the magnitude of this moment in which Love comes to her with an offering of oleanders. *Love and the Maiden* is considered John Roddam Spencer Stanhope's great masterpiece. A later-generation Pre-Raphaelite artist, Stanhope absorbed the influence of Botticelli, as seen in his palette and the modeling of the figures. Edward Burne-Jones (see cat. no. 4) called him "the finest colorist in Europe," while an early twentieth-century writer praised his "dainty imagery which drifted into fairy-tales."

34 | John Roddam Spencer Stanhope (English, 1829–1908), *Love and the Maiden*, 1877
Oil and gold leaf on canvas, 55 ½ x 81 in. (141 x 205.7 cm)
Museum purchase, European Art Trust Fund, Grover A. Magnin Bequest Fund and Dorothy Spreckels Munn Bequest Fund, 2002.176

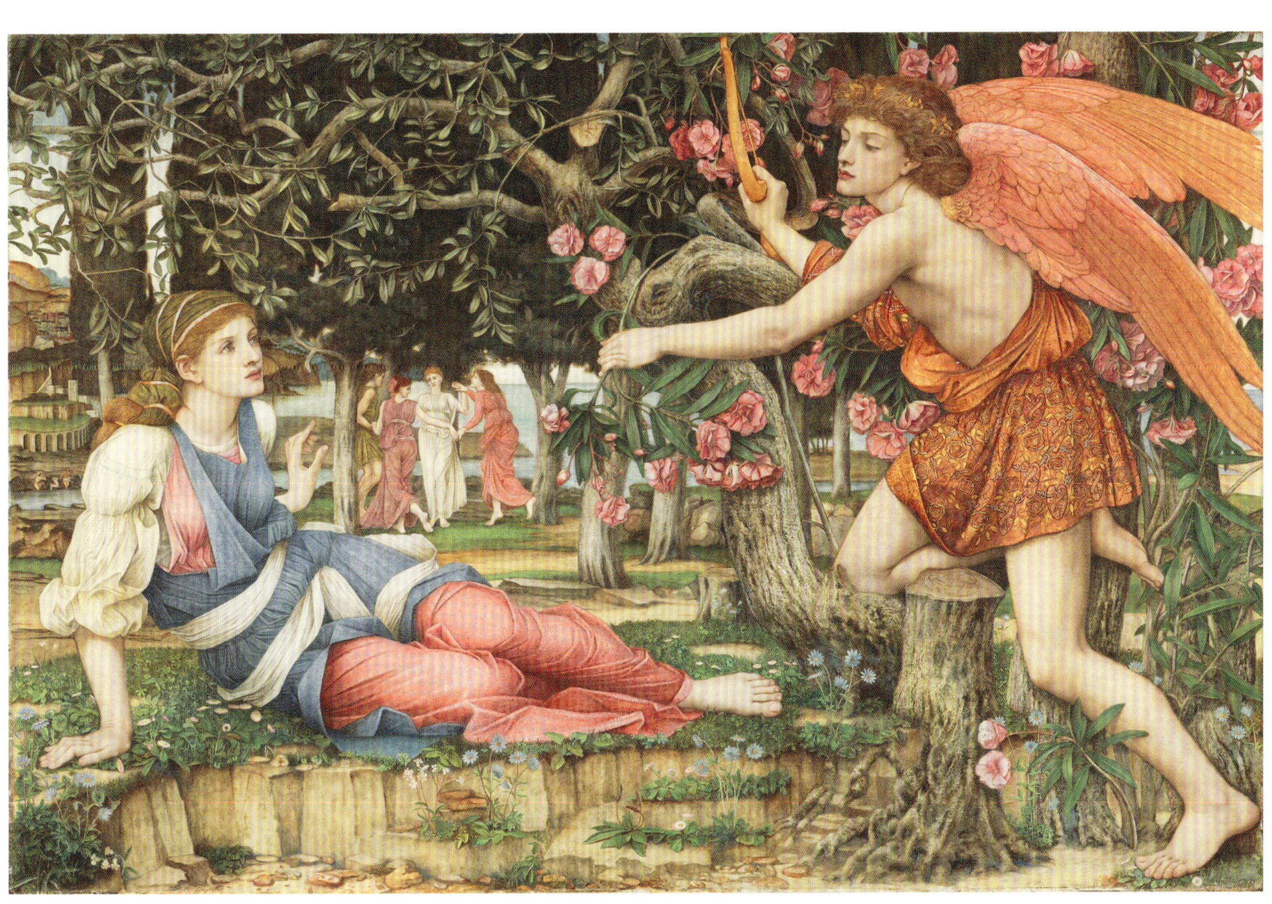

Orchid

A belle, sexuality, virility

ALTHOUGH EXOTIC orchids gained popularity as a scientific subject in the nineteenth century, they rarely featured as a subject in the fine arts. While the orchid (*ran*) was historically used on family crests in Japan, its rarity in Western art may be attributed to its lack of strong religious or symbolic associations and its sexual overtones (it was supposedly used in ancient Greece as a charm for seduction). On the rare occasion that the orchid was included in a Victorian flower dictionary, it was vaguely characterized as symbolizing "a belle." Even as global orchid trading networks proliferated, orchids remained largely absent from the culture of floriography.

American artist Martin Johnson Heade was exceptional in his dedication to orchids. *Orchid and Hummingbird* demonstrates Heade's skill in blending tropical landscape with still life: a sweeping view of a tropical body of water is pushed to the background, giving attention to the dramatic pink *Cattleya* orchid and tiny bird in the foreground. This *Cattleya* is cast in a light that reveals the delicate colors and ruffled edges of its unblemished petals. Heade studied this subject from life, as the artist made three trips to Brazil, Colombia, Panama, and Jamaica between 1863 and 1870. During his first trip in 1863, Heade likely saw orchids in the wild for the first time, and he went on to paint numerous studies for compositions that he later completed in the studio. He often repeated his use of an orchid study multiple times, repositioning the same mesmerizing flower again and again.

35 | Martin Johnson Heade (American, 1819–1904), *Orchid and Hummingbird*, ca. 1885
Oil on canvas, 15 ⅛ x 20 ¼ in. (38.4 x 51.4 cm)
Gift of Mr. and Mrs. John D. Rockefeller 3rd, 1979.7.49

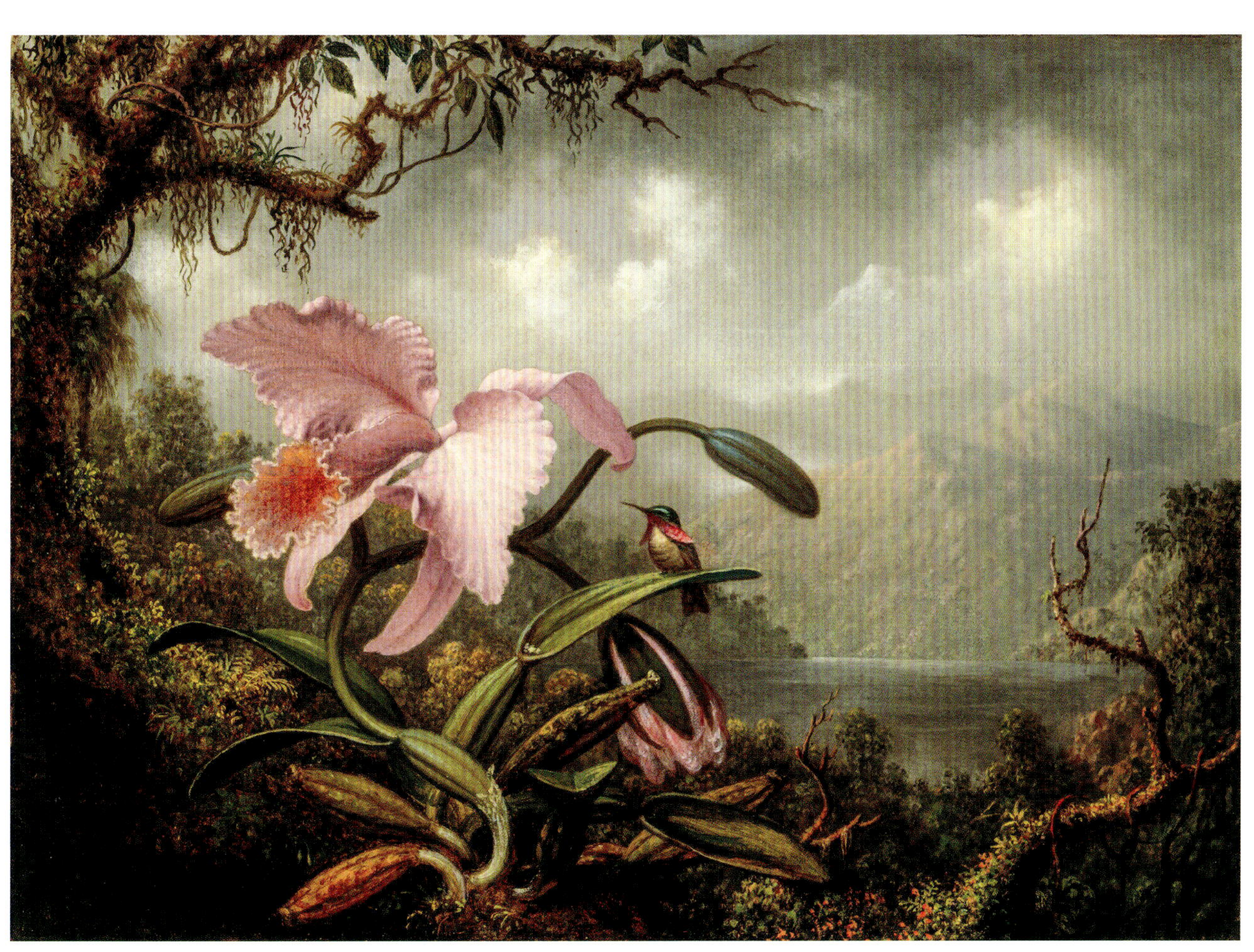

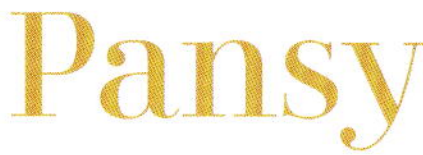

Pansy

Thoughts; you occupy my thoughts

"There are pansies, they're for thoughts."
— William Shakespeare, *Hamlet* (Act 4, Scene 5), ca. 1600

THE WORD "PANSY" is derived from the French *pensée* ("thought"), and in the language of flowers, pansies mean "I'm thinking of you." Among spring's earliest flowers, pansies bring a burst of color wherever they appear — thanks to modern horticulture, they come in a rainbow of hues. Many feature markings resembling a smiling face, while the pansy's form recalls the Holy Trinity, with its central golden eye surrounded by bright petals. Because its petals are heart-shaped, the pansy was also associated with romance: the Celts used it to brew a charmed tea that served as a love potion.

With their paintbox colors and joyful appearance, pansies possess obvious appeal as a decorative feature in fashion. This midcentury hat was an authorized reproduction of a design by French couturier Hubert de Givenchy for the famed San Francisco department store City of Paris. Flowers are a traditional millinery trimming; in 1889, a communiqué sent to the American *Millenary Trade Review* from Paris noted, "Very small velvet pansies, such as are to be found growing wild . . . are favorite blossoms for the moment." About fifty years later, the Los Angeles writer, gardener, and artist Olive Percival wore a notable pansy number to a garden party. It was, according to poet Hildegarde Flanner, "a hat extraordinary in its crowded tumult of velvet pansies . . . a beautiful, even a terrifying hat. It completed Miss Percival's dignity on top of Miss Percival, in a way that left the rest of us breathing hard with pride of Los Angeles County."

36 | City of Paris (American, 1850–1976), maker, Hubert de Givenchy (French, 1927–2018), designer
Woman's hat, mid-20th century
Synthetic velvet, synthetic faille, cotton/synthetic grosgrain ribbon, buckram, and plastic comb; inked and starched cotton/synthetic pile weave, painted composite, flocked paper, and wire, 3¾ x 7½ x 7 11/16 in. (9.5 x 19 x 19.5 cm)
Gift of Mr. E.J. Larson, 1984.24.31

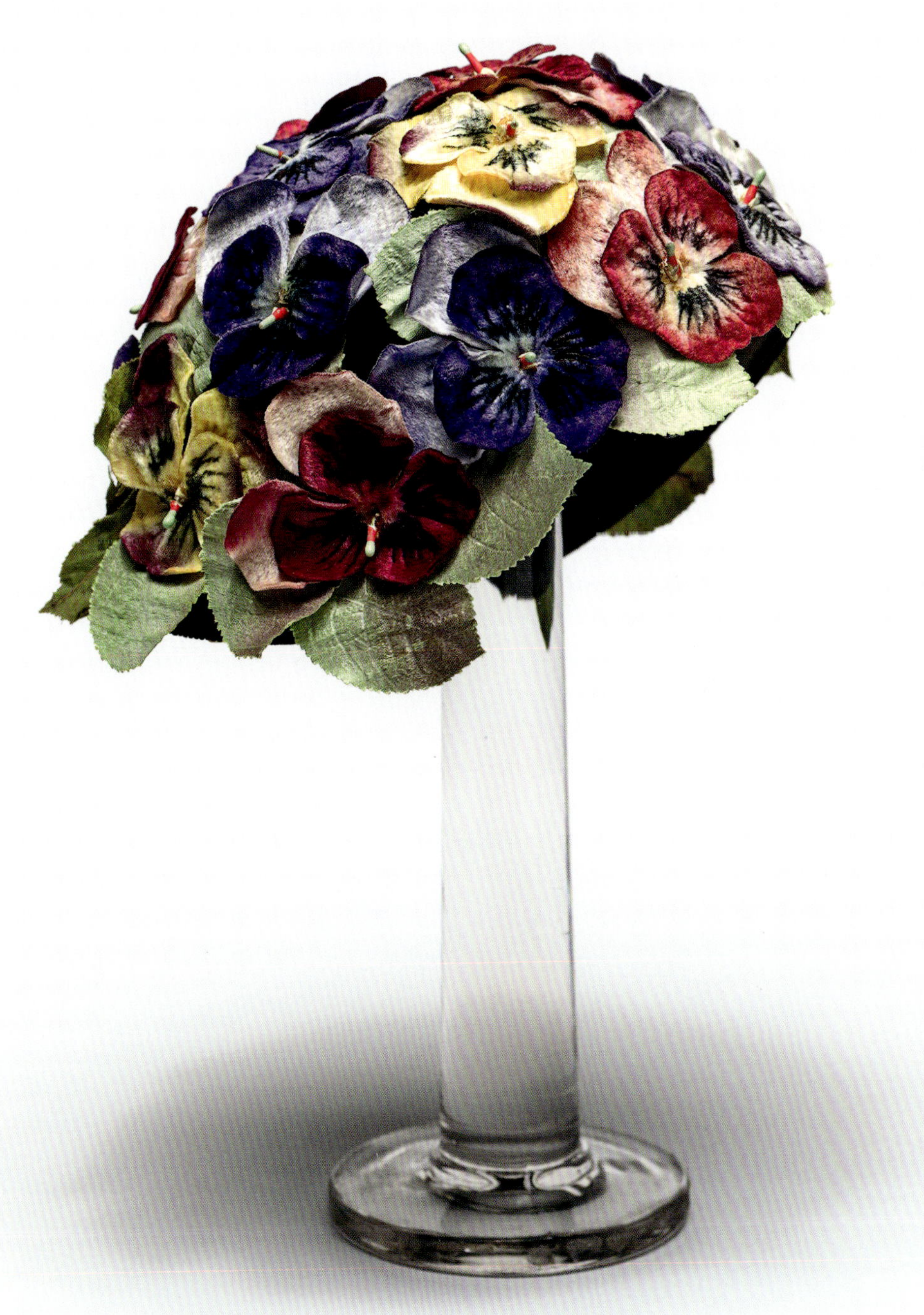

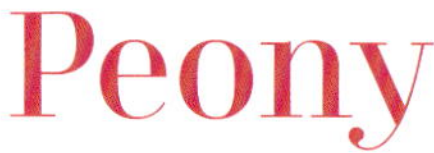

Peony

Bashfulness, shame, ostentation

THE LUSH PEONY is named for Paeon, Greek god of medicine and healing. Paeon received the flower on Mt. Olympus and used it to cure Hades of a wound inflicted by Herakles. Another myth associates this bloom with the shy, blushing shepherdess Paeonia, whose charms attracted Apollo. In a likely tribute to Paeonia, the peony signifies bashfulness in the Victorian language of flowers. The earliest recorded peonies were discovered in a first-century Chinese tomb, providing evidence of this flower's traditional importance in China, where it is called "*sho yu*," or "most beautiful," and the pharmacopeia of Chinese medicine includes peony roots. The peony was introduced to Japan for its medicinal properties in the Nara period (ca. 710–794 CE). There, it developed popularity as an ornamental plant, and it is said that Japanese horticulturists cultivated hundreds of new varieties.

In this rapturous still life, pink and cream-colored peonies stand out from the arrangement, staggering downward from the center of the composition. Jan Frans van Dael belonged to a notable circle of Flemish flower painters who were working in Paris, and he is said to have represented this group's most ambitious efforts. Born in Antwerp, Van Dael later moved to Paris, where he went on to earn royal commissions for his paintings. This early work demonstrates Van Dael's ability to capture texture and light, revealing the distinctive detail of each flower. Interestingly, this selection of flowers also includes varieties that bloom at different times throughout the year, creating a floral arrangement made possible only by the artist's imagination.

37 | Jan Frans van Dael (Flemish, 1764–1840), *Flowers Before a Window*, 1789
Oil on canvas, 36⅜ x 31¼ in. (92.4 x 79.4 cm)
Museum purchase, Mildred Anna Williams Collection, 1952.79

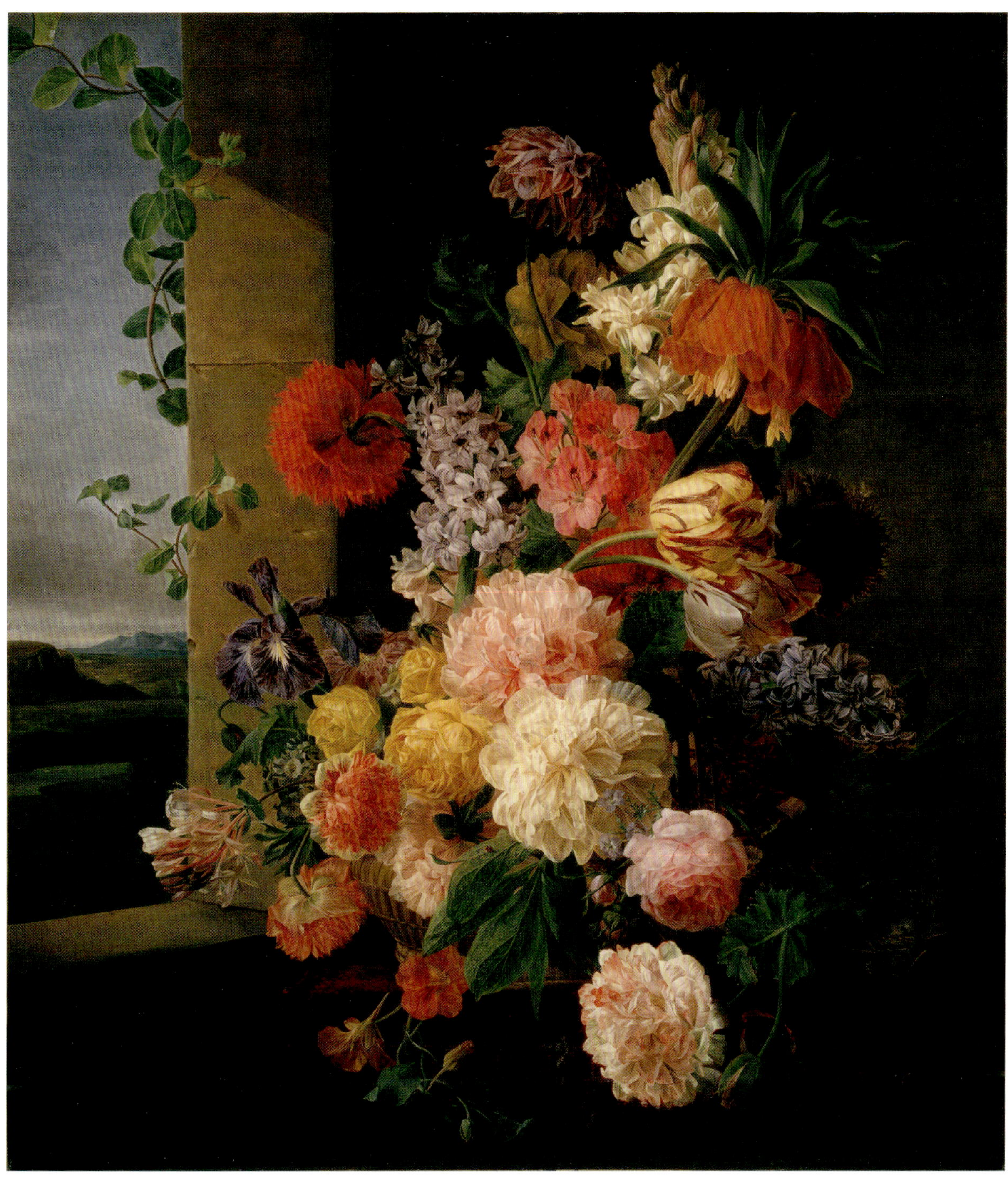

Petunia

Your presence soothes me

THE CHEERY PETUNIA is part of the nightshade family (*Solanaceae*), along with chiles, tomatoes, potatoes, and tobacco. In fact, the name "petunia" comes from *petun*, an indigenous Brazilian word for tobacco. Native to South America, petunias were found in the early sixteenth century by Spanish explorers near Argentina's coast. They were eventually popularized in Europe, where horticulturists cultivated additional hybrids. Like many flowers, the petunia possesses divergent associations: in Victorian floral dictionaries, it is often linked with the sentiment "Your presence soothes me." However, it may also signify anger, resentment, disdain, and "I am not proud." Because of these discrepancies, it is best to make your intentions especially clear when sending a gift of petunias.

Georgia O'Keeffe's captivating flower paintings are characterized by their heightened sense of observation. She later wrote, "Nobody sees a flower — really — it is so small — we haven't time — and to see takes time, like to have a friend takes time." *Petunias* (1925) emblematizes O'Keeffe's intense exploration of the color and texture of these vibrant blossoms, bridging the divide between representation and abstraction. This work is one of a dozen of various sizes and perspectives inspired by petunias O'Keeffe planted at the Stieglitz family estate at Lake George in New York's Adirondack region in the summer of 1925. This composition is the most elaborate in the petunia series: featuring six blossoms at different angles and at various stages of blooming, its magnified flowers fill the canvas, each purple petal brought to life.

38 | Georgia O'Keeffe (American, 1887–1986), *Petunias*, 1925
Oil on hardboard, 18 x 30 in. (45.7 x 76.2 cm)
Museum purchase, gift of the M.H. de Young Family, 1990.55

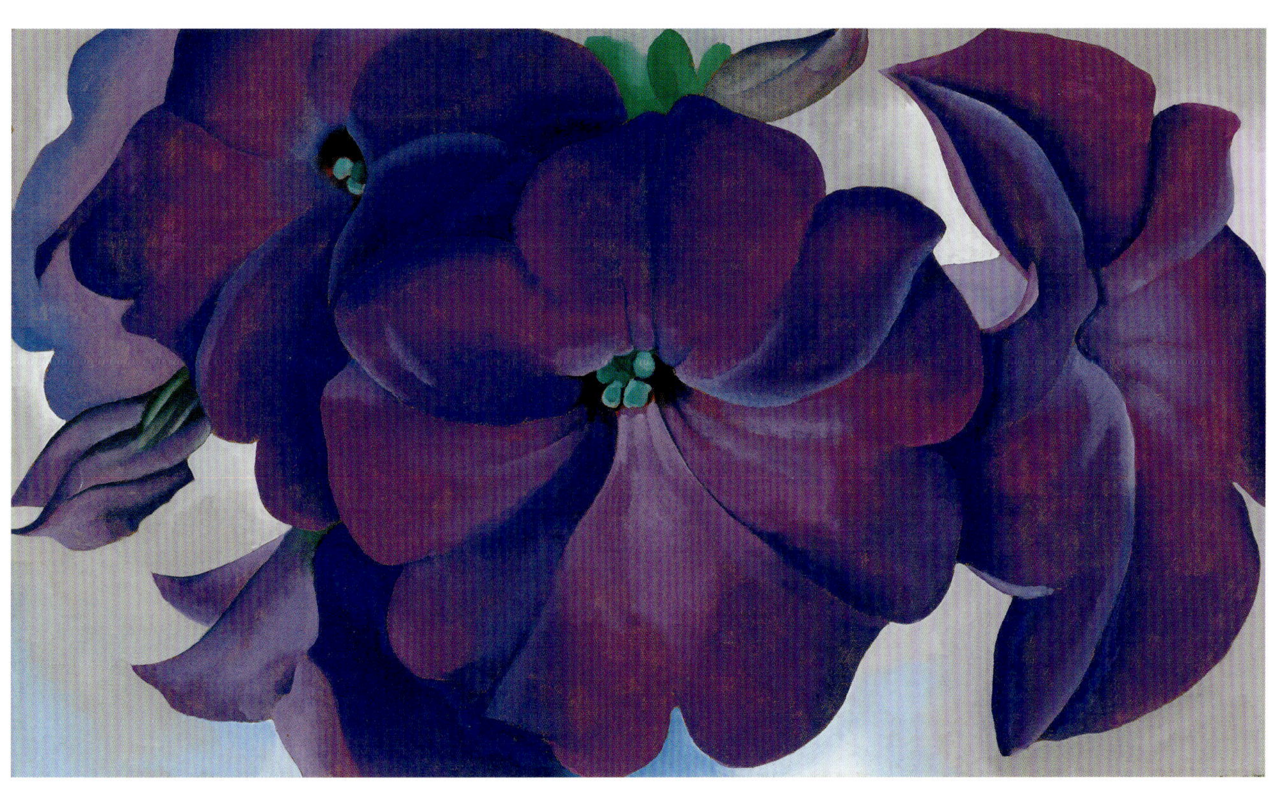

Phlox

Unanimity; our hearts are united

ONCE POPULAR in cottage gardens, phlox is admired for its sweet perfume and vivid appearance. Native to the eastern and central United States, ornamental phlox was introduced to Great Britain in the eighteenth century. Later, upon seeing a patch of phlox in New Jersey in 1831, the eminent British collector Thomas Drummond exclaimed, "The beauty of that alone is worth coming to America to see, it is so splendid!" Although they come in many colors, the word "phlox" comes from a Greek word meaning "flame," likely inspired by a red variety. While a gift of phlox in medieval times meant wishes for sweet dreams or signaled a proposal of love, by the Victorian era they came to signify unanimity or "our hearts are united."

Featuring an overflowing arrangement of pink, purple, orange, and red phlox, Florine Stettheimer's *Still Life with Flowers* offers a compelling example of the artist's inimitable approach to floral subjects. Two arrangements are framed by curtains, as if placed on a stage. Attention is paid primarily to the sensation of viewing the bouquet as one joyous arrangement. Stettheimer called her floral still lifes "eyegays," a word she derived from the term "nosegay" to convey her view that these paintings were intended to please the eye. Stettheimer took great pleasure in arranging bouquets for her own enjoyment, and photographs of her Bryant Park studio show flower arrangements placed throughout the space. Her birthday bouquets were particularly noteworthy: her annual ritual involved picking a bouquet of seasonal flowers that she would note in her journals and paint for posterity.

39 | Florine Stettheimer (American, 1871–1944), *Still Life with Flowers*, 1921
Oil on canvas mounted on hardboard, 25¾ x 29⅝ in. (65.4 x 75.2 cm)
Gift of Miss Ettie Stettheimer to the California Palace of the Legion of Honor, 1955.24

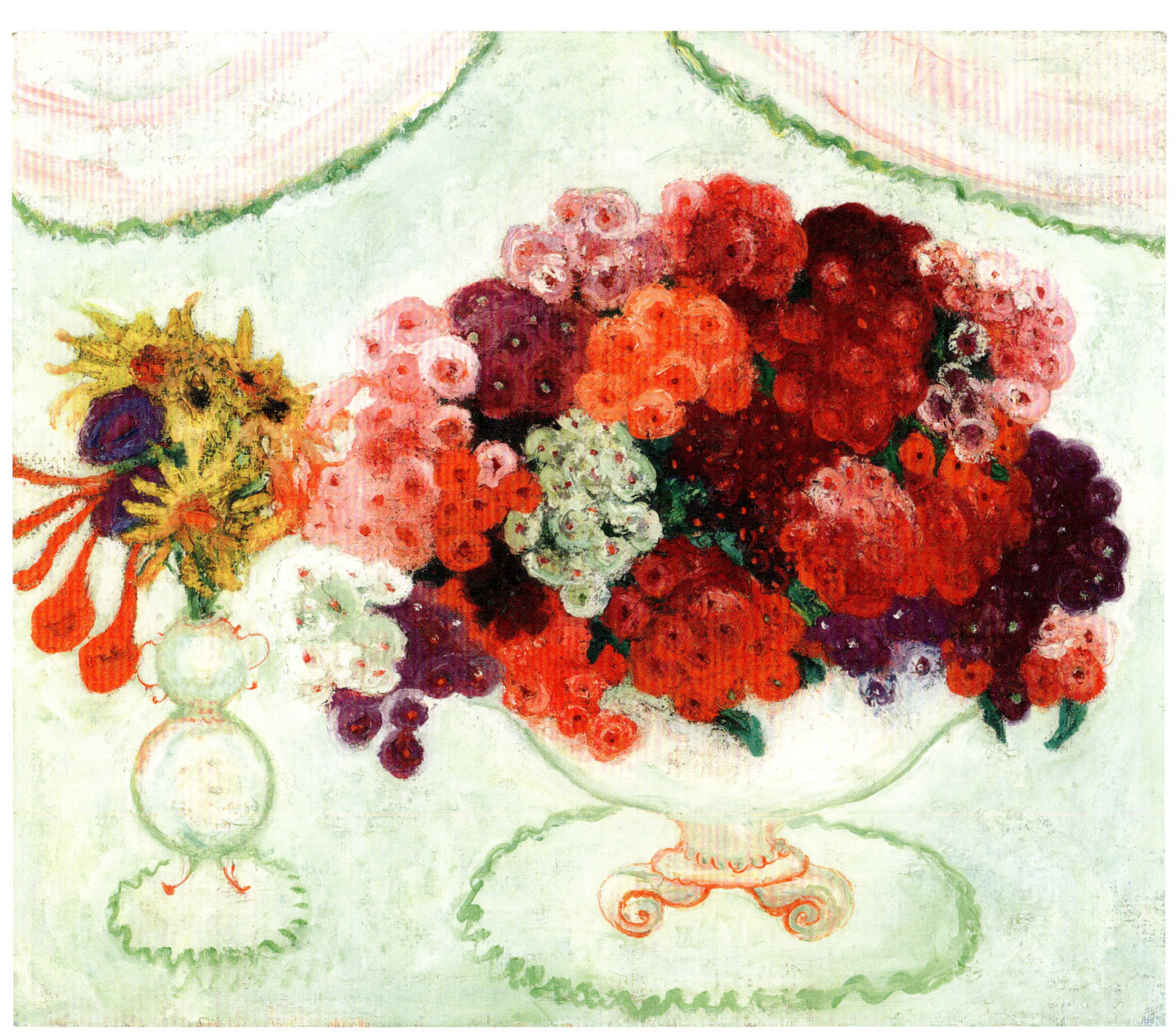

Plum Blossom

Fidelity; keep your promises

IN THE VICTORIAN language of flowers, the plum tree represents fidelity and keeping promises. Perhaps these associations come from how this tree bears fruit: every year the plum blooms profusely, but it will not always yield a harvest unless a devoted gardener faithfully prunes and maintains the tree. In Chinese culture, plum blossoms signify strength, endurance, renewal, and winter, due to how their pretty flowers erupt on gnarled branches before the winter snow melts. The plum tree also features in the ancient Chinese text, the *I Ching*, or *Book of Changes*, which notes that its blossoms are of the *Yang* principle, associated with heaven, while the wood of its trunk and branches are of the *Yin* principle, associated with the earth.

The plum blossom was once the flower most frequently described in Japanese poetry, noted for its delicate appearance and sweet fragrance. Utagawa Hiroshige's woodcut *The Plum Orchard at Kameido* celebrates what was once the most revered plum tree in Japan — the "Sleeping Dragon Plum" (*garyūbai*), found in the garden of Kameido Tenjin Shrine, Tokyo. According to one guidebook, its blossoms were "so white when full in bloom as to drive off the darkness." The foreground is filled by a dark, flowering tree, which blocks the view of the immense plum grove in the background. Tiny figures along the horizon may be admirers who have come to enjoy the bloom. Vincent van Gogh later copied this composition directly, translating the palette with even deeper intensity in *Flowering Plum Tree (after Hiroshige)* (1887).

40 | Utagawa Hiroshige (Japanese, 1797–1858), *The Plum Orchard at Kameido (Kameido Umeyashiki)*, no. 30 from the series *One Hundred Views of Famous Places in Edo (Meisho Edo hyakkei)*, 1857
Color woodcut with mica, 13 5⁄16 x 8 13⁄16 in. (33.8 x 22.4 cm)
Published by Uoya Eikichi, Edo (Tokyo), Gift of Miss Carlotta Mabury, 54755.752

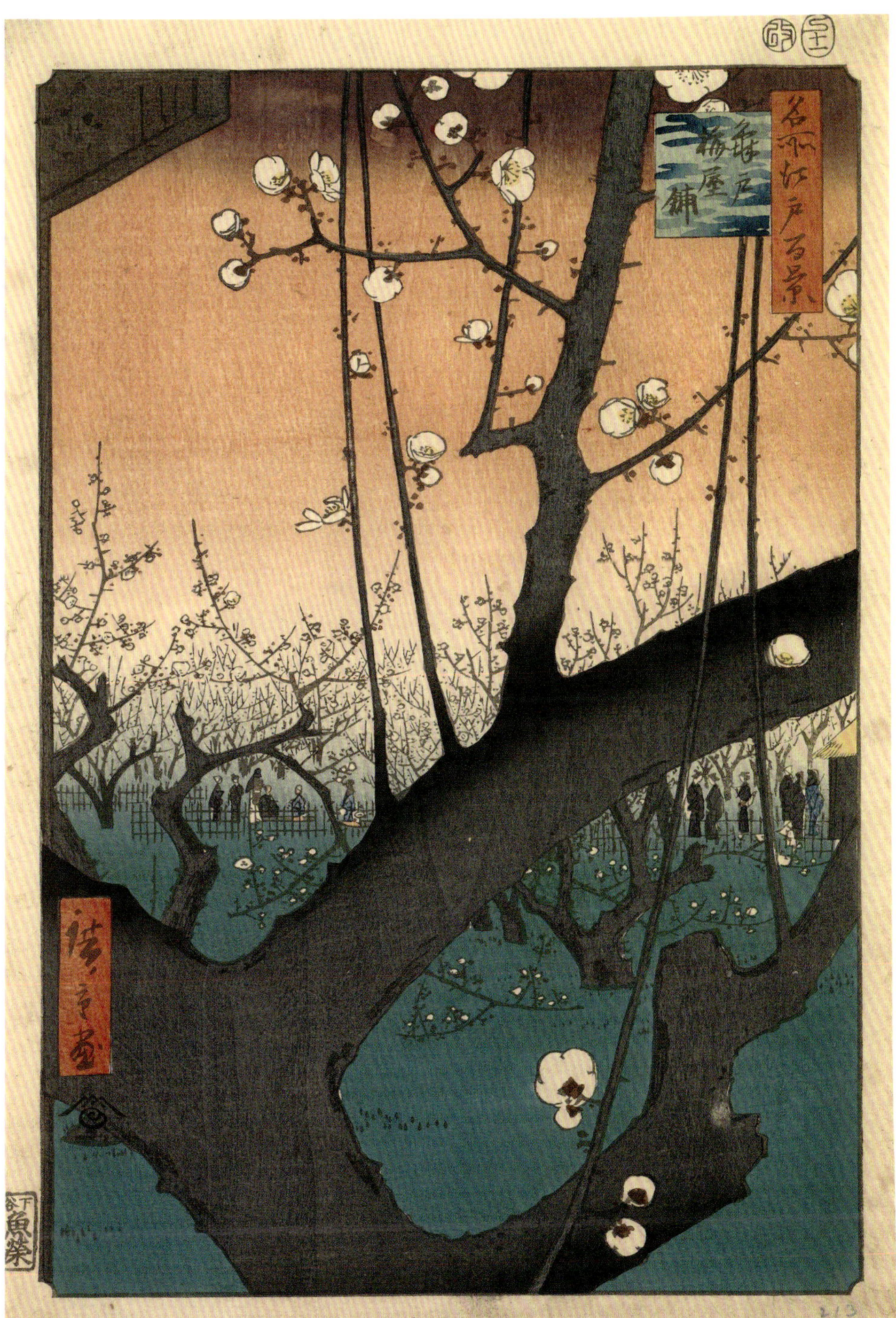
名所江戸百景
亀戸梅屋舗
広重画
下谷
魚栄

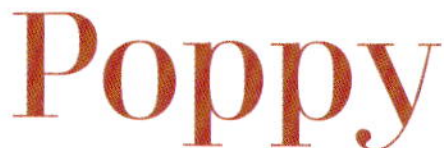

Poppy

Consolation, sleep, remembrance

IN GREEK MYTHOLOGY, the poppy was said to have been created by Demeter, who partook of the poppy's sleep-inducing narcotic properties in order to soothe her grief over her daughter, Persephone. This helps explain the poppy's associations with consolation and slumber, the latter an effect of the opium derived from this plant. Ancient Romans used poppy juice to ease the pains of love, and poppy syrup was used in Elizabethan England to relieve discomfort and induce sleep. After the First World War, thousands of blood-red poppies grew around the bodies of fallen soldiers on the front lines of France and Flanders (northern Belgium). Some believed the flowers grew from the spilled blood of war, making the red poppy the flower of remembrance for those lost in battle.

Mary Frank's poetic color monotype captures the poppy's associations with remembrance and mourning. Depicted against a flat black ground, her poppies dance upward, as if captured in a moment of metamorphosis. This sense of transformation is heightened by the open red flower, its petals presenting a stark contrast with the unopened poppy heads beside it. Widely acclaimed for her sculptures, Frank's distinctive monoprints appear to reveal a sculptor's tactile approach. American art critic Carter Ratcliff writes, "Her touch has the power to animate. . . . Frank's monotypes show her rushing form into existence and doing it with such delicate aggressiveness that the very conditions of existence — space and time among them — seem to be defined by the intensities of her gesture."

41 | Mary Frank (American, b. 1933), *Untitled*, 1978
Color monotype, 40⅛ x 50⅛ in. (101.9 x 127.3 cm)
Anderson Graphic Arts Collection, gift of the Harry W. and Mary Margaret Anderson Charitable Foundation, 1996.74.132

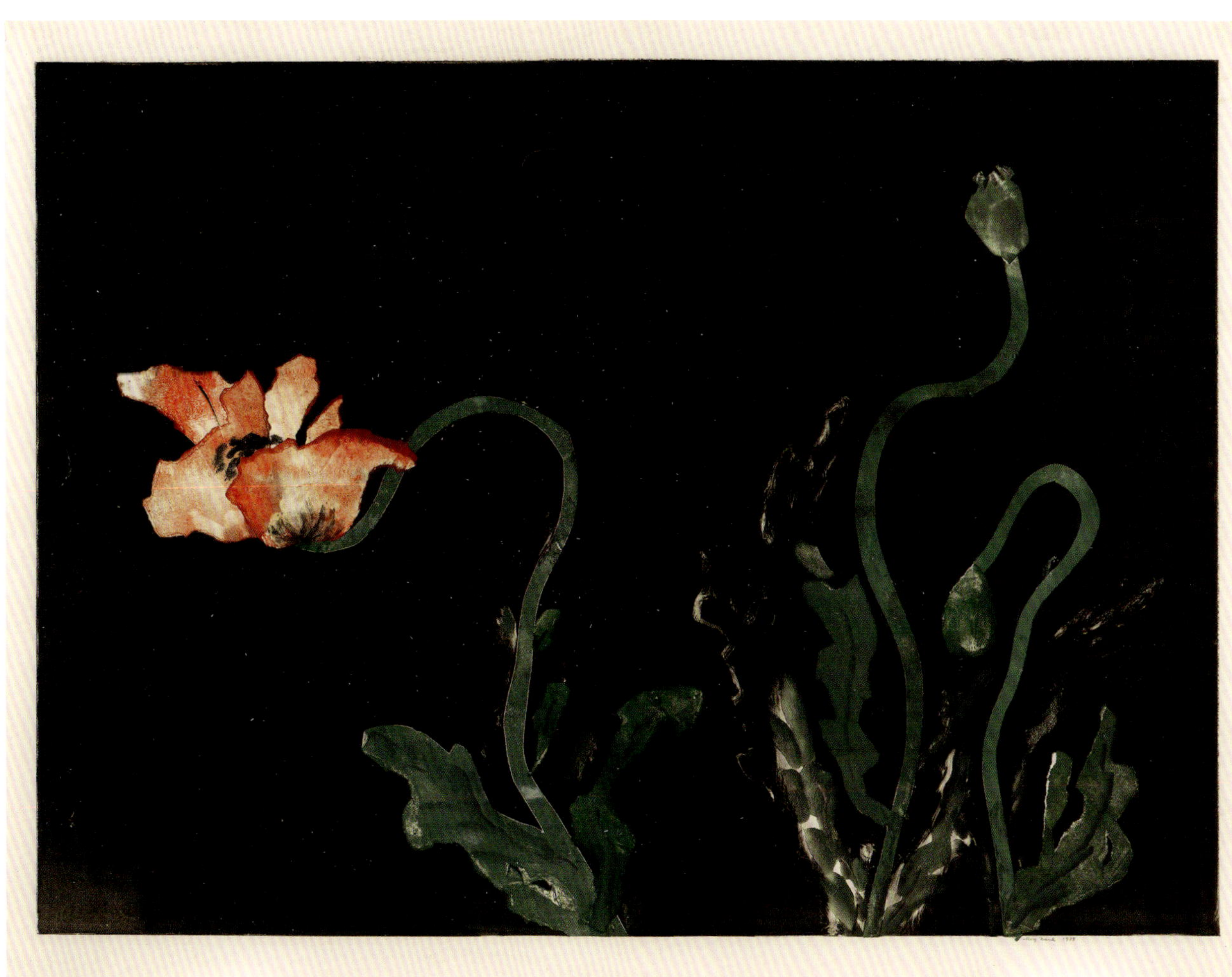

Quince Blossom

Temptation

"And suddenly, from out of nowhere, whirls the pear-bloom /
upon us, and apple- and almond- and apricot- and quince-blossom, /
storms and cumulus clouds of all imaginable blossom /
about our bewildered faces, / though we do not worship."
— D.H. Lawrence, "Craving for Spring," 1917

A RELATIVE OF THE APPLE, the quince belongs to the rose family. An ancient fruit known in the Middle East since the first millennium BCE, the quince, not the apple, is thought to be the original fruit of knowledge that tempted Eve in the Garden of Eden. Some also believe that the mythical golden apple of Hesperides given by Paris to Aphrodite, which led to Troy's downfall, was also a quince. Perhaps both of these stories explain why the Victorian language of flowers associates this fruit and its flowers with temptation.

With its sense of spontaneity and "naturalness," Philip Dolan's *A Bird's Nest and Blossom* depicts a nest alongside a branch of flowers that strongly resemble quince blossoms. Dolan takes on the compositional format most closely associated with the British watercolorist William Henry Hunt, whose birds'-nests still lifes earned him the nickname "Bird's Nest Hunt." Such realistic images of nests and flora in nature were largely influenced by the prominent English art critic John Ruskin, who implored young artists to "go to nature in all singleness of heart . . . having no other thoughts but how best to penetrate her meaning rejecting nothing, selecting nothing . . . and rejoicing always in the truth."

42 | Philip Dolan (English, active 1867–1877), *A Bird's Nest and Blossom*, mid-19th century
Watercolor and opaque watercolor with scraping, sheet: 10 3/16 x 13 1/16 in. (25.9 x 33.2 cm)
Museum purchase, Achenbach Foundation for Graphic Arts Endowment Fund, 1979.2.19

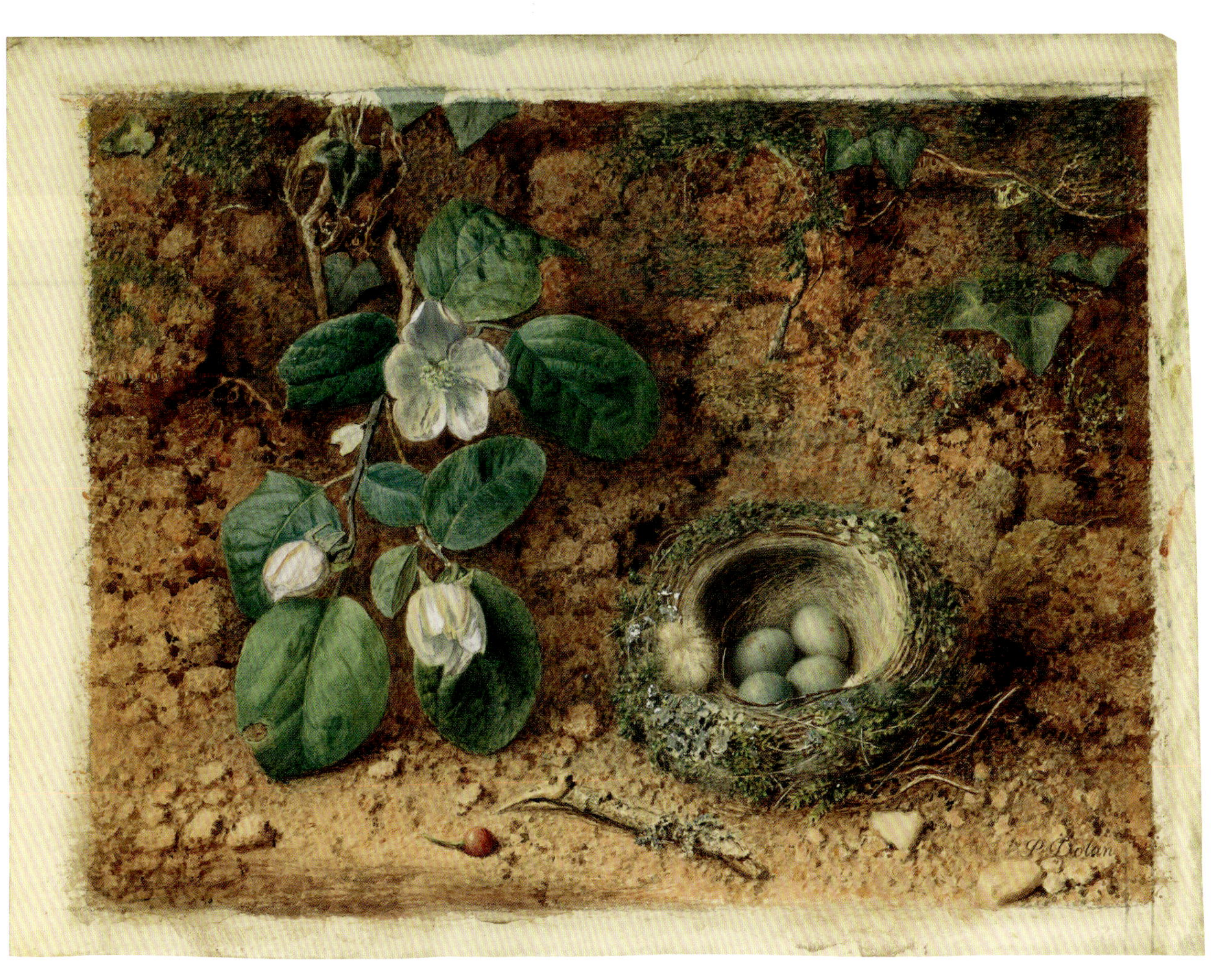
P. Dolan

Rose

Love, beauty

A TRADITIONAL EMBLEM of love and beauty, the rose is one of the oldest cultivated flowers. Tended in ancient gardens of western Asia and northeastern Africa, the rose also featured in Greek mythology and the Roman Empire: Chloris, the Greek goddess of flowers, was credited with creating the rose, while ancient Romans associated roses with women, wine, and indulgence. While the rose symbolized amorousness, its color could be used to indicate the seriousness of one's ardor: yellow stood for friendship, secret love, and admiration; white symbolized innocent love; and light pink represented the beginning of a relationship, according to the Victorian language of flowers. Deep red stood for passionate romance, while the flower's thorns suggest the threat of heartbreak.

The rose is also included among symbols associated with the Grateful Dead, the iconic San Francisco Bay Area band (est. 1965) that embodied 1960s counterculture. This promotional poster depicting a skeleton crowned with red roses was designed in 1966. Legendary artist and poster designer Stanley Mouse first encountered the image with collaborator Alton Kelley: "We would go to the San Francisco library and peruse the books on poster art . . . and found this thing and thought, this says Grateful Dead all over it." Mouse repurposed the original Edmund Sullivan illustration from the 1913 edition of *The Rubáiyát of Omar Khayyám*. Heavily influenced by Art Nouveau and Symbolism, Mouse and his peers mined and manipulated images from the past to create the psychedelic posters now inextricable from Bay Area cultural history.

43 | Stanley Mouse (American, b. 1940)
"Skeleton and Roses,"— Grateful Dead, Oxford Circle, September 16 & 17, Avalon Ballroom, 1966
Color offset lithograph poster, 19 15/16 x 14 in. (50.7 x 35.6 cm)
Published by Family Dog Productions, San Francisco. Museum purchase, Achenbach Foundation for Graphic Arts Endowment Fund, 1974.13.100

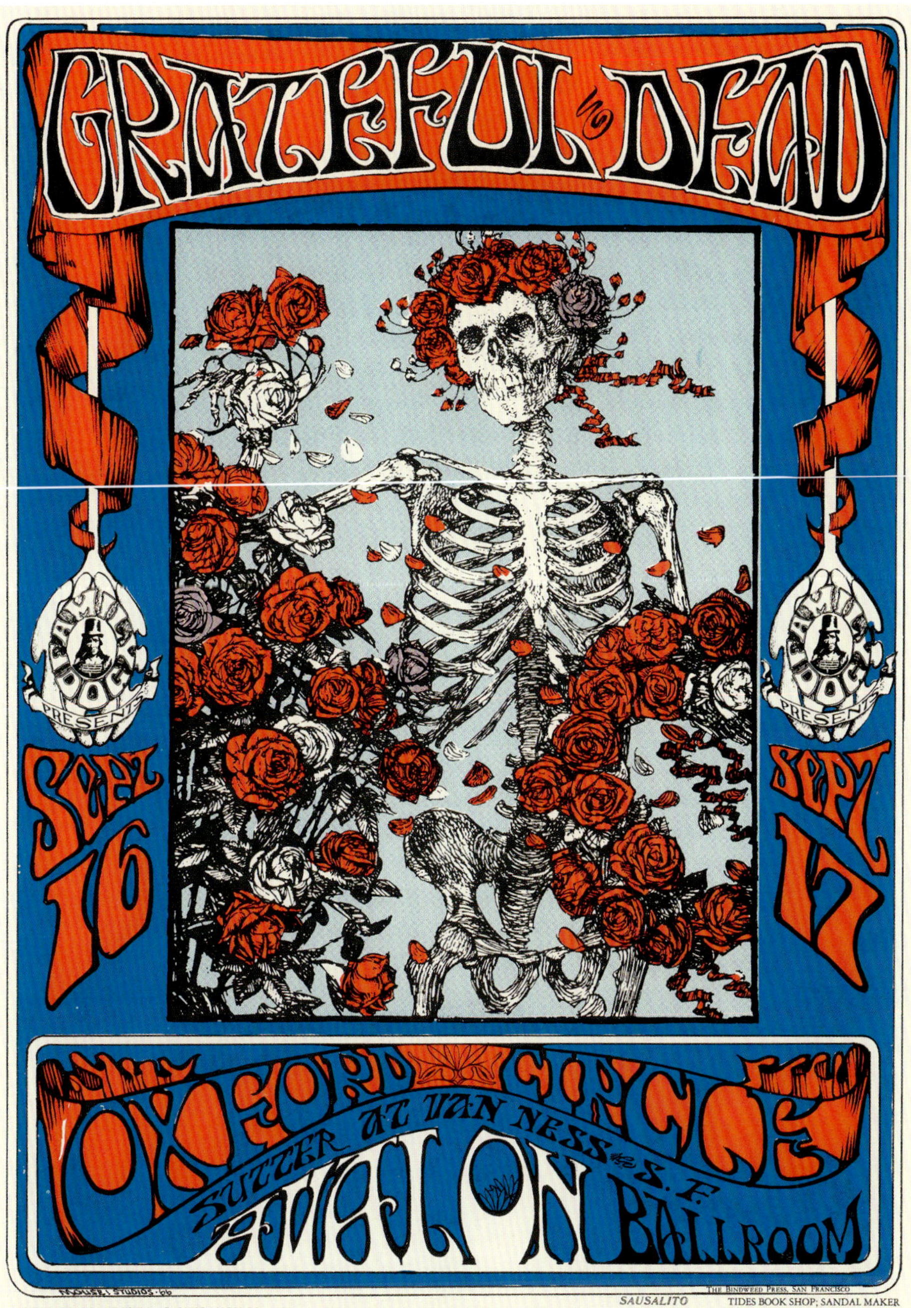

TICKET OUTLETS: *SAN FRANCISCO* THE PSYCHEDELIC SHOP; CITY LIGHTS BOOKS; BALLY LO; CEDAR ALLEY COFFEE HOUSE; MNASIDIKA; DISCOUNT RECORDS (North Beach); SANDAL MAKER (North Beach)

SAUSALITO TIDES BOOK SHOP; SANDAL MAKER

BERKELEY RECORD CITY, 234 Telegraph Avenue

MENLO PARK KEPLER'S BOOK STORE

26(3) , 639 GOUGH ST., San Francisco, Calif. 94102

Sunflower

Haughtiness, adoration, lofty thoughts

AS THEIR NAME indicates, sunflowers constantly turn to face the sun. The name also describes the flower's appearance, with its halo of dozens of golden petals. Its genus name, *Helianthus*, is derived from the Greek words *helios* (sun) and *anthos* (flower). Native to the Americas, the sunflower was symbolic for the Inca people, who called themselves "the children of the sun." Spanish explorers brought sunflowers to Europe around 1500, and they grew to be a popular cultivated plant in the eighteenth century. They became even more common after tsar Peter the Great brought them to Russia, where they were farmed at commercial scale. In the Victorian language of flowers, sunflowers are associated with haughtiness, adoration, and lofty thoughts, suggested by the flower's towering stature.

This immersive view of sunflowers in a riverside garden belongs to a group of canvases representing the gardens of Gustave Caillebotte's estate at Petit Gennevilliers, along the River Seine. In the foreground, sunflowers crowd the view of the promenade d'Argenteuil and the reflections on the water's surface. A leading member of the Impressionists, Caillebotte was singular for the degree of realism in his work. Like other Impressionist painters, such as his friend Claude Monet, Caillebotte was an avid gardener who designed colorful scenes to translate to his canvases. In 1881, he purchased the Petit Gennevilliers property and built a house surrounded by formal gardens. Assisted by two full-time gardeners, Caillebotte laid out his flower gardens by species and cultivated additional exotic varieties inside his greenhouse.

44 | Gustave Caillebotte (French, 1848–1894), *Sunflowers along the Seine*, ca. 1885–1886
Oil on canvas, 35½ x 28 in. (90.2 x 71.1 cm)
Estate of Diana Dollar Knowles, 2013.45.3

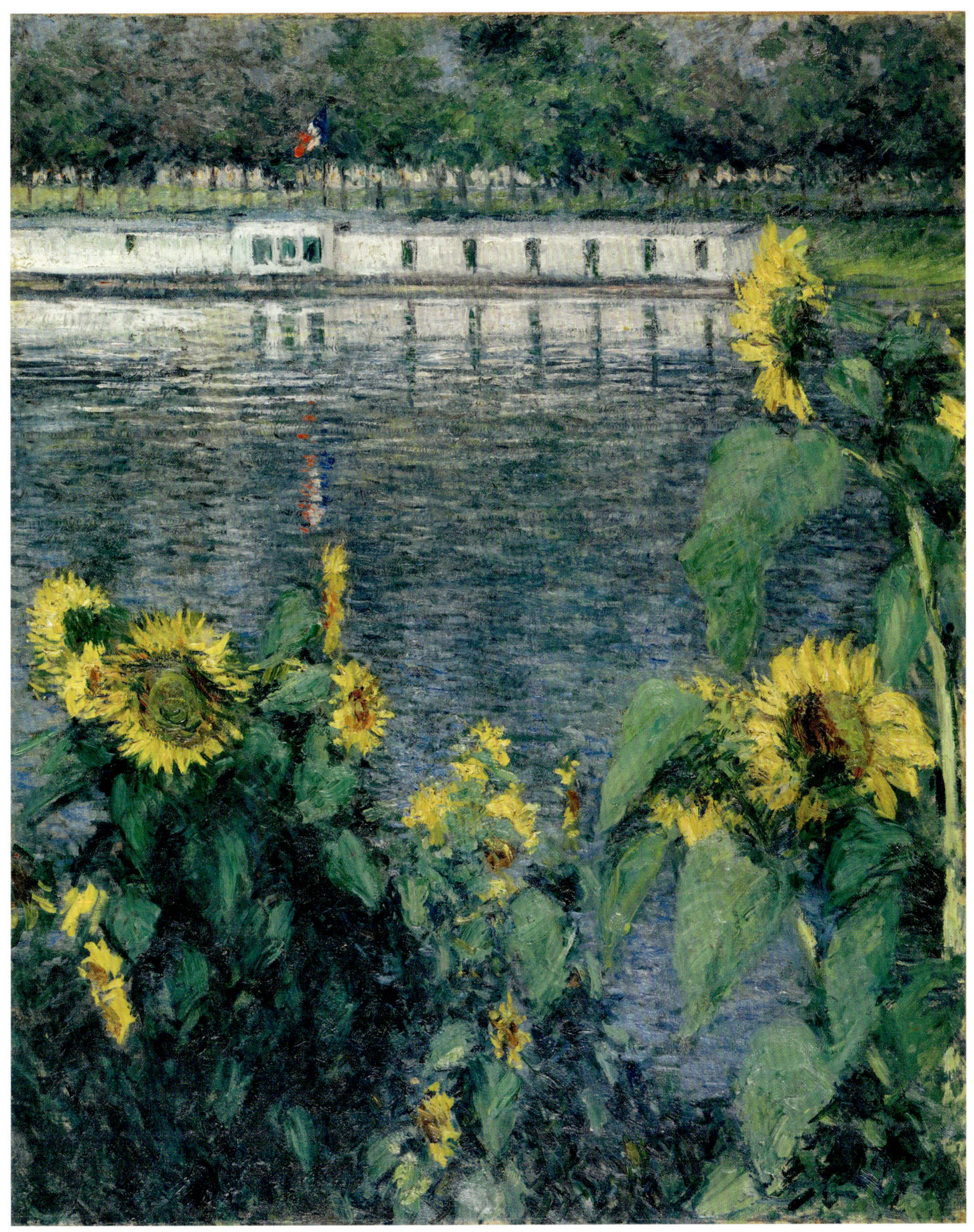

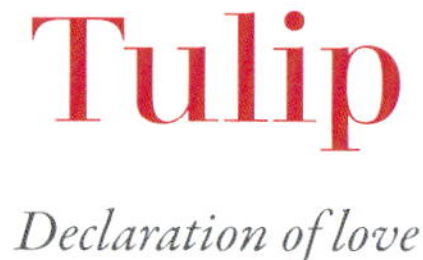

Tulip

Declaration of love

WITH THEIR LARGE, colorful oval-shaped blossoms, tulips may be one of the earliest flowers cultivated for appearance alone. Native to Central Europe and Southern Asia, tulips are believed to have been named *tulipan*, or "turban" by the Persians after their distinctive shape. In the early 1500s, European travelers admired the tulips they saw growing in Turkish gardens, and the so-called "tulipomania" in Europe began in earnest after some Turkish bulbs were given to the Flemish botanist Charles de l'Écluse, who laid the foundations for the Dutch tulip craze. From 1634 to 1637, tulips fetched enormous prices in the Netherlands: one collector exchanged twelve acres of land for a single bulb. In light of the tulip's historical value and refined beauty, the Victorian language of flowers regards it as a "declaration of love."

The English writer Sacheverell Sitwell described this print, which "displays the flower in its forgotten faculties after two centuries of performance in the hands of Dutch, English, and French florists, and puts to shame the tame colors of the tulip as it is known today." Published as the first print in Robert J. Thornton's *The Temple of Flora*, this image of seemingly monumental flowers perfectly capture's Thornton's aims for this ambitious project, with which he sought to create the most dazzling botanical work ever produced. As art director, Thornton collaborated with reputable artists, such as the English painter Philip Reinagle, as well as mezzotint masters like Richard Earlom. The resulting prints depict plants, both common and exotic, set against romantic landscapes.

45 | Richard Earlom (English, 1743–1822), after Philip Reinagle (English, 1749–1833)
Tulips, from *The Temple of Flora or Garden of Nature*, by Robert J. Thornton (London: 1799)
Mezzotint with hand coloring, 18¾ x 14 in. (47.5 x 35.5 cm)
California State Library long loan, L534.1966

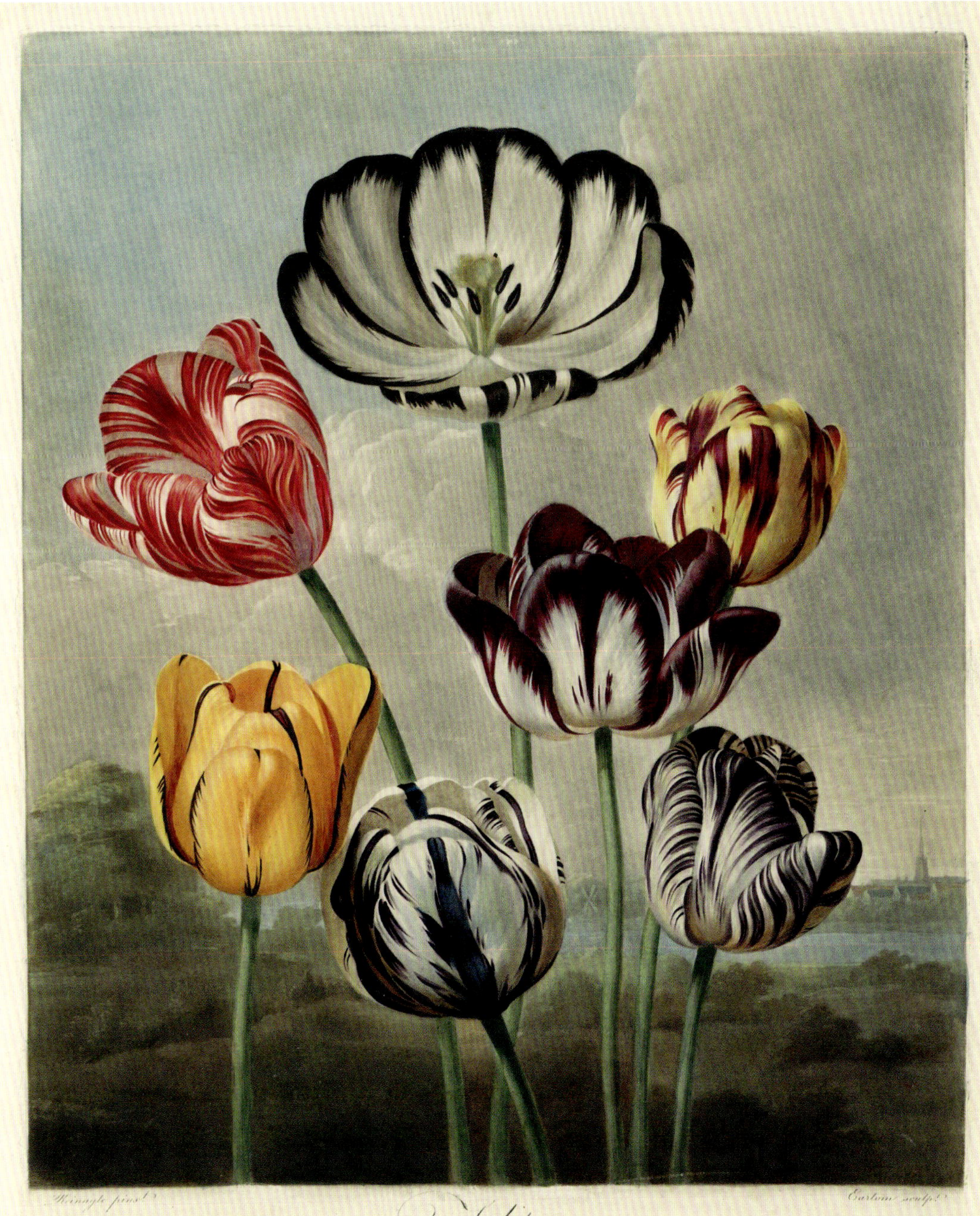

Reinagle pinx^t *Earlom sculp^t*

Tulips

London, Published May 1 1798, by Dr Thornton

Viburnum

A token, "I die if neglected," a delicate friendship

"The woodland borders are wreathed with bloom — elder, viburnum, rose; / The young trees yearn on the breast of the wind that sighs of love as it goes."
— Schuyler Van Rensselaer, "Under Two Windows," from *Poetry: A Magazine of Verse*, November 1912

VARYING IN HEIGHT, flower shape, and leaves, viburnum enjoys diverse appearances. Some are evergreen, and some produce berries that are favored by birds in winter. Because viburnum requires diligent attention, its symbolic meanings include "I die if neglected" and "a delicate friendship." As one Victorian flower guide advises, "The Viburnum assumes a rather straggling shape if left entirely to itself, but with a little attention and pruning can be trained into a well-shaped bush [that] harmonizes well with the delicate and simple tints of the lilac and other spring flowers." When the flowers initially appear in early spring, many begin as small green clusters, turning a creamy white as summer nears.

Viburnum, which appears in many Dutch still lifes, represents just one of the many floral varieties included in Willem van Aelst's striking tabletop arrangement. Van Aelst trained in Delft with his uncle, a still-life painter, and traveled to France and Italy, where he worked as a court painter before settling in Amsterdam. Celebrated for his ornate still lifes featuring luscious, asymmetrical floral arrangements, precious silver objects, and ornate timepieces, Van Aelst is also remembered as a teacher who instructed other leading still-life artists of the Dutch Golden Age, including Maria van Oosterwijck (1630–1693) in Delft and Rachel Ruysch (1664–1750) in Amsterdam.

46 | Willem van Aelst (Dutch, 1627–1683), *Flowers in a Silver Vase*, 1663
Oil on canvas, 26 5⁄8 x 21 1⁄2 in. (67.6 x 54.6 cm)
Gift of Dr. and Mrs. Hermann Schuelein, 51.21

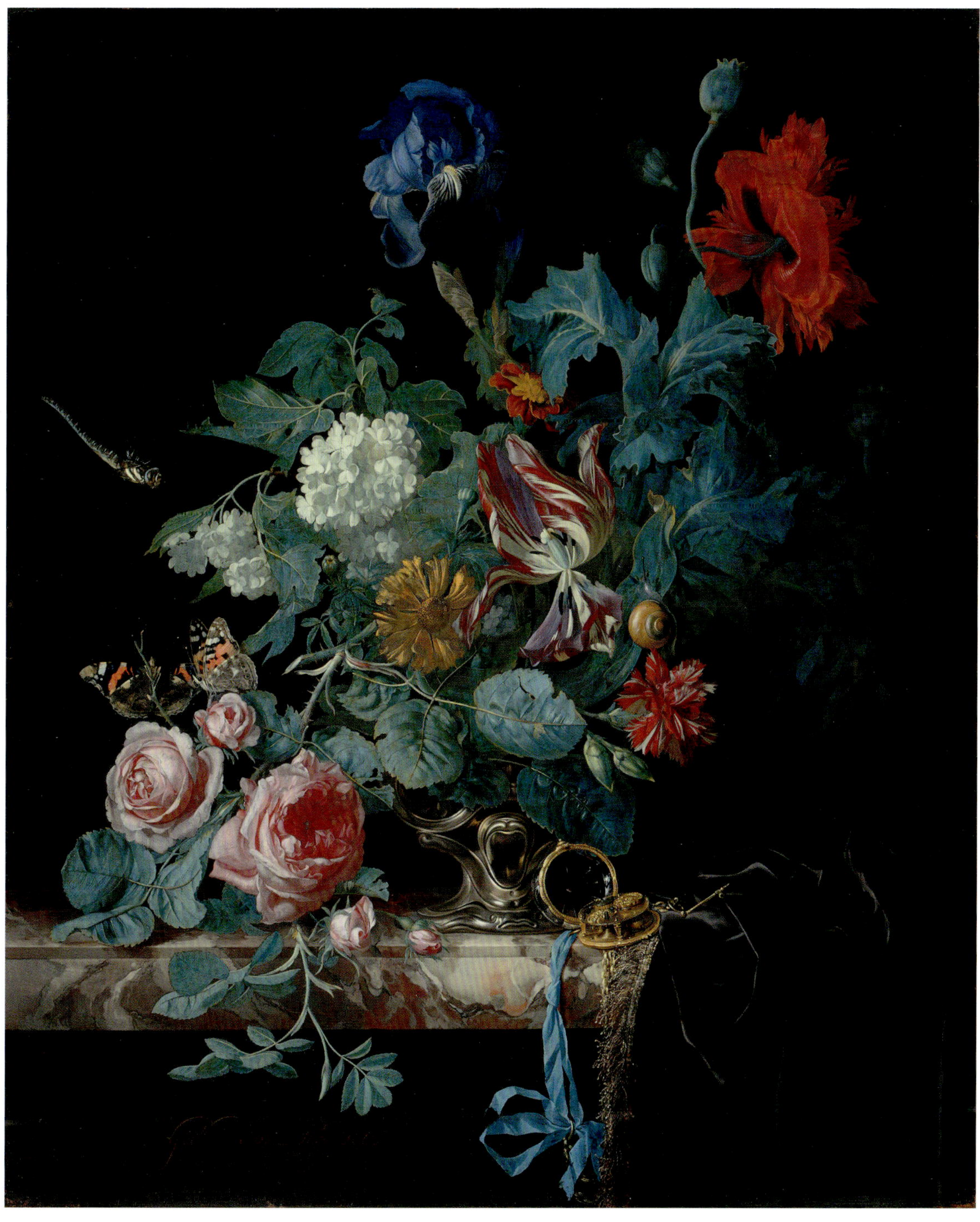

Violet

Modesty, faithfulness

"If some invisible power should suddenly sweep away from the earth every tuft of violets . . .
the very soul of Spring would have passed away with them."
— Miss Ildrewe, *The Language of Flowers,* 1875

VIOLETS WERE HELD in high regard in centuries past: in ancient Rome, violet offerings were made to the dead during the feast of Feralia, and in ancient Greece, Athens was "the city of the violet crown." Empress Joséphine and Napoleon Bonaparte adored violets, which their supporters wore even after Napoleon's exile to Elba, and he promised to return to France when the violets blossomed. Violets symbolize modesty or faithfulness, and their sweet perfume has long inspired literature from Homer and Shakespeare to Tennyson and Wilde.

In the 1860s, candied violets began to be produced commercially in Toulouse, France, nicknamed "la Cité des violettes." European and American perfumers began introducing more violet fragrances, such as Lundborg's Vio-Violet (1895), Coty's La Violette Pourpre (1906), and Mühlens & Kropf's Rhine Violets (1910). In this Vio-Violet advertisement, designer Louis J. Rhead captures the romance of the violet's essence in an image demonstrating the influence of Art Nouveau on American poster design. Born in England, Rhead was influenced by French Art Nouveau designer Eugène Grasset and later moved to the United States, where he enjoyed a successful commercial career. "The pictorial advertising of this firm is perfectly *en rapport* with the article advertised," and Rhead's work for Lundborg was praised for its ability to convey "the smell of sweet flowers."

47 | Louis J. Rhead (American, 1858–1926), *Vio-Violet, A Perfume,* 1895
Color lithograph poster, sheet: 17 ½ x 12 in. (44.5 x 30.4 cm)
Bequest of Arthur W. Barney, 1974.13.561

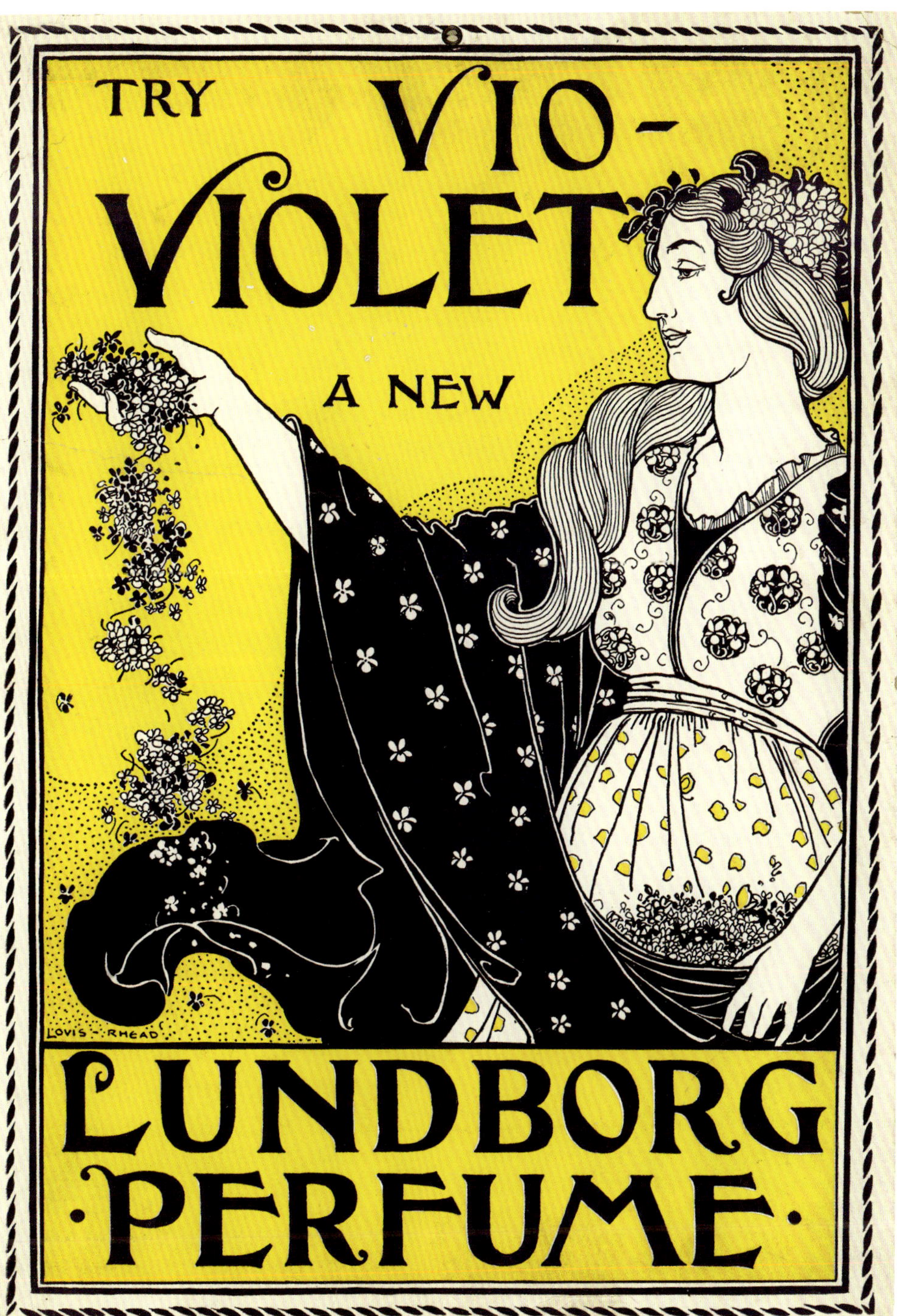
TRY
VIO-
VIOLET
A NEW
LOUIS - RHEAD
LUNDBORG
·PERFUME·

Water Lily

Eloquence, purity of heart

"How significant that the rich black mud of our dead stream produces the water lily — out of that fertile slime springs this spotless purity."
— Henry David Thoreau, 1853

THE ELEGANT WATER LILY traditionally symbolizes eloquence and purity of heart. Like the lotus (cat. no. 28), its flowers grow above the water's surface, while its underwater stems are buried deep in the mud below. The rosette-shaped flowers have pointed petals that curve, cuplike, toward the center. In northern European lore, water lilies are linked with the Undines, water spirits said to make their homes in the heart of these flowers, where they rise with the morning sun as the petals open.

No other Western artist is as closely associated with the water lily as French Impressionist Claude Monet. In 1890, Monet purchased property in the Normandy village of Giverny. He set to work redesigning the gardens and in 1893 purchased additional land that allowed him to create a water lily pond. The pond became central to his impressive garden, and he devoted himself to painting its reflective surface, capturing the changing effects of light and the color of the lilies — as Monet claimed, "Nothing in the whole world is of interest to me but my painting and my flowers." The pond was enlarged in 1900, allowing more lilies to be planted and enabling Monet to paint larger expanses of the pond's mirrorlike surface. In the top-right corner of this canvas from the series, the water reflects a single white cloud in the sky above.

48 | Claude Monet (French, 1840–1926), *Water Lilies*, ca. 1914–1917
Oil on canvas, 65⅜ x 56 in. (166 x 142.2 cm)
Museum purchase, Mildred Anna Williams Collection, 1973.3

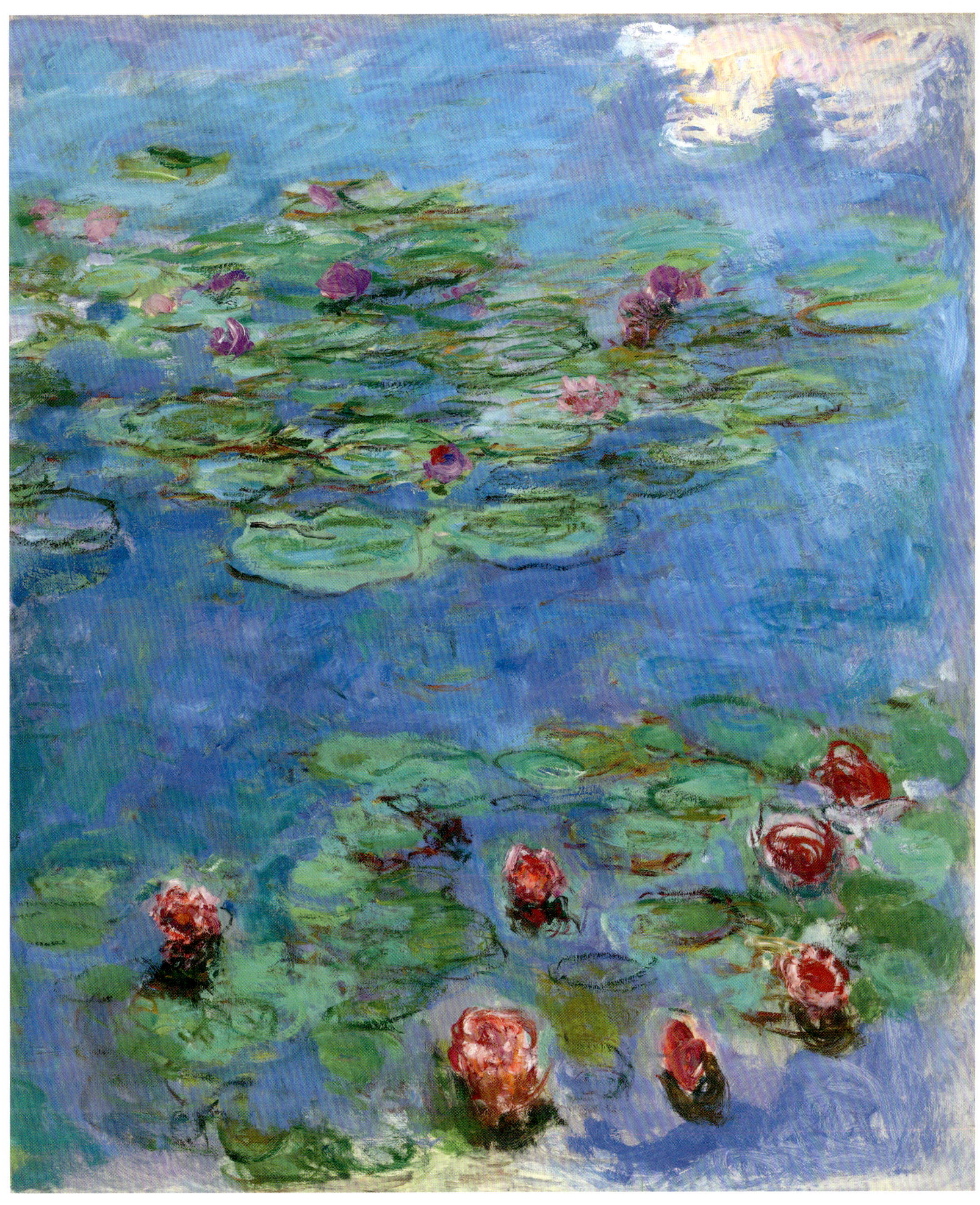

Wisteria

Welcome, fair stranger

"[Cherry blossoms] . . . are so quick to run off and leave you. And then just when your regrets are the strongest the wisteria comes into bloom, and it blooms on into the summer . . . Even the color is somehow companionable and inviting."
— Murasaki Shikibu, *The Tale of Genji,* ca. 1000

THE GENUS *Wisteria* comprises species native to Asia and the United States. It was named in 1818 by Thomas Nuttal, curator of Harvard's botanical garden, in memory of Casper Wistar (1761–1818), an anatomy professor at the University of Pennsylvania. In the Victorian language of flowers, wisteria expresses the sentiment "Welcome, fair stranger," perhaps since it often adorns arbors and doorways (constructing trellises to support wisteria is believed to have originated in the late seventeenth century).

In Japan, the wisteria (*fuji*) was originally a mountain plant that could be found climbing trees. It was then domesticated and trained, and by the late Heian period (794–1185), members of the Japanese elite would gather for wisteria viewing parties. Particularly beautiful vines became popular tourist attractions, such as those found at the Kameido Tenjin Shrine in present-day Tokyo, famously depicted in Utagawa Hiroshige's *Precincts of the Tenjin Shrine at Kameido (Kameido Tenjin keidai).* Like *The Plum Orchard at Kameido (Kameido Umeyashiki),* of 1857 (cat. no. 40), this image belongs to Hiroshige's famous series *One Hundred Views of Famous Places in Edo,* an effort produced late in the artist's life. Celebrated for its drum-shaped bridge, visitors still flock to this shrine each spring to enjoy the wisteria in full bloom.

49 | Utagawa Hiroshige (Japanese, 1797–1858), *Precincts of the Tenjin Shrine at Kameido (Kameido Tenjin keidai),* no. 57 from the series *One Hundred Views of Famous Places in Edo (Meisho Edo hyakkei),* 1856. Color woodcut, 13 7/16 x 8 3/4 in. (34.2 x 22.2 cm) Published by Uoya Eikichi, Edo (Tokyo). Gift of Miss Carlotta Mabury, 54755.761

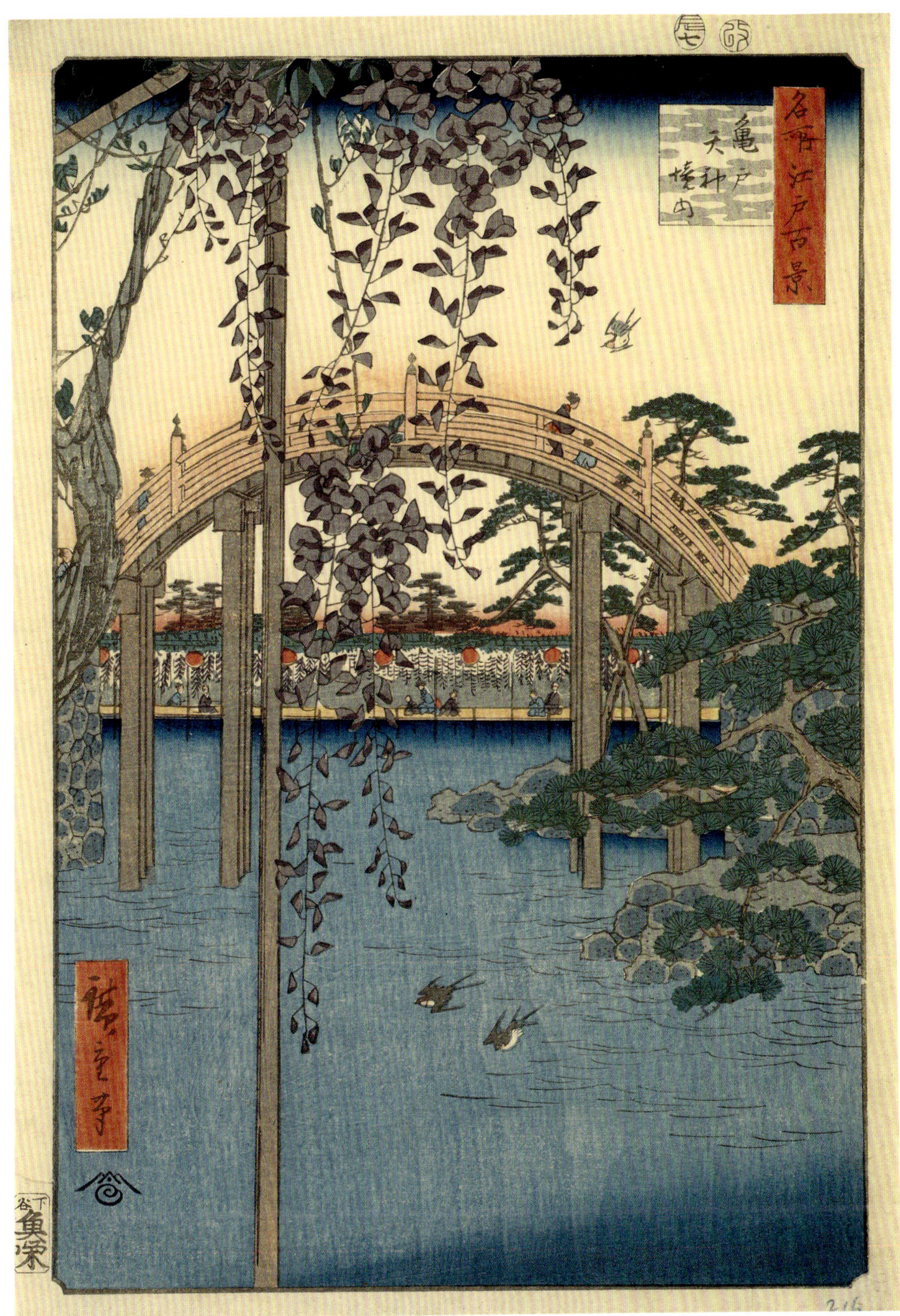
名所江戸百景
亀戸天神境内
廣重画
下谷
魚栄

Zinnia

Thoughts of absent friends

MANY ZINNIA ENTRIES in Victorian flower dictionaries feature the same anonymous verse: "The zinnia's solitary flower, / Which blooms in forests lone and deep, / Are like the visions fresh and bright, / That faithful, absent hearts will keep." These lines refer to the flower's associations with friendship and remembrance; often employed as an emblem of "thoughts of absent friends," zinnias were a common Victorian gift to a departing friend. Native to Mexico, Central America, and the American Southwest, zinnias were collected by Spanish conquistadors in the early sixteenth century, and the flower was later named in honor of the German botanist Johann Gottfried Zinn (1727–1759). Modern horticulturists bred new, colorful varieties with distinctive names like 'Giant Mammoth,' 'Double Lilliput,' 'Dwarf Fireball,' 'Peppermint Stick,' and 'Persian Carpet,' and in the early 1920s, Luther Burbank developed the first dahlia-type zinnia in Santa Rosa, California.

Paul Wonner's *Zinnia* depicts this stem set within an ambiguous space, its softly defined orange blossom surrounded by an enigmatic, radiating ocher halo. Unlike Wonner's *Still Life with Fruit and Flowers* (cat. no. 21), which integrates various flowers within an arrangement of everyday objects, this work takes the solitary zinnia as its subject. It fits critic Kenneth Baker's assessment that "[Wonner's] mature pictures distinctively portray things as separated by almost surrealistically vacant distended spaces." Artist Bruce Cohen, whom Wonner mentored, notes that his work exudes a "poetic magic that can really move you." With its quiet veneration of its solitary flower, *Zinnia* fully expresses this poetic magic.

50 | Paul Wonner (American, 1920–2008), *Zinnia*, ca. 1969
Opaque watercolor and graphite, 23 x 18 in. (58.4 x 45.7 cm)
Gift of Barbara and William G. Hyland, 2017.59.2.7

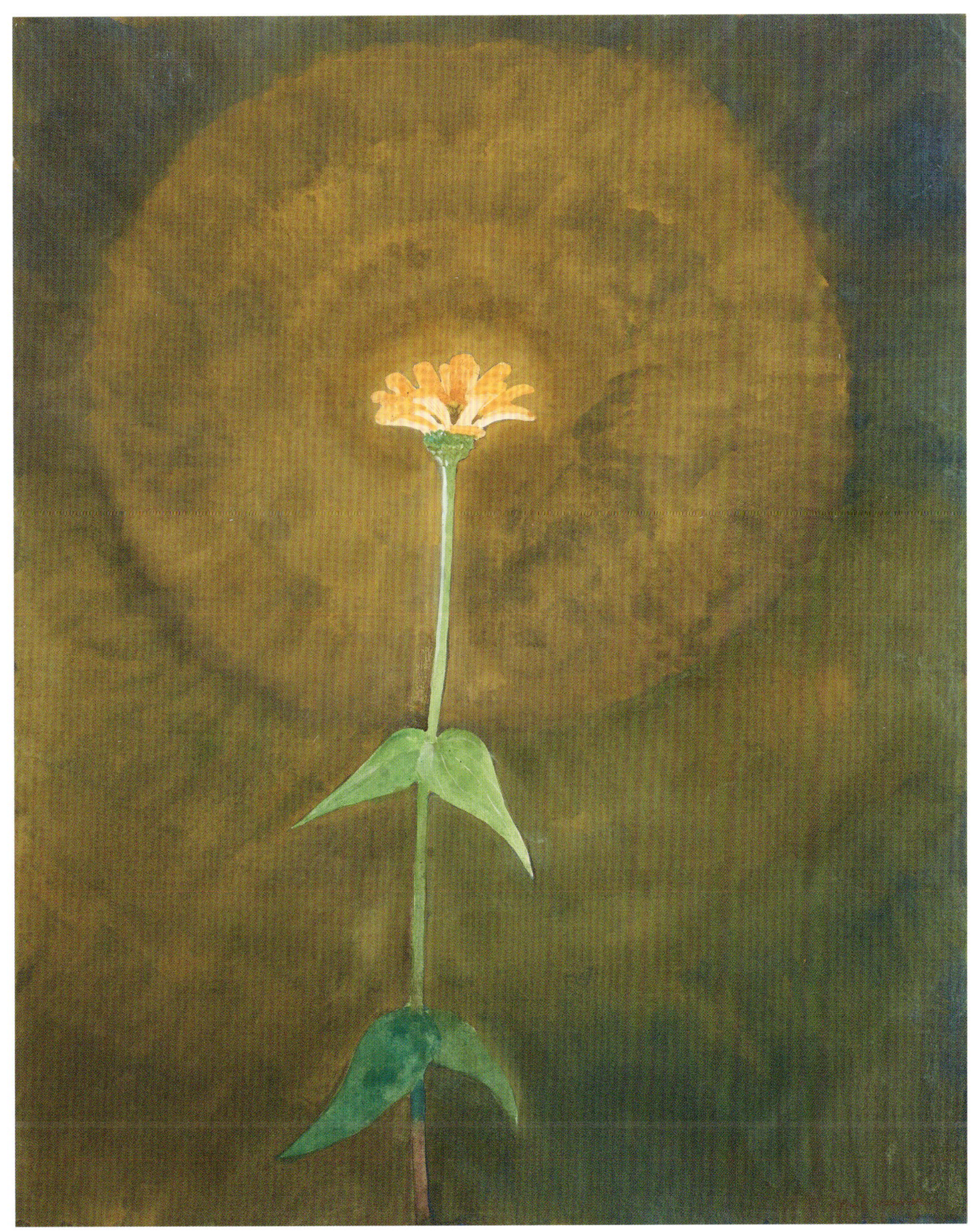

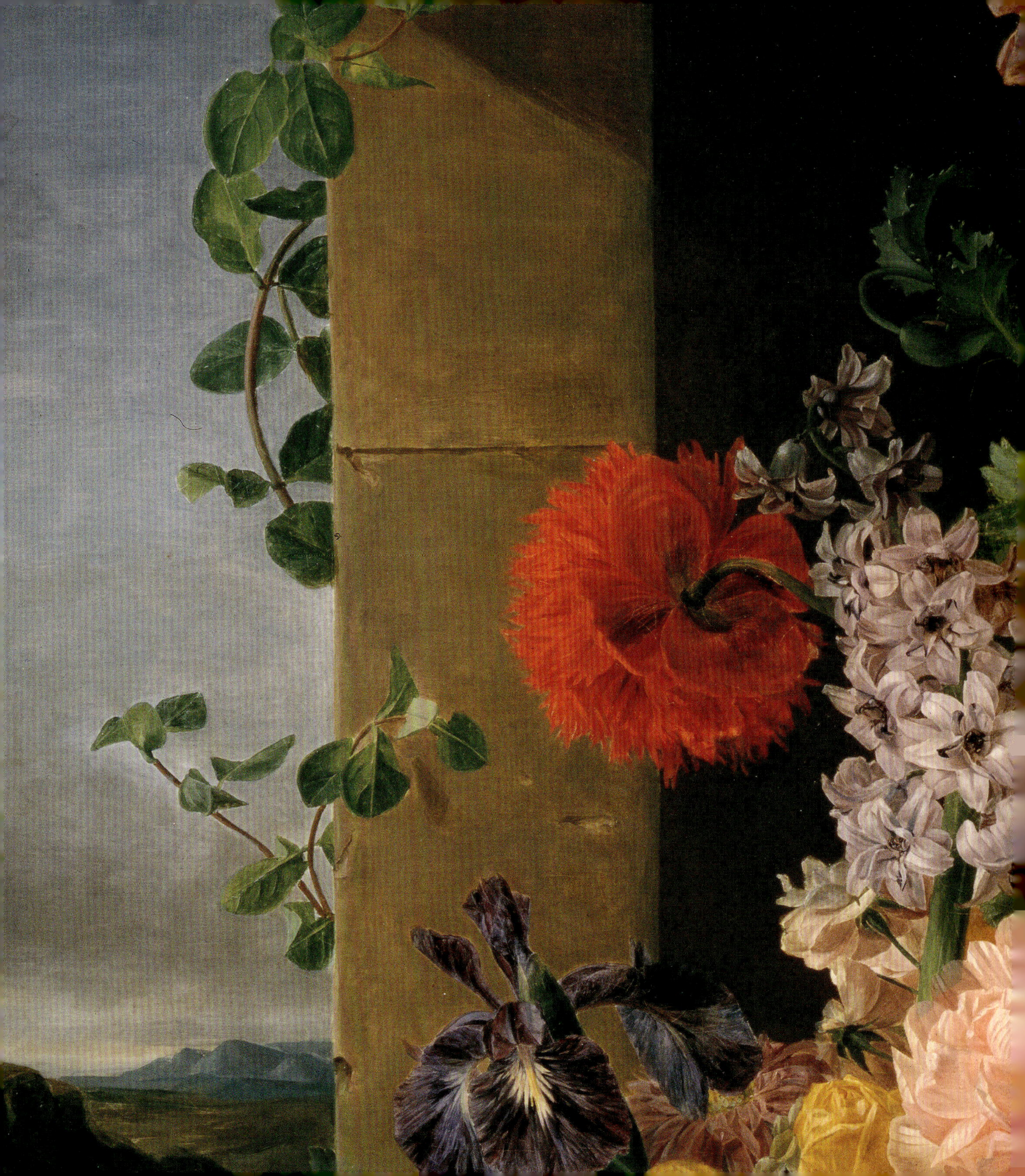

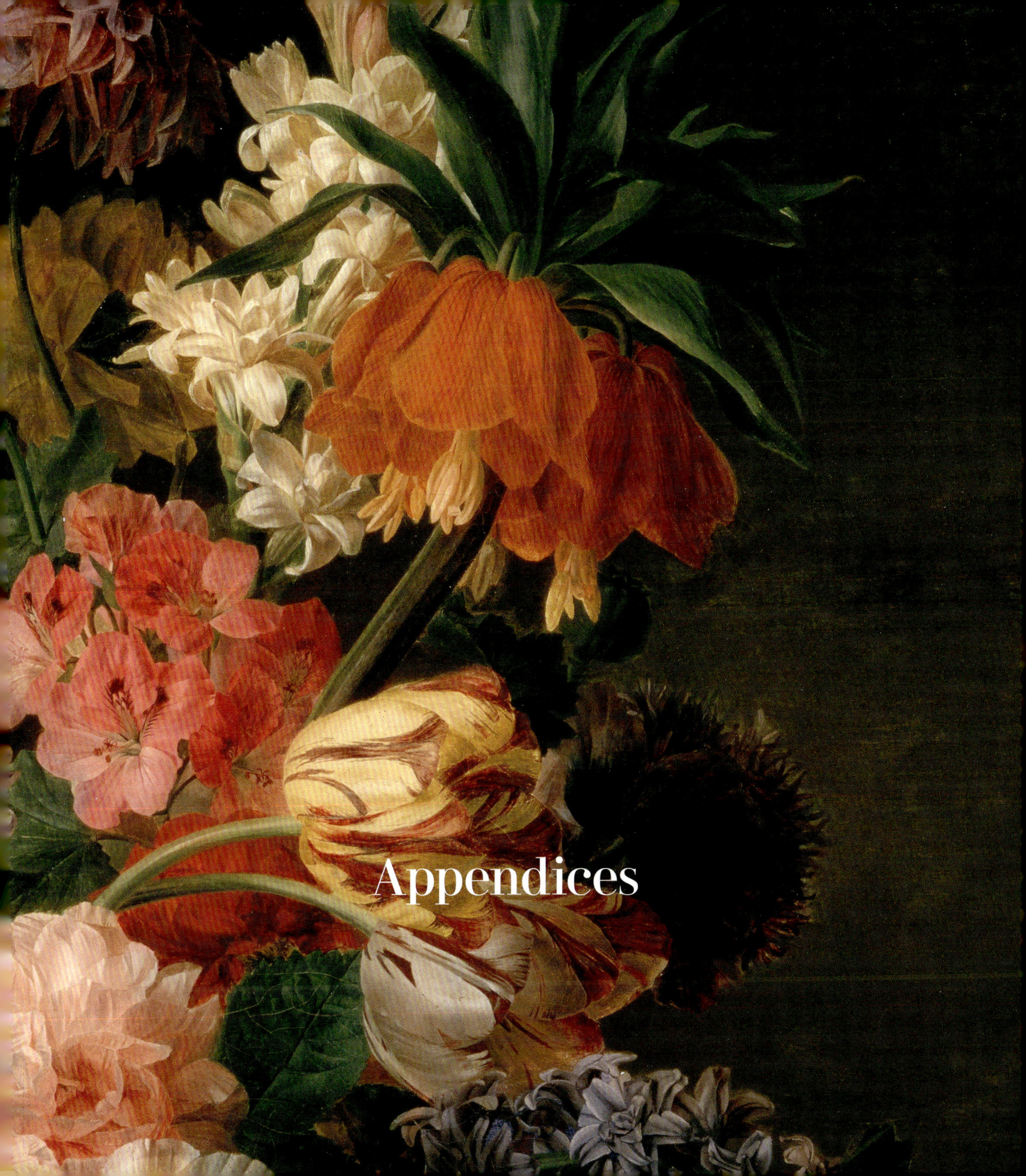

Appendices

An Index of Flowers

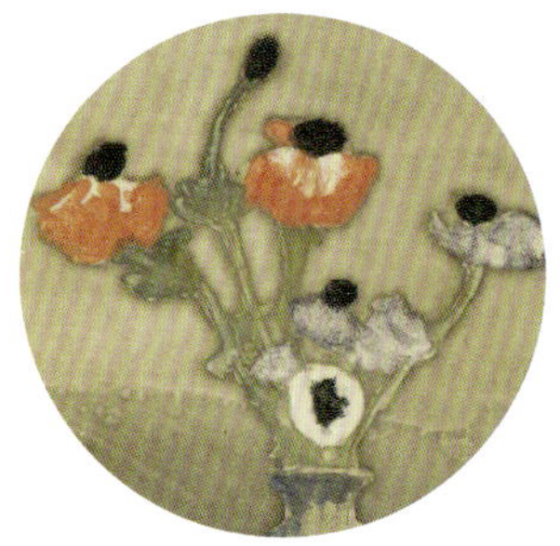

Anemone
Expectation, anticipation

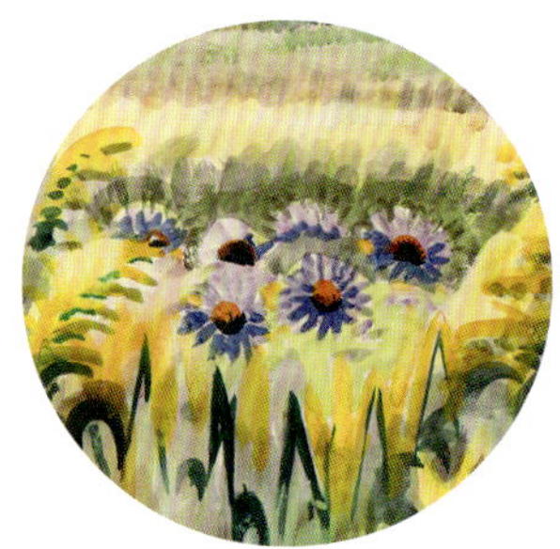

Aster
Afterthought, variety

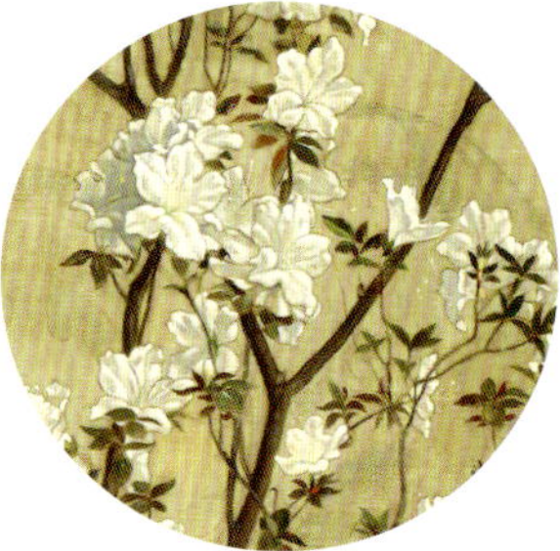

Azalea
Temperance

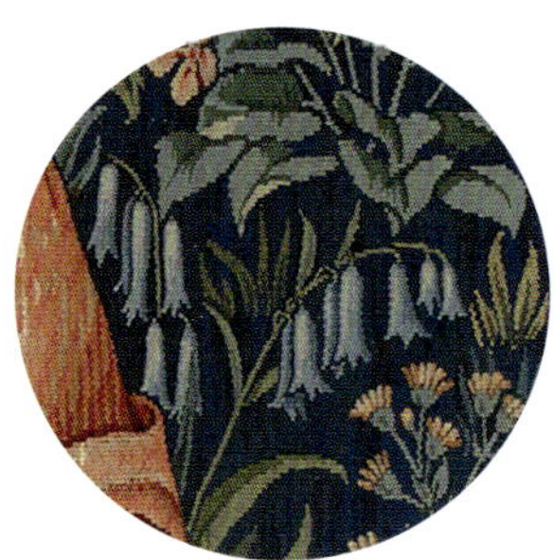

Bluebell
Constancy, sorrowful regret

Bleeding Heart
Love

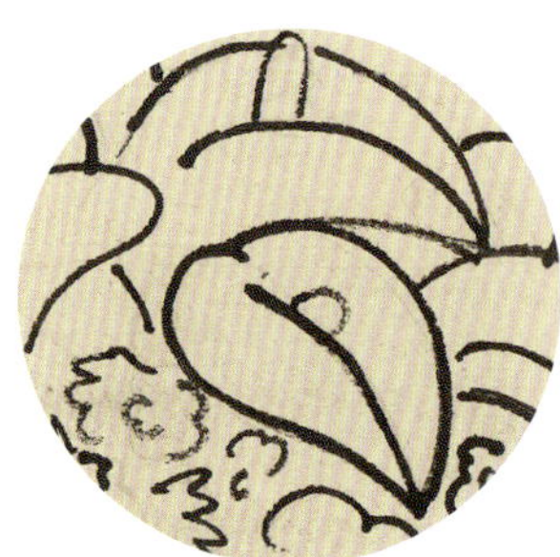

Calla Lily
Feminine beauty, modesty

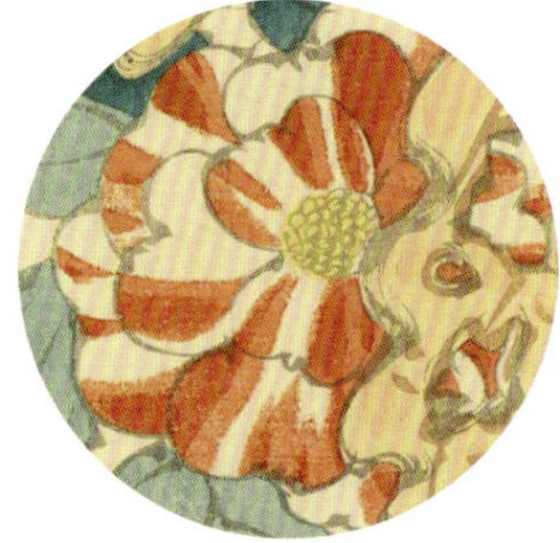

Camellia
Unpretending excellence, perfect loveliness

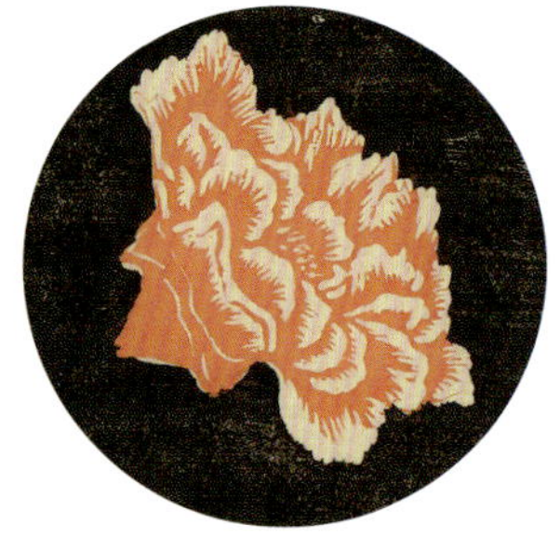

Carnation
Disdain, antipathy, admiration

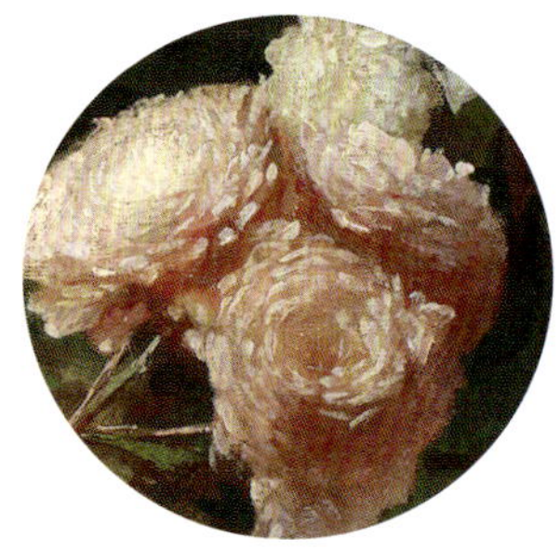

Chrysanthemum
Love, truth, slighted affection

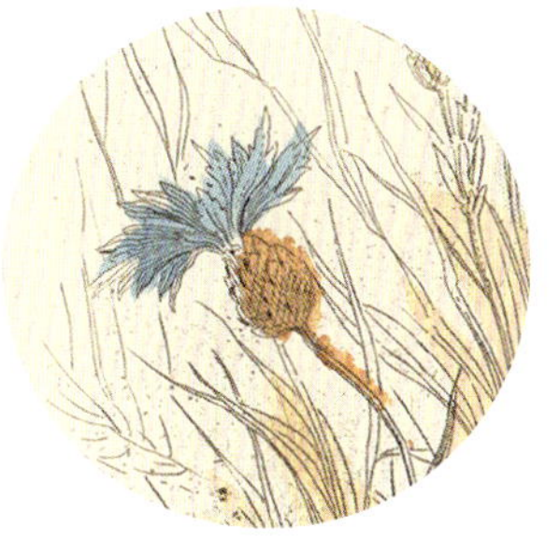

Cornflower
Delicacy, celibacy

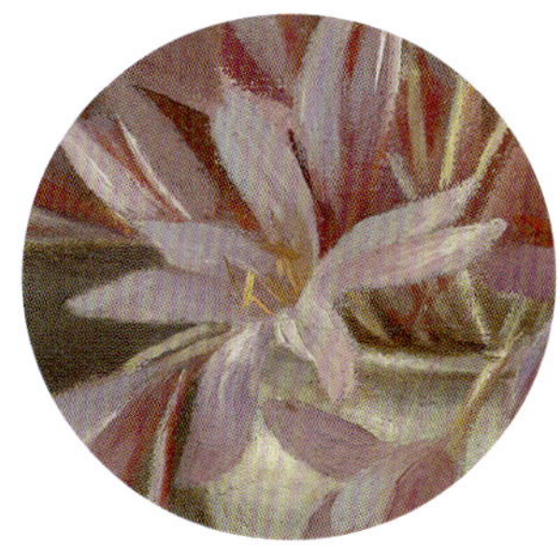

Crocus
Cheerfulness, mirth

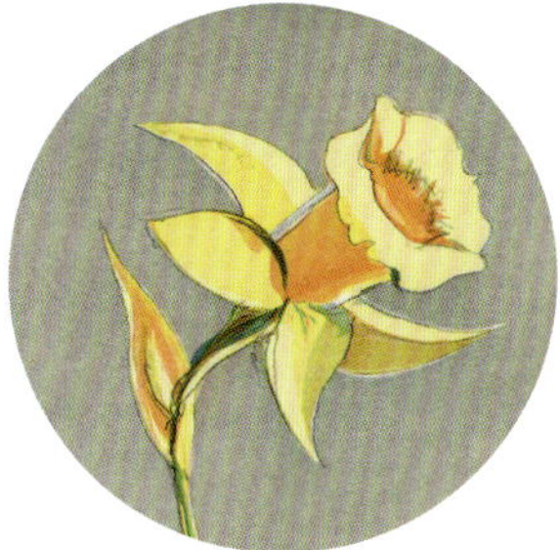

Daffodil
Regard, unrequited love

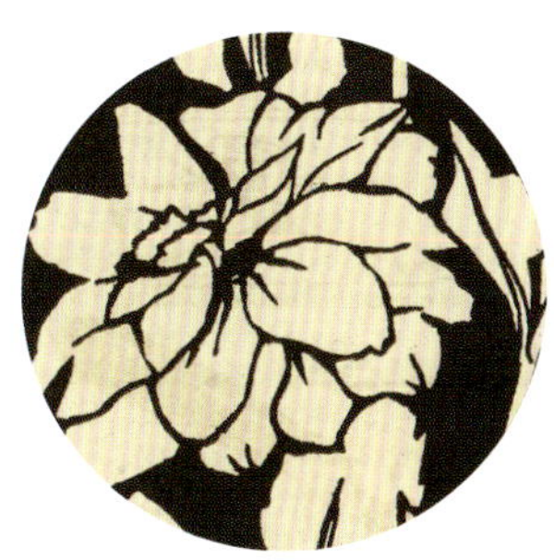

Dahlia
Heartless beauty, dignity, instability, pomp

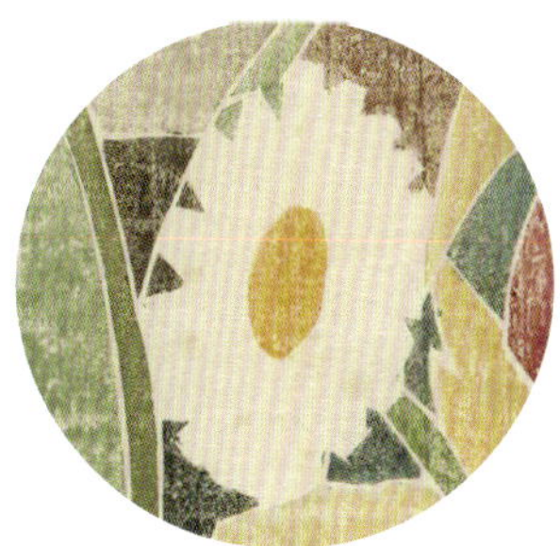

Daisy
Innocence

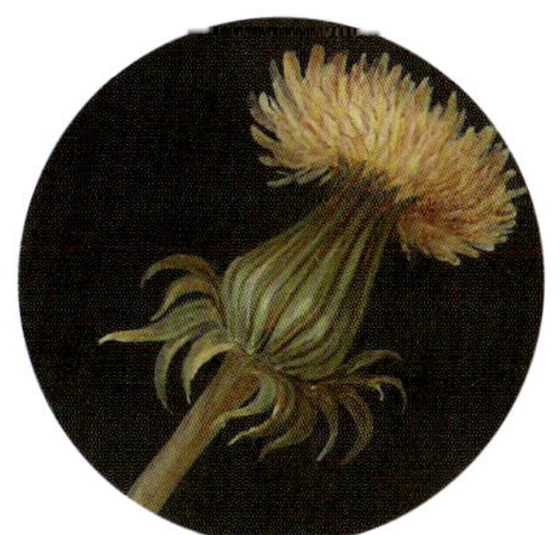

Dandelion
Oracle

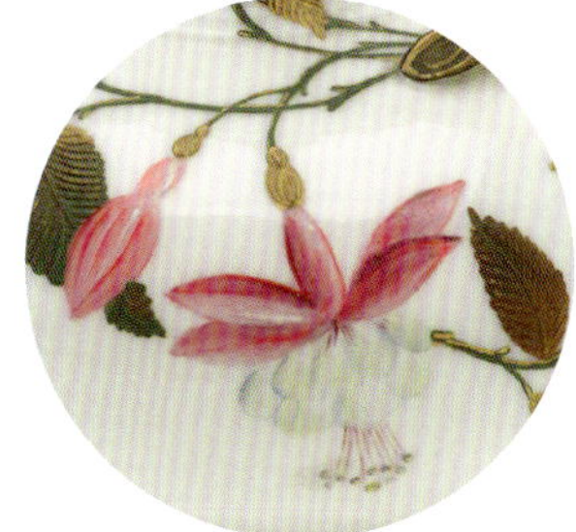

Fuschia
Taste

Geranium
Preference, folly, deceit

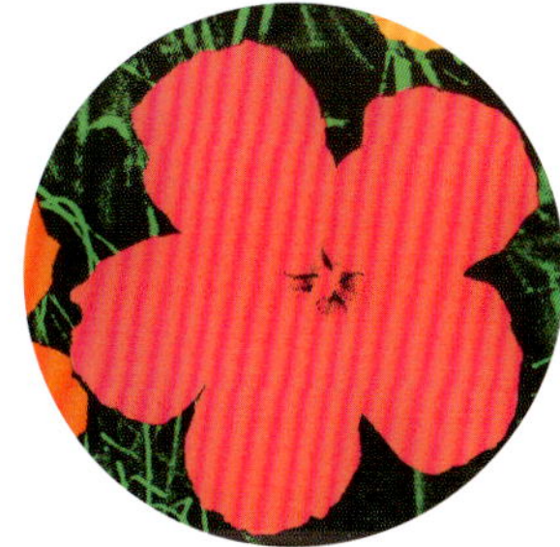

Hibiscus
Deliccate beauty

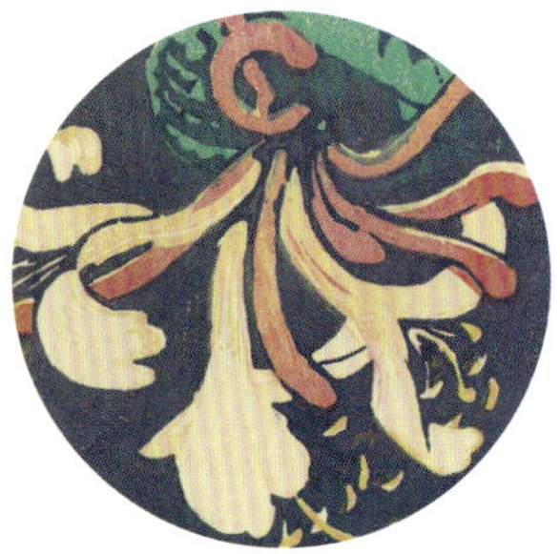

Honeysuckle

Devoted affection

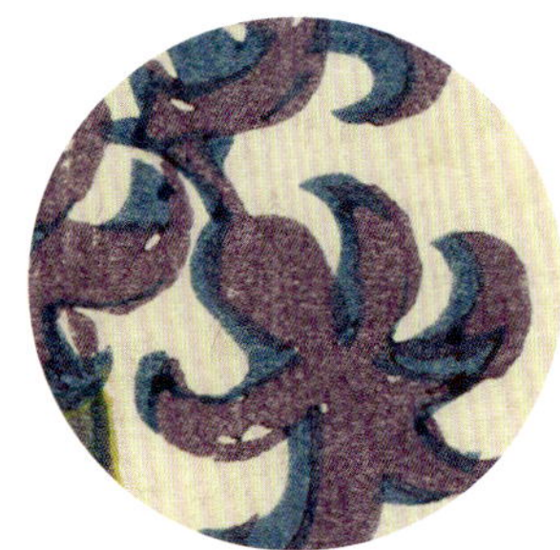

Hyacinth

Sport, play

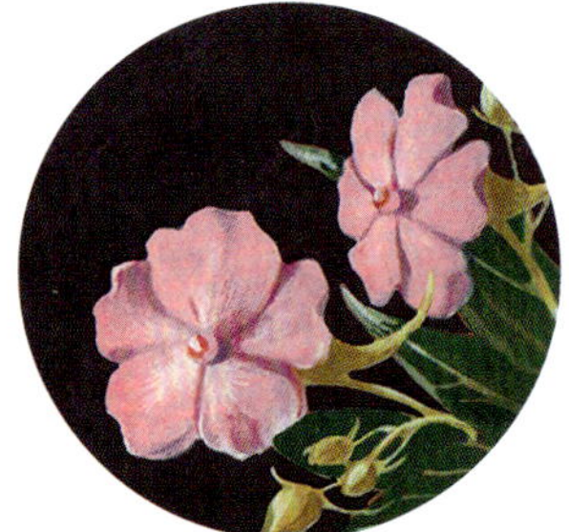

Impatiens

Impatience

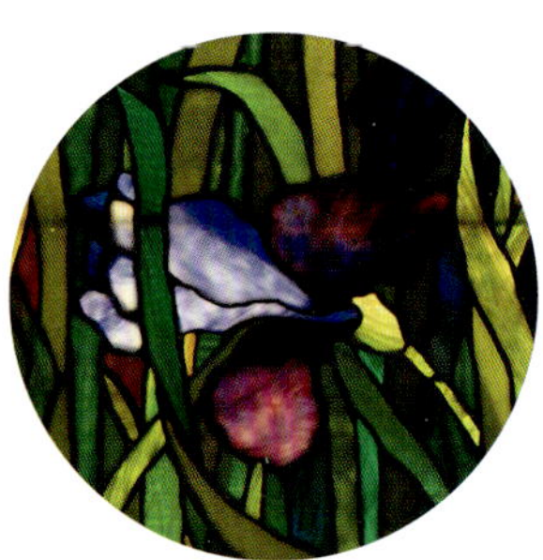

Iris

Message

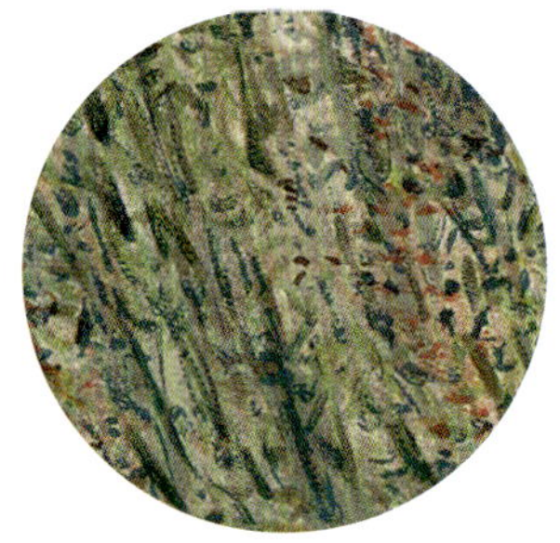

Larkspur

Levity, lightness

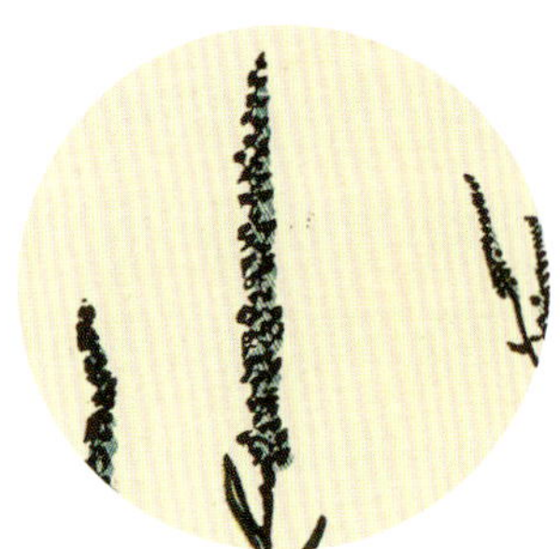

Lavender

Mistrust, calmeness

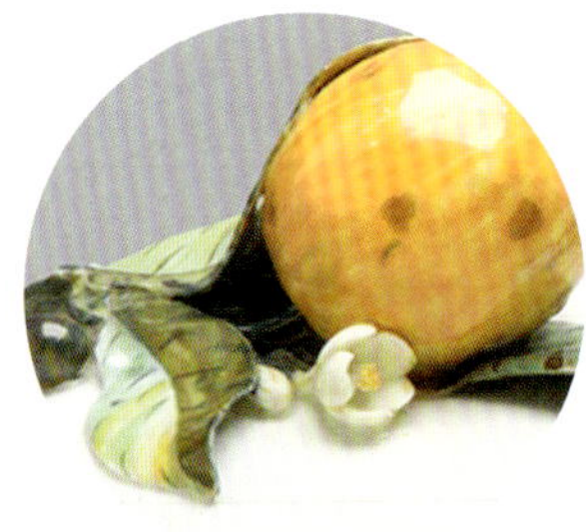

Lemon Blossom

Fidelity in love

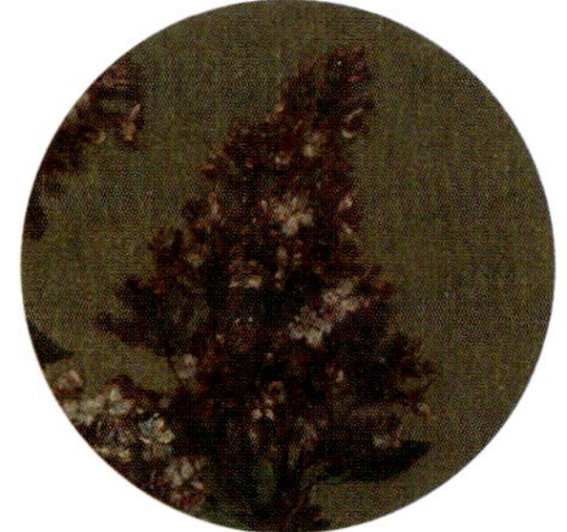

Lilac

First emotions of love

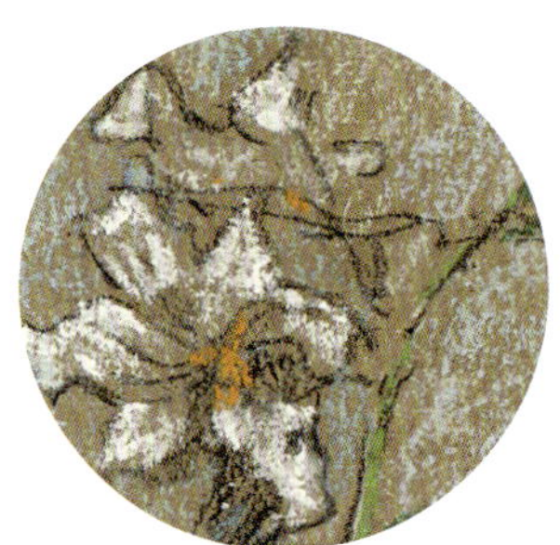

Lily

Purity, majesty, sweetness

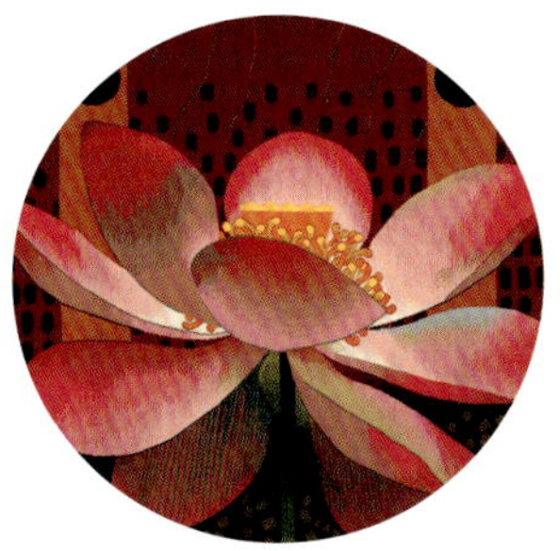

Lotus Flower

Purity, rebirth, estranged love

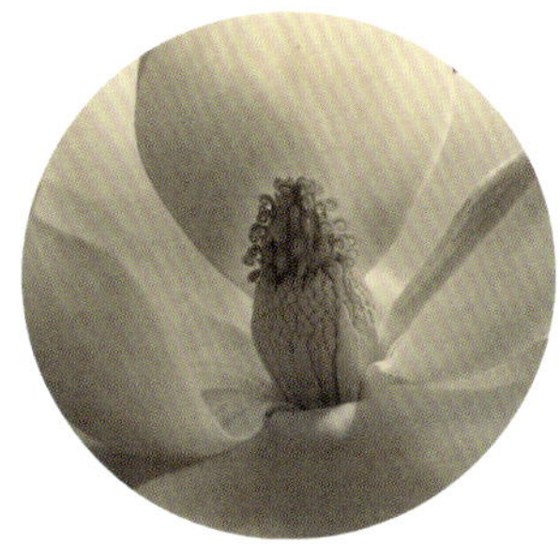

Magnolia

Love of nature, magnificence

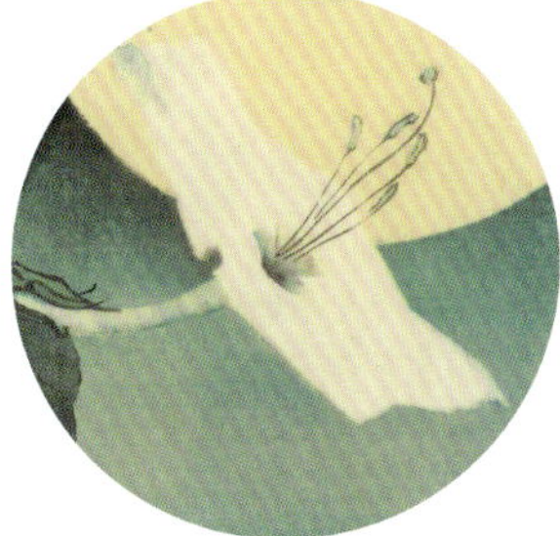

Moonflower

Dreaming of love, night

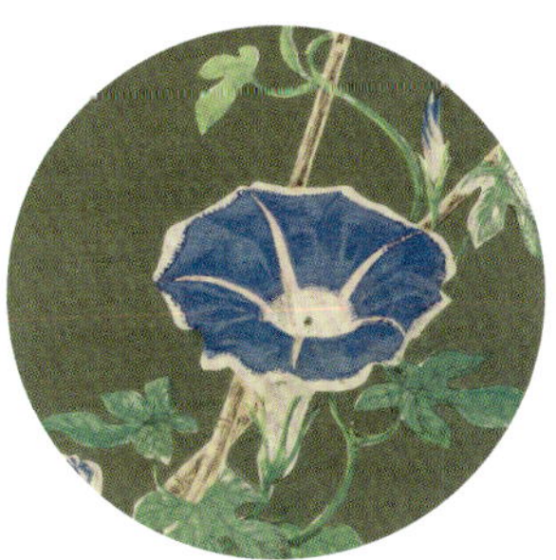

Morning Glory

Affectation, repose

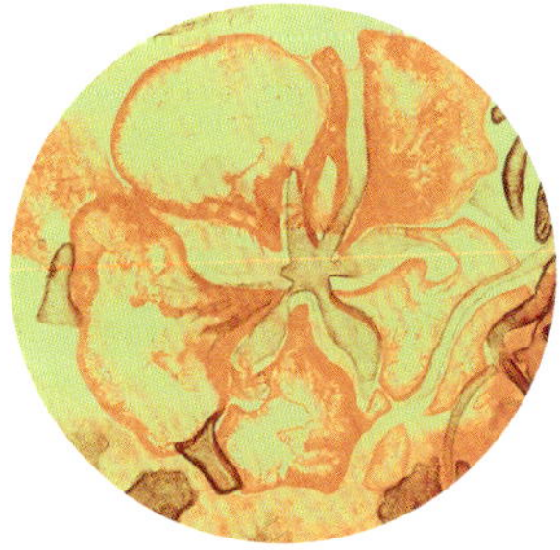

Nasturtium

Patriotism, heroism

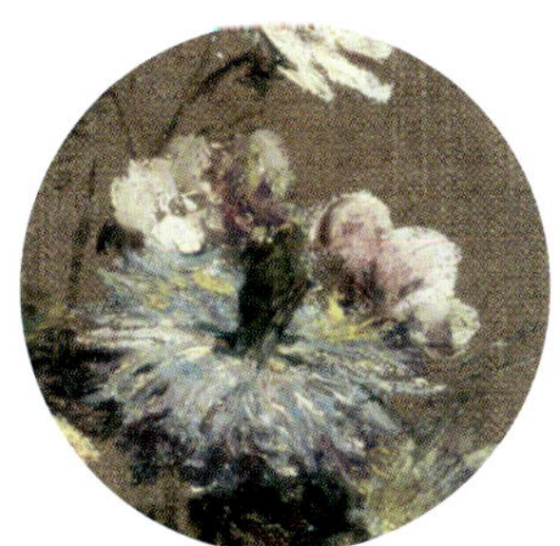

Nigella

Perplexity

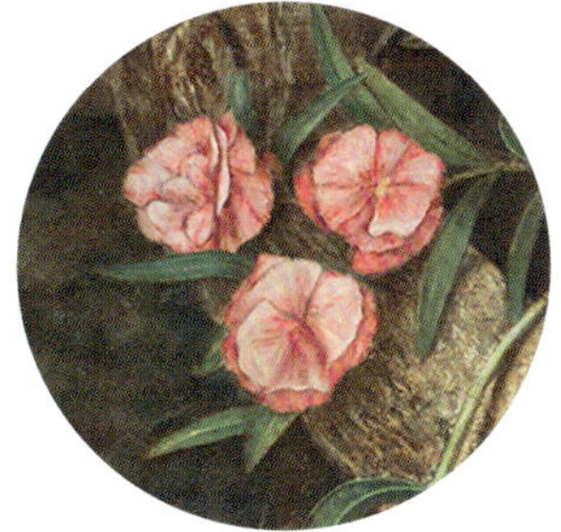

Oleander

Caution, beware!

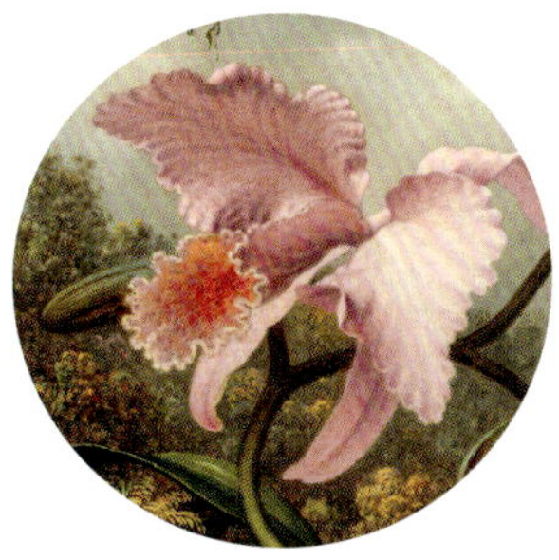

Orchid

A belle, sexuality, virility

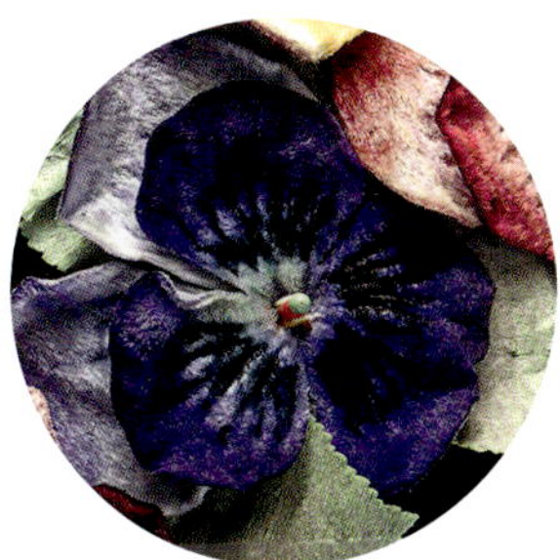

Pansy

Thoughts; you occupy my thoughts

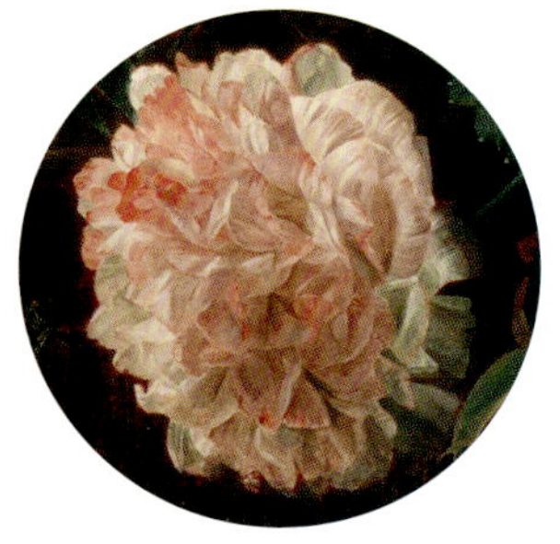

Peony

Bashfulness, shame, ostentation

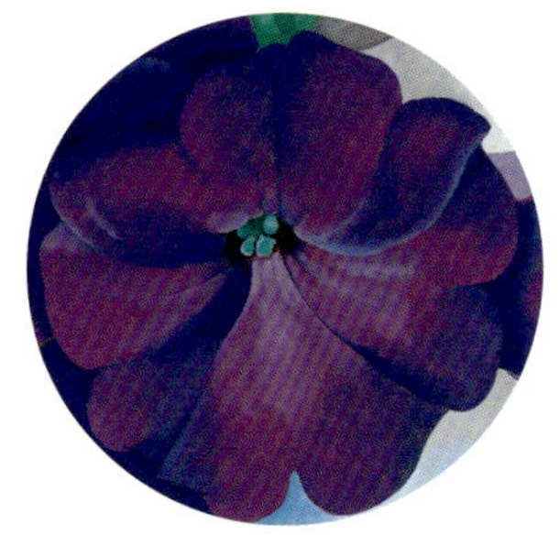

Petunia

Your presence soothes me

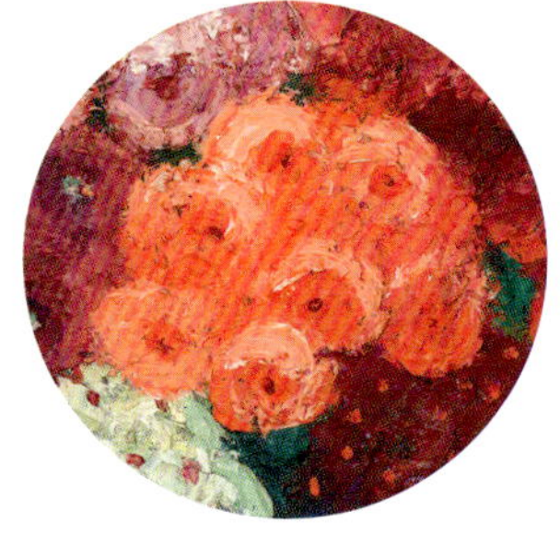

Phlox

Unanimity; our hearts are united

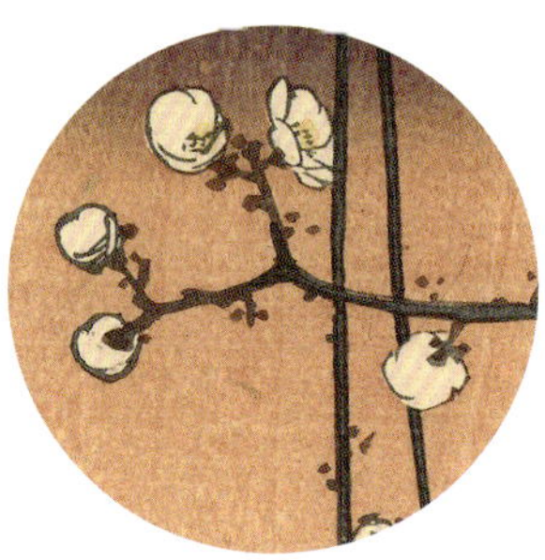

Plum Blossom

Fidelity; keep your promises

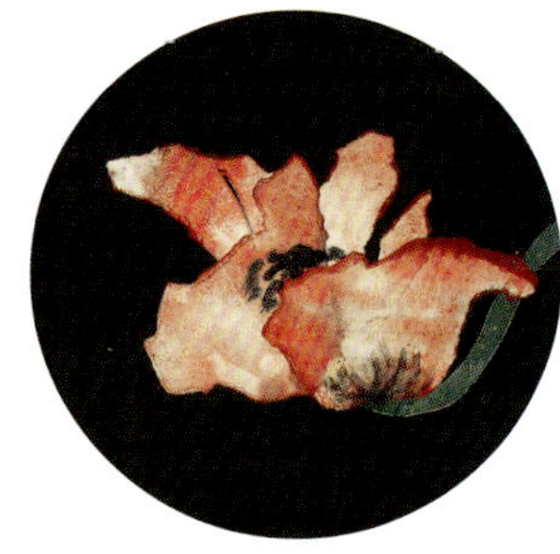

Poppy

Consolation, sleep, remembrance

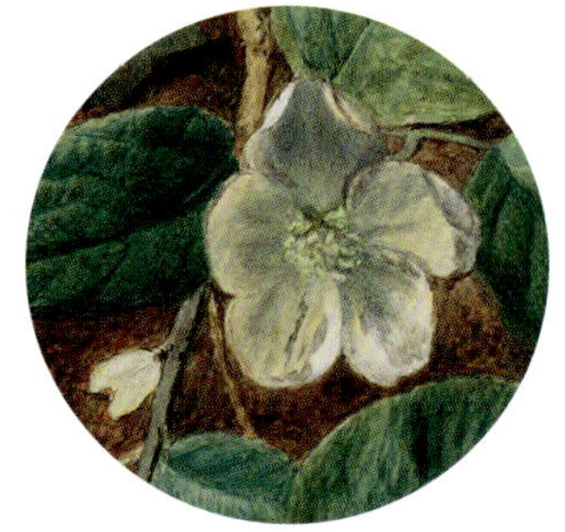

Quince Blossom

Temptation

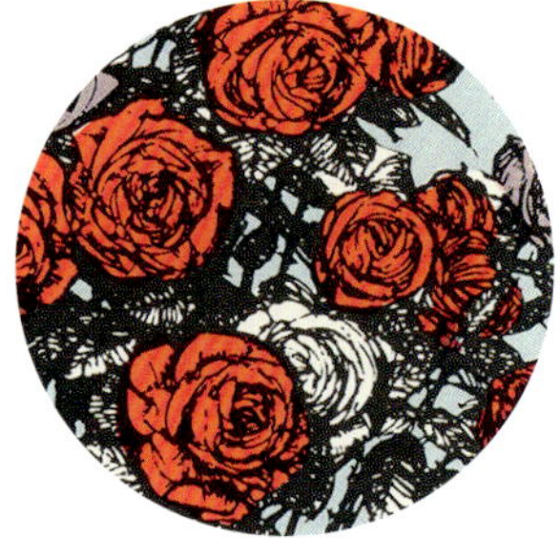

Rose

Love, beauty

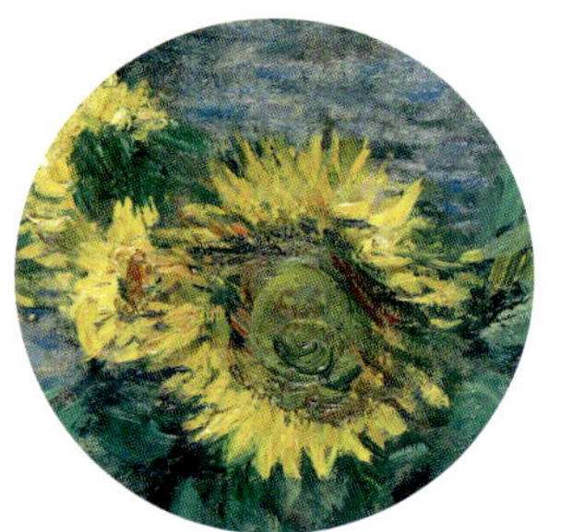

Sunflower

Haughtiness, adoration, lofty thoughts

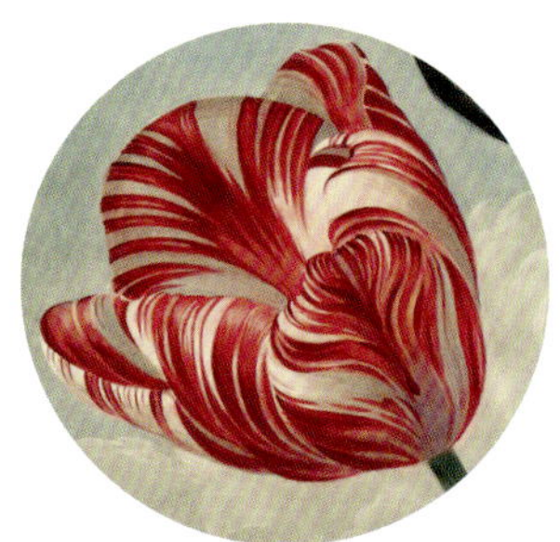

Tulip

Declaration of love

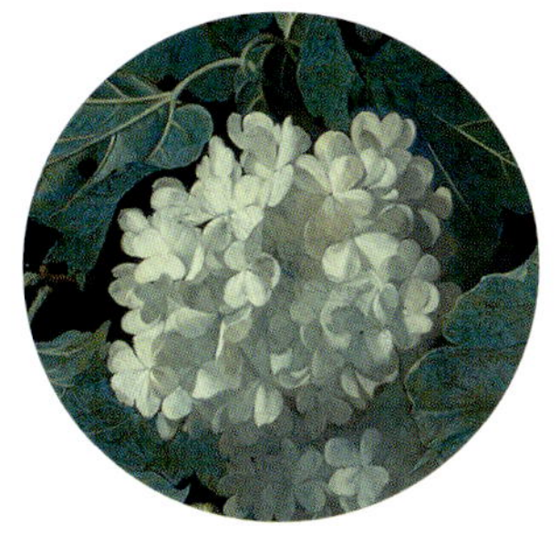

Viburnum

A token, "I die if neglected," a delicate friendship

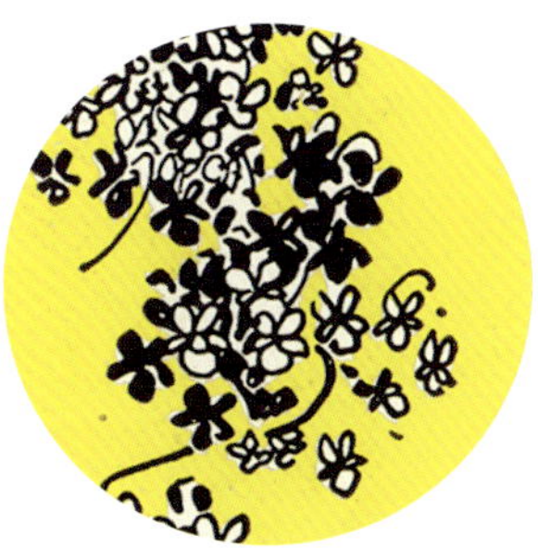

Violet

Modesty, faithfulness

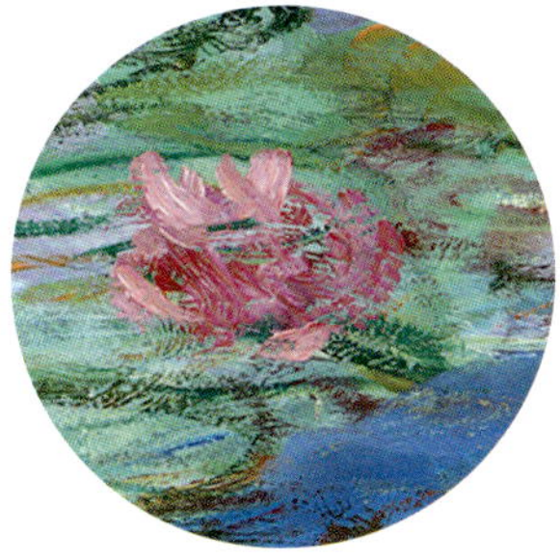

Water Lily

Eloquence, purity of heart

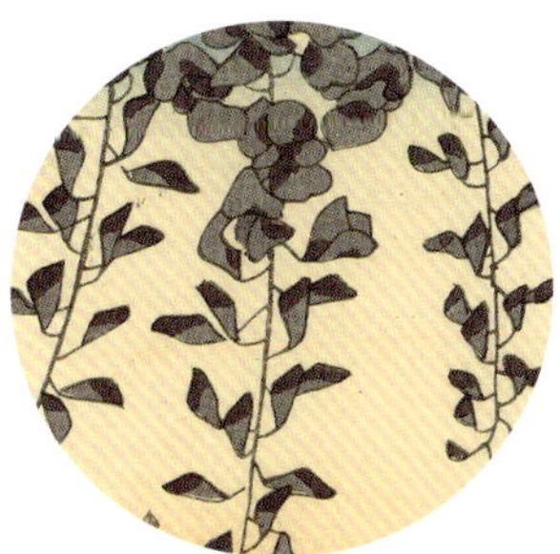

Wisteria

Welcome, fair stranger

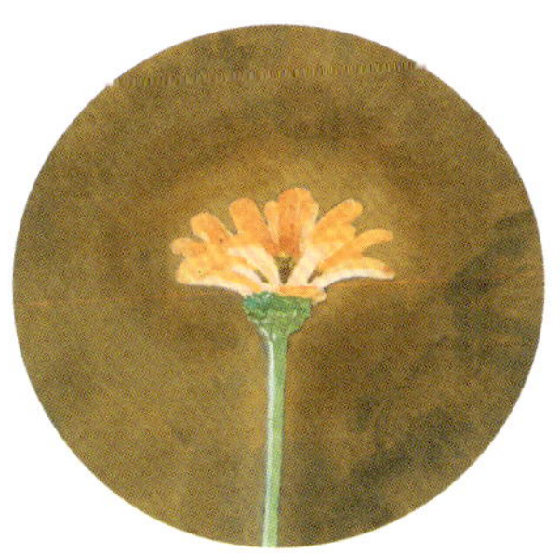

Zinnia

Thoughts of absent friends

Selected Bibliography

Adamich Laufer, Geraldine. *Tussie-Mussies: The Victorian Art of Expressing Yourself in the Language of Flowers*. New York: Workman Publishing Company, 1993.

Baird, Merrily C. *Symbols of Japan: Thematic Motifs in Art and Design*. New York: Rizzoli, 2001.

Begay, Odessa. *A Fully Illustrated Compendium of Meaning, Literature, and Lore for the Modern Romantic*. New York: Harper Design, 2020.

Bell, Adrienne Baxter. "Charles Caryl Coleman: Transnational American Artist." *American Arts Quarterly* 32, no. 1 (Winter 2015): 31–40.

Boddy, Kasia. *Blooming Flowers: A Seasonal History of Plants and People*. New Haven, CT: Yale University Press, 2020.

Bradler, Christine M. and Joachim Alfred P. Scheiner. *Feng Shui Symbols: A User's Handbook*. New York: Sterling Publishing Co., Inc., 1999.

Braswell, Suzanne. "Mallarmé, Huysmans, and the Poetics of Hothouse Blooms." *French Forum* 38, nos. 1/2 (Winter/Spring 2013): 69–87.

Buchmann, Stephen L. *The Reason for Flowers: Their History, Culture, Biology, and How They Change Our Lives*. New York: Scribner, 2016.

Burke, L. *The Miniature Language of Flowers*. London: George Routledge and Sons, Broadway, Ludgate Hill, 1865.

Campbell, Elizabeth A. "Don't Say It with Nightshades: Sentimental Botany and the Natural History of 'Atropa Belladonna.'" *Victorian Literature and Culture* 35, no. 2 (2007): 607–615.

Cargill, Lafayette F. *The Language of Flowers*. Michigan City, IN: L.F. Cargill, 1937.

Carruthers, [Miss]. *Flower Lore: The Teachings of Flowers, Historical, Legendary, Poetical & Symbolical*. Belfast: McCaw, Stevenson & Orr, 1879.

Chwalkowski, Farrin. *Symbols in Arts, Religion and Culture: The Soul of Nature*. Newcastle upon Tyne: Cambridge Scholars Publishing, 2016.

Cumo, Christopher, ed. *Encyclopedia of Cultivated Plants: From Acacia to Zinnia*. Santa Barbara, CA: ABC-CLIO, 2013.

Deas, Lizzie, Anne Renier, and Fernand G. Renier. *Flower Favourites: Their Legends, Symbolism and Significance*. London: George Allen, 1898.

Dietz, S. Theresa. *The Complete Language of Flowers: A Definitive and Illustrated History*. New York: The Wellfleet Press, 2020.

Eldredge, Charles C. "Calla Moderna: Such a Strange Flower." *Georgia O'Keeffe and the Calla Lily in American Art, 1860–1940*. Edited by Barbara Buhler Lynes. New Haven, CT: Yale University Press, 2002.

Elliott, Brent. "The Victorian Language of Flowers." *Occasional Papers from the RHS Lindley Library* 10 (December 2013). London: The Lindley Library, the Royal Horticultural Society: 3–131.

Fish, David Taylor. *Bulbs and Bulb Culture*. London: L. Upcott Gill, 1885.

Fisher, Celia. *Flowers in Medieval Manuscripts*. Toronto: University of Toronto Press, 2004.

Flora's Pocket Dictionary: A Lexicon of the Language and Sentiment of Flowers. Philadelphia: Porter & Coates, 1870.

Flowers, Their Language, Poetry, and Sentiment. Philadelphia: Porter & Coates, 1870.

Giesecke, Annette. *The Mythology of Plants: Botanical Lore from Ancient Greece and Rome*. Los Angeles: J. Paul Getty Museum, 2014.

Goody, Jack. *The Culture of Flowers*. Cambridge, UK: Cambridge University Press, 1993.

Gülçin Ambros, Edith. "The 'Language of Flowers' and Ottoman Don Juans (*Zenpāres*)." *Wiener Zeitschrift für die Kunde des Morgenlandes* 95 (2005): 19–43.

Haig, Elizabeth. *The Floral Symbolism of the Great Masters*. London: Kegan Paul, Trench, Trübner & Co. Ltd., 1913.

Hibberd, James Shirley. *The Fuchsia, Pansy, and Phlox: Their History, Properties, Cultivation, Propagation, and General Management in All Seasons*. London: Groombridge and Sons, 1858.

Hooper, Lucy. *The Lady's Book of Flowers and Poetry: To Which Are Added, a Botanical Introduction, a Complete Floral Dictionary; and a Chapter on Plants in Rooms.* New York: J.C. Riker, 1842.

Howell, Catherine Herbert. *Flora Mirabilis: How Plants Have Shaped World Knowledge, Health, Wealth, and Beauty*. Washington, DC: National Geographic Society, 2009.

Hyde, Elizabeth. *Cultivated Power: Flowers, Culture, and Politics in the Reign of Louis XIV.* Philadelphia: University of Pennsylvania Press, 2005.

Ildrewe, [Miss]. *The Language of Flowers.* Boston: Lee and Shepard, 1865.

Impelluso, Lucia. *Nature and Its Symbols.* Los Angeles: J. Paul Getty Museum, 2004.

Jewell, Jennifer. *The Earth in Her Hands: 75 Extraordinary Women Working in the World of Plants.* Portland, OR: Timber Press, 2020.

Johnson, Robert F., and Joseph R. Goldyne. *Master Drawings from the Achenbach Foundation for Graphic Arts, the Fine Arts Museums of San Francisco*. San Francisco: Fine Arts Museums of San Francisco; Geneva, Switzerland: R. Burton, 1985.

Kingsbury, Noël. *Garden Flora: The Natural and Cultural History of the Plants in Your Garden*. Portland, OR: Timber Press, 2016.

Kirkby, Mandy. *A Victorian Flower Dictionary: The Language of Flowers Companion.* New York: Ballantine Books, 2011.

Kirtland, C.M. *Poetry of the Flowers.* New York: Thomas Y. Crowell and Co., 1848.

Lehner, Ernst, and Johanna Lehner. *Folklore and Symbolism of Flowers, Plants and Trees: With Over 200 Rare and Unusual Floral Designs and Illustrations.* Mineola, NY: Dover Publications, 2004.

Loewer, H. Peter. *Loves Me, Loves Me Not: The Hidden Language of Flowers*. New York: Skyhorse Publishing, 2018.

Looby, Christopher. "Flowers of Manhood: Race, Sex and Floriculture from Thomas Wentworth Higginson to Robert Mapplethorpe." *Criticism* 37, no. 1 (Winter 1995): 109–156.

The Man'yōshū: The Nippon Gakujutsu Shinkokai Translation of One Thousand Poems. New York: Columbia University Press, 1969.

Martin, Laura C. *Garden Flower Folklore*. Chester, CT: The Globe Pequot Press, 1987.

Mendonça de Carvalho, Luís Manuel. "The Symbolic Uses of Plants." *Ethnobiology*. Edited by E.N. Anderson, Deborah M. Pearsall, Eugene S. Hunn, and Nancy J. Turner. Hoboken, NJ: Wiley-Blackwell, 2011.

Merritt, Helen, and Nanako Yamada. *Guide to Modern Japanese Woodblock Prints: 1900–1975*. Honolulu: University of Hawai'i Press, 1992.

Olderr, Steven. *Symbolism: A Comprehensive Dictionary*. Jefferson, NC: McFarland & Co., 2012.

Osgood, Frances S., ed. *The Poetry of Flowers and Flowers of Poetry: To Which Are Added, a Simple Treatise on Botany, with Familiar Examples, and a Copious Floral Dictionary*. New York: Derby & Jackson, 1860.

Prettejohn, Elizabeth. *The Cambridge Companion to the Pre-Raphaelites*. Cambridge, UK: Cambridge University Press, 2012.

Saberi, Helen. *Tea: A Global History*. London: Reaktion Books, 2010.

Seaton, Beverly. *The Language of Flowers: A History.* Charlottesville, VA: University Press of Virginia, 1995.

Sheley, Nancy Strow. "The 'Language of Flowers' as Coded Subtext: Conflicted Messages of Domesticity in Mary Wilkins Freeman's Short Fiction." *Working Papers on Design* 2 (2007): 5–14.

Shoberl, Frederic. *The Language of Flowers: With Illustrative Poetry; to Which Are Now Added the Calendar of Flowers and the Dial of Flowers*. Philadelphia: Lea & Blanchard, 1839.

Statler, Oliver. *Modern Japanese Prints: An Art Reborn*. Rutland, VT: Charles E. Tuttle Company, 1956.

Stuart-Smith, Sue. *The Well-Gardened Mind: The Restorative Power of Nature*. New York: Scribner, 2020.

Tebbitt, Mark C., Magnus Lidén, and Henrik Zetterlund. *Bleeding Hearts, Corydalis, and Their Relatives*. Brooklyn: Brooklyn Botanic Garden; Portland, OR: Timber Press, 2008.

Thiselton Dyer, Thomas Firminger. *The Folk-Lore of Plants*. New York: D. Appleton and Company, 1889.

Tomasi, Lucia Tongiorgi. *An Oak Spring Flora: Flower Illustration from the Fifteenth Century to the Present Time: A Selection of the Rare Books, Manuscripts, and Works of Art in the Collection of Rachel Lambert Mellon.* New Haven, CT: Yale University Press, 1997.

Trenton, Patricia, Susan Landauer, and William H. Gerdts. *The Not-So-Still Life: A Century of California Painting and Sculpture.* Berkeley: University of California Press, 2003.

Turner, Cordelia Harris. *The Floral Kingdom, Its History, Sentiment and Poetry*. Chicago: Moses Warren, 1877.

Tyas, Robert. *The Language of Flowers; or, Floral Emblems of Thoughts, Feelings, and Sentiments*. London: George Routledge and Sons, 1875.

Watts, D.C. *Elsevier's Dictionary of Plant Lore*. Burlington, MA: Academic Press, 2007.

Weekly, Nancy. *Charles E. Burchfield: The Sacred Woods*. Albany, NY: State University of New York Press, 1993.

Wildman, Stephen, and John Christian. *Edward Burne-Jones, Victorian Artist-Dreamer*. New York: Abrams, 1998.

Williams, C.A.S. *Outlines of Chinese Symbolism and Art Motives: An Alphabetical Compendium of Antique Legends and Beliefs, as Reflected in the Manners and Customs of the Chinese*. New York: Dover Publications, 1976.

Wirt, Elizabeth Washington Gamble. *Flora's Dictionary*. Baltimore: Fielding Lucas, 1832.

Picture Credits

Figure Illustrations 1: © Kehinde Wilsey. Courtesy of the National Portrait Gallery, Smithsonian Institution, Washington, DC. 2: Courtesy of the Dumbarton Oaks Archives, Ephemera Collection, Washington, DC. 3: Copyright © Fine Arts Museums of San Francisco; photograph by Randy Dodson. 4: Digital image courtesy of the Getty's Open Content Program, J. Paul Getty Museum, Los Angeles. 5: Courtesy of the Metropolitan Museum of Art, New York. 6: Drew Altizer Photography.

Plate Illustrations Unless otherwise noted, all plate illustrations are copyright © Fine Arts Museums of San Francisco; photograph by Randy Dodson. Unless otherwise noted, all photographs are by Randy Dodson. 2: Reproduced with permission from the Charles E. Burchfield Foundation and the Burchfield Penney Art Center, Buffalo, New York. 3, 37: Copyright © Fine Arts Museums of San Francisco; photograph by Joseph McDonald. 5: Courtesy of the artist and Jessica Silverman, San Francisco. 6: 2022 Banco de México Diego Rivera Frida Kahlo Museums Trust, Mexico, D.F. / Artists Rights Society (ARS), New York. 8: © Sayaka Kawakami. 12: © 2022 Wayne Thiebaud / Licensed by VAGA at Artists Rights Society (ARS), New York. 13: Courtesy of the Estate of William Seltzer Rice. 14: Courtesy of the Lazzell Family. 17: © 2021 Figge Art Museum, successors to the Estate of Nan Wood Graham / Licensed by VAGA at Artists Rights Society (ARS), New York. 18: © 2022 The Andy Warhol Foundation for the Visual Arts, Inc. / Licensed by Artists Rights Society (ARS), New York. 19: © Estate of Mabel Allington Royds. 20: © Onchi Koshiro Estate. 21: Copyright Estate of Paul Wonner and Theophilus Brown, Crocker Art Museum, Sacramento. 26: Copyright © Fine Arts Museums of San Francisco; photograph by Joseph McDonald; transparency scan by Krause Johansen, Light Source. 28: © Estate of Mark Adams. 29: © 2022 Imogen Cunningham Trust. 32: © 2022 Estate of Ruth Asawa / Artists Rights Society (ARS), New York; photograph by Jorge Bachman. 33: Copyright © Fine Arts Museums of San Francisco; transparency scan by Krause Johansen, Light Source. 35: Copyright © Fine Arts Museums of San Francisco; photograph by Joseph McDonald; transparency scan by Light Source. 38: © 2022 Georgia O'Keeffe Museum / Artists Rights Society (ARS), New York. 41: © Mary Frank; courtesy of DC Moore Gallery, New York. 43: © 1966, 1984, 1994 Rhino Entertainment Company. Used with permission. All rights reserved. www.familydog.com. 45: Courtesy of the California State Library. 50: Copyright Estate of Paul Wonner and Theophilus Brown, Crocker Art Museum, Sacramento; photograph by Jorge Bachmann.

Decorative Illustrations pp. ii–iii: Grand Duchess Kyril, *Still Life—Flowers*, late 19th century (detail of pl. 11). p. iv: Mark Adams (designer), Phoebe McAfee (weaver), and Rudi Richardson (weaver), *Lotus, Sumatra*, 1989 (detail of pl. 28). pp. 18–19: Florine Stettheimer, *Still Life with Flowers*, 1921 (detail of pl. 39). pp. 120–121: Jan Frans van Dael, *Flowers Before a Window*, 1789 (detail of pl. 37). pp. 134–135: Claude Monet, *Water Lilies*, ca. 1914–1917 (detail of pl. 48).

Acknowledgments

IN THE VICTORIAN LANGUAGE OF FLOWERS, a variety of blossoms are associated with sentiments of thankfulness and acknowledgment. Dark pink roses convey "thank you," and peach roses signal appreciation. Agrimony, Canterbury bells, bellflower, common bluebell, yellow lily, and Bells-of-Ireland all serve as emblems of gratitude. This publication is the result of various efforts from the staff of the Fine Arts Museums of San Francisco, and to the following individuals we extend a bouquet comprising the aforementioned flowers:

We are grateful to Thomas P. Campbell, director and CEO, for supporting diverse projects that deepen engagement with the Museums' collections. As ever, we thank our board of trustees, led by Jason Moment, president, and Diane B. Wilsey, chair emerita, for their sustaining advocacy of all of our museum endeavors.

This book was inspired by Bouquets to Art, a beloved annual event at the Fine Arts Museums, and originated through the exceptional efforts of the staff throughout the institution. We are also grateful for the guidance of the members of the curatorial team who care for the objects featured on these pages and who contributed their insights and assistance. We offer bouquets of peach roses to Karin Breuer, curator in charge of the Achenbach Foundation for Graphic Arts; Martin Chapman, curator in charge of European decorative arts and sculpture; and Jill D'Alessandro, curator in charge of costume and textile arts for the Caroline and H. McCoy Jones Department of Textile Arts; as well as to Laura L. Camerlengo, associate curator, costume and textile arts; Furio Rinaldi, curator, Achenbach Foundation for Graphic Arts; Isabella Holland, curatorial assistant, European paintings; and Thomas Wu, curatorial assistant, European decorative arts and sculpture.

A special arrangement of bluebells and yellow lilies is dedicated to Timothy Anglin Burgard, distinguished senior curator and Ednah Root Curator in Charge of American Art, and Emma Acker, associate curator of American art, for their thoughtful vetting and review of the various materials prepared for this publication. We also express our appreciation to Melissa E. Buron, director of curatorial affairs, for her early support of the project.

The concept for this book developed through the collaboration of a number of museum staff members whose efforts are deserving of dark pink roses, including Leslie Dutcher, director of publications, and Stuart Hata, director of retail operations, who endorsed this undertaking from its inception and helped shape it. The expert editing was the work of Trina Enriquez, editor. Leslie Dutcher and Matt Mayerchak created the beautiful design. The management of photography assets and new object photography was overseen by Sue Grinols, director of photo services, and prepared by Randy Dodson, head photographer. Robert Carswell, digital assets and rights manager, and José Jovel, publications associate, researched and secured the image rights. The prepress work, printing, and binding was completed by Conti Tipocolor, Florence, Italy, with the oversight of Roberto Conti, Marta Conti, Laura Cuccoli, and Lucia Conti. The book is distributed by Cameron + Company under the superb guidance of Chris Gruener and Jan Hughes.

We also wish to thank other staff members whose work behind the scenes has enabled the flowering of this publication and the annual event that inspired it: Jason Seifer, chief financial officer; Megan Bourne, chief of staff; Susan McConkey, chief administrative officer; Krista Brugnara, director of exhibitions, with Kimberley Montgomery, chief registrar; Patricia Buffa, director of digital strategy; Linda Butler, director of marketing, communications, and visitor experience; Patty Lacson, director of facilities; Amanda Riley, director of development; and Jane Williams, director of conservation, with Victoria Binder, head of paper conservation, and Elise Effmann Clifford, head of paintings conservation. Abigail Dansiger, head of library and archives, and Araceli Bremauntz-Enriquez, former archives assistant and Logan Fellow, offered meaningful support. We also acknowledge the efforts of Douglas DeFors, associate registrar; Rebecca Burton, assistant registrar; and Egle Mendoza, assistant registrar. A special sprig of agrimony goes to Debra Evans, former head of paper conservation, for the many works on paper she cared for throughout her tenure with the Museums.

Most of all, we wish to acknowledge all who have worked so hard to make the Fine Arts Museums of San Francisco a place for flowers. We acknowledge the efforts of Elizabeth Hundt, former associate director of special events; Cheyenne Tang, events manager; Meghan McCauley, director of membership; and Danielle Hobart, former assistant director of membership, who have helped ensure the ongoing success of Bouquets to Art. Most important, we dedicate a basket of bellflowers to the members of the San Francisco Auxiliary of the Fine Arts Museums, whose long-standing commitment to Bouquets to Art deeply enriches the museum experience for visitors and staff alike.

Finally, I would like to conclude with a personal dedication to my son, Asher, who blossomed in tandem with this book. To you, I offer an entire garden, always in full bloom.

LAUREN PALMOR
Assistant Curator of American Art, Fine Arts Museums of San Francisco

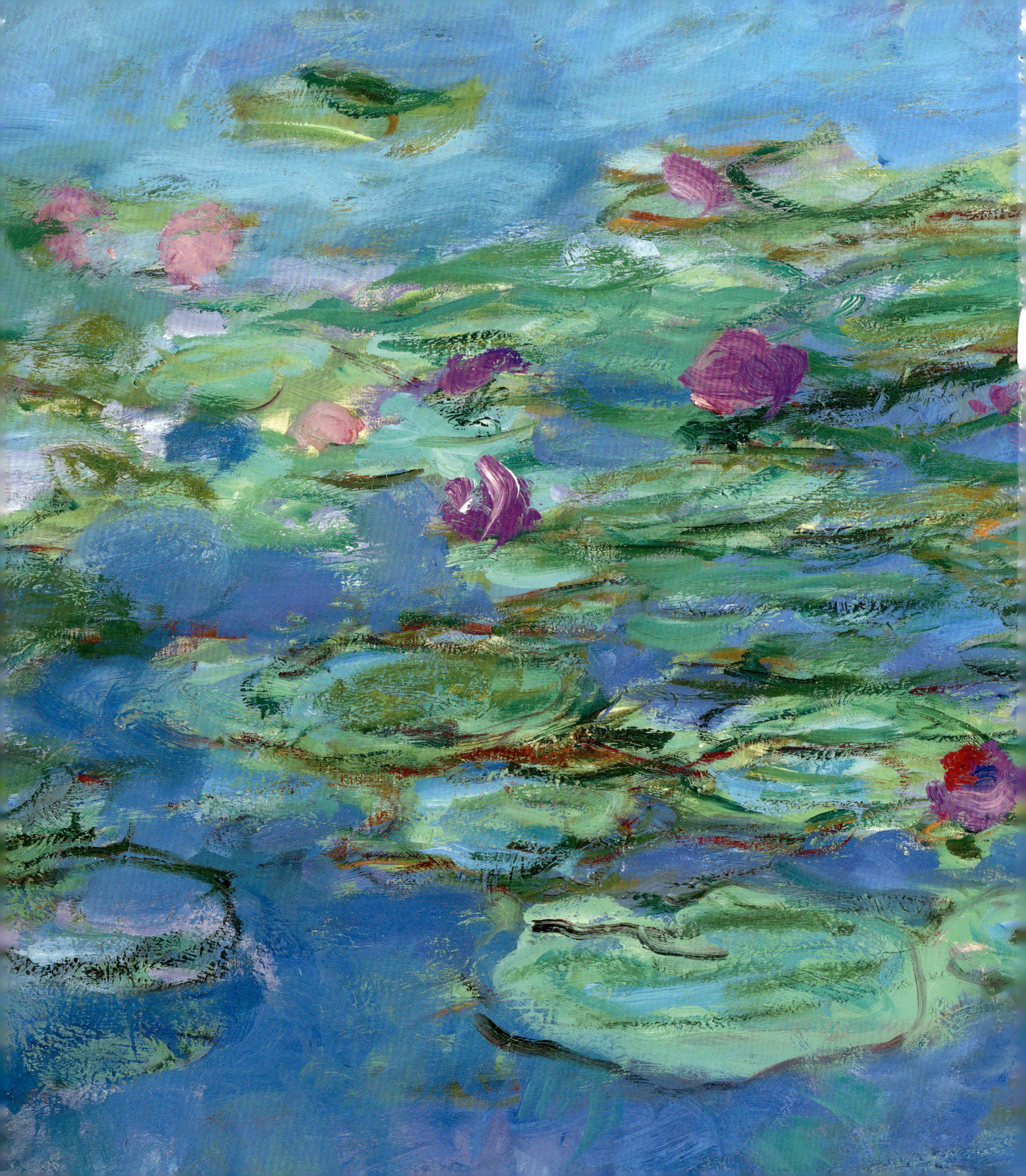

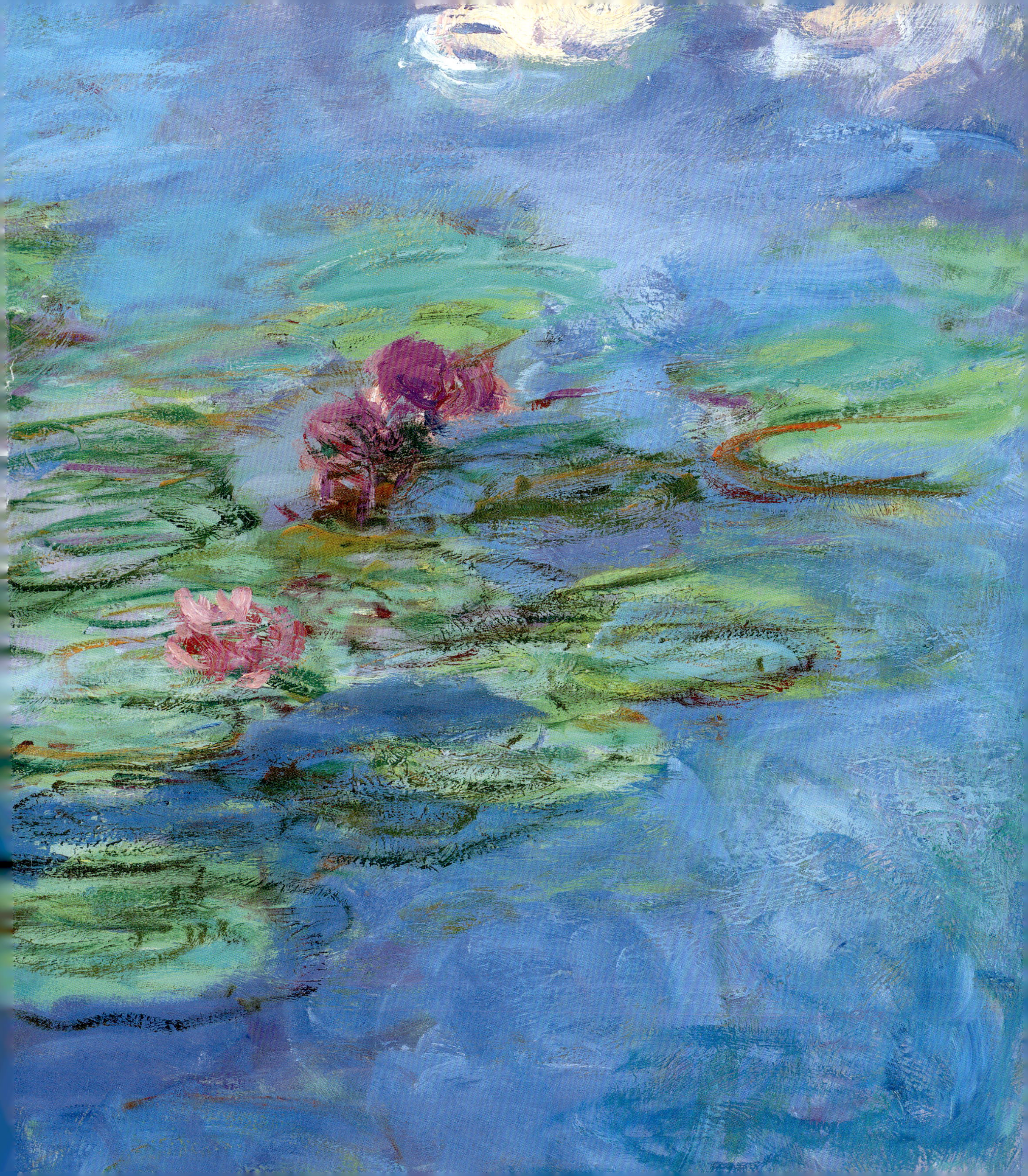

Bouquets of Art

A FLOWER DICTIONARY
from the
FINE ARTS MUSEUMS OF SAN FRANCISCO

This catalogue is published to celebrate the Fine Arts Museums of San Francisco's beloved annual event Bouquets of Art, held at the de Young and organized by the San Francisco Auxiliary of the Fine Arts Museums.

Library of Congress control number: 2021950680
ISBN: 978-1-951836-83-2

Front cover image: Willem van Aelst, *Flowers in a Silver Vase*, 1663 (detail of pl. 46). © FAMSF, photograph by Randy Dodson
Back cover image: Andy Warhol (artist), Leo Castelli Gallery (publisher), and Total Color (printer), *Flowers*, 1964 (pl. 18). © 2022 The Andy Warhol Foundation for the Visual Arts, Inc. / Licensed by Artists Rights Society (ARS), New York. Photograph by Randy Dodson / FAMSF

de Young \ \ Legion of Honor fine arts museums of san francisco

Fine Arts Museums of San Francisco
de Young, Golden Gate Park
50 Hagiwara Tea Garden Drive
San Francisco, CA 94118-4502
www.famsf.org

Leslie Dutcher, director of publications
Lesley Bruynesteyn, editor
Trina Enriquez, editor
Victoria Gannon, editor
José Jovel, publications associate

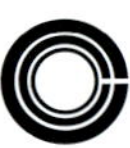

CAMERON + COMPANY
a division of ABRAMS
149 Kentucky Street, Suite 7
Petaluma, CA 94952
www.cameronbooks.com

Project management and editing by Trina Enriquez
Proofread by Lesley Bruynesteyn
Picture research by José Jovel
Designed by Leslie Dutcher and Matt Mayerchak
Color separations by Rusty Sena, Art Product, LA
Printing and binding by Conti Tipocolor, Italy

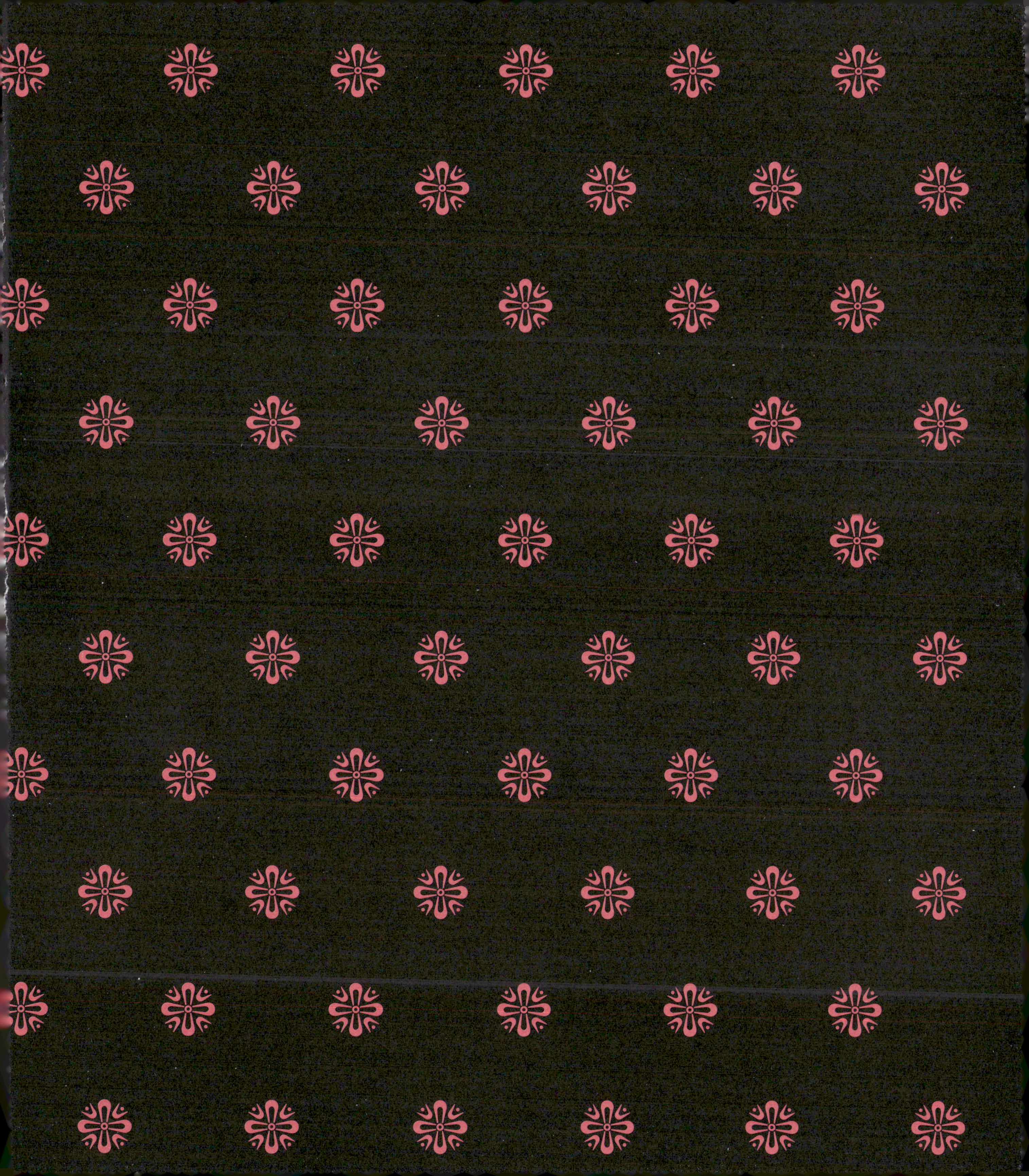

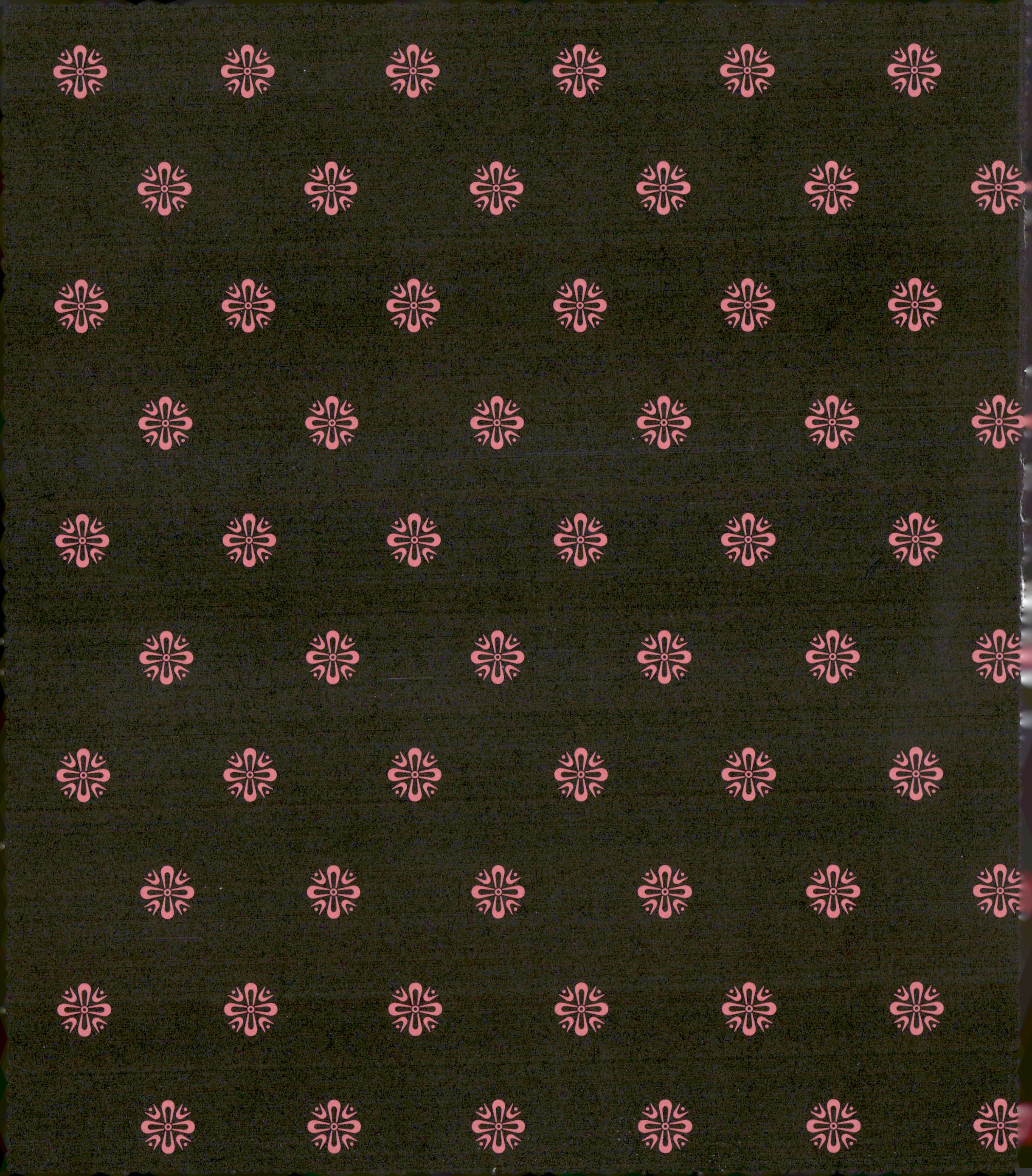